WESTMIDLANDS

WESTMIDLANDS

A history of West Midlands Passenger Transport Executive
Malcolm Keeley

Capital Transport

Contents

Introduction

to secure or promote the provision of a properly integrated and efficient system of public passenger transport to meet the needs of that area with due regard to the town planning and traffic and parking policies of the councils of constituent areas and to economy and safety of operation

This piece of convoluted English was the first commandment for the elected representatives who comprised the Passenger Transport Authorities and for the professional officers of the Passenger Transport Executives, set up under the Transport Act 1968.

The PTAs and PTEs came into operation in 1969 and their tools for the job were the municipal bus undertakings handed over to them. The rest of the integration brief, involving bus companies and local railways, had to be achieved by negotiation.

The dominant contribution to the West Midlands Passenger Transport Executive in terms of staff and vehicles came from Birmingham City Transport. Rather smaller, even added together, were the municipal bus undertakings of Walsall, West Bromwich and Wolverhampton. Real bus integration became possible after 1973 upon control of Midland Red's local services whilst, in 1974, local government re-organisation saw the PTA/PTE boundaries changed and Coventry Corporation's bus fleet added.

This book charts the course of the West Midlands Passenger Transport Executive from its inception. It follows the spread of the WMPTE image and the integrated network, not only between buses but with trains too. It then describes the changing political thought leading up to the Transport Act 1985, which separated the bus operations into a new company, West Midlands Travel, upon national de-regulation of bus services.

The Transport Act 1985 removed the Executive's role as effective integrator of public passenger services although it retains its co-ordination brief and continues to support local rail services. The 'new' Executive fills the gaps in the commercial network by offering socially necessary services through competitive tender, it administers concessionary fares revenue and generally promotes bus and rail travel in the West Midlands.

It is very easy to make judgements with the benefit of hindsight. It was very difficult initially to see the value of the newly-created PTEs. Ten years later, after the integration exercises and the introduction of new tickets available for use on all buses and trains in the County, the advantages were obvious. Today it is difficult to see why the integrated system has been abandoned under the 1985 Act. Perhaps in ten years time we will see that, having earlier created logical order out of the previous self-contained systems, the de-regulated industry has been able to use its competitive edge to make the most of that order.

The writer's lifelong interest has been in the buses themselves. This book, therefore, is inevitably a vehicle history but showing their part in the creation of an integrated transport network. There are, however, shifts of emphasis as the story proceeds. The early years review the movements of the many interesting buses inherited by the PTE. The emphasis changes, after the influx of Midland Red routes and the agreement with British Rail, to cover the thorough service revisions that lasted throughout the second half of the 1970s. The extent of these revisions was such that there

Front Cover Upper The old municipal liveries could be seen alongside the advancing PTE blue and cream for a number of years. The former Coventry colours lasted longest as that fleet was not absorbed until 1974. Daimler CVG6 255Y leaves Pool Meadow bus station, Coventry, in March 1978. *M.R. Keeley*

Front Cover Lower The modern image achieved. Metrobuses 2538 and 2473 are seen at Kings Norton Station, Cotteridge in August 1983. The blue applied to the Metrobuses with WMPTE was a shade lighter than that used on its other vehicles. *M.R. Keeley*

Back Cover The solid traditional Guys and Daimlers acquired from Birmingham City Transport greatly assisted the Executive in its earlier years, even if their image was rather dated. Guy Arab IV 3011, in PTE colours, was 20 years old when photographed in Bradford Street, Birmingham, in June 1973. Those who remember these Guys will readily imagine the exhaust rasping as 3011 accelerates up the slight incline from the junction with Camp Hill in the background. This Ethel Street journey was a once a day short working on the 32 service. *M.R. Keeley*

First published 1988

ISBN 1 85414 100 7

Published by Capital Transport Publishing
38 Long Elmes, Harrow Weald, Middlesex

Printed by Staples Printers St Albans Ltd
The Priory Press, London Road, St Albans, Herts

© Malcolm Keeley 1988

Frontispiece Fleetline 6980 at Colmore Circus, Birmingham. This particular vehicle was fitted with deflecting strips, visible at the top of the front offside blue panels, in an attempt to reduce the problem of dirt being sprayed onto the driver's window. *M.R. Keeley*

Facing Contents Page South Division meets North Division at Hamstead village in October 1971. Ex-Birmingham City Transport 1953 Crossley-bodied Daimler CVG6 3112 turns at the Birmingham boundary, whilst Daimler Fleetline/Northern Counties 4006 loads in the background for West Bromwich. A Birmingham City Transport Bundy time recording clock, requiring each Birmingham driver to register his departure time with an individual key, stands near the West Bromwich version of a Ministry of Transport stop plate. Divisional boundaries in some cases proved almost as impenetrable as municipal ones — the South Division service from Birmingham centre did not reach the northern part of Hamstead until December 1982. Below this picture is a busy scene at Walsall bus station with a number of ex-Walsall Fleetlines and ex-West Bromwich Daimler CVG6 buses in evidence and, most prominent, 1961 Metro-Cammell bodied AEC Regent V 891L overhauled into blue and cream. *M.R. Keeley/T.W. Moore*

Contents Page The Bull Ring Bus Station was under repair in July 1980 and its services were terminating in nearby streets, including Smallbrook Queensway. An exaggerated demonstration of the disparity of vehicle ages in the North and South Divisions is provided by this scene. The four modern Fleetlines, led by 6362, wait to work North Division services to the Black Country. Passing by is South Division Fleetline 3394, one of the first ten buses with new style windscreens built for Birmingham City Transport in 1964. This disparity was largely caused by the poorer quality stock inherited by the North Division, giving it priority in replacements. *M.R. Keeley*

Opposite Bristol VRT 4366 leaves the bus station in Walsall, rebuilt in 1975, on the service to Boney Hay formerly numbered 85. *T.W. Moore*

can only be space to refer to the most significant ones. The road to an integrated network was largely complete by 1980, by which time most of the fleet comprised standard PTE vehicles. At this point the political climate changed and, quite separately, recession hit the West Midlands very hard. Inevitably the remainder of the book deals increasingly with political moves.

West Midlands Passenger Transport Executive was the most efficient operator of its type – trade press figures confirmed it. There is sufficient scope for the writer to heap unstinting praise on the organisation but, in doing so, the book would lose all credibility. There are too many outside factors to allow all the best laid plans to function correctly. For instance, no operator chasing a modern image would *plan* to run 25-year old buses and I shall no doubt cause frothing at some mouths for stressing the role of these veterans. I hope that I have made clear the reasons why these buses continued to run; it enhances the PTE's reputation that it was both able to keep them going and yet still win through to that desired image.

The writer is conscious of the politicians and PTE personnel left unmentioned in this book, and this is not to belittle their hard work on behalf of West Midlands passengers and ratepayers. To avoid too great a proliferation of names, however, a decision had to be taken to restrict generally reference to the top layer. Great camaraderie exists, however, at all levels within an industry which has required its employees to work at times under appalling conditions for often moderate reward. It is a pity there is no proper manner to record the innumerable charitable efforts made by WMPTE employees over the years for outside organisations and for colleagues whose health has broken before their expected retirements. There is no convenient chapter either to record the amusing coincidences that occasionally crop up in a large organisation, such as Horace Hastings receiving roll number 1066 or the East Division's senior management including Messrs Penny and Shilling!

The information contained in this book has been drawn from press cuttings, WMPTE annual reports, the former staff magazine 'Fare' and the news pages of the preservation societies BaMMOT (promoters of the Midland Bus & Transport Museum) and the 1685 Group. The book is in no way an official publication of West Midlands PTE or West Midlands Travel and any views are those of the writer alone. Those wishing to keep up-to-date with the activities of West Midlands Travel are advised to join BaMMOT, if your interests also happen to embrace vehicle preservation, or the Omnibus Society or PSV Circle. Readers are also recommended to purchase 'Major Bus Operators The Midlands', published by Capital Transport, for a West Midlands Travel fleet list.

I owe thanks to a large number of people, beginning with the photographers whose contributions have brought to life the progress of the PTE. I am indebted to those who have provided information and/or checked the manuscript including Peter Jaques, Stewart King, David Kirk and Monty Russell. Assistance in other ways came from Paul Gray, Jean Langton, Stan Letts and my wife Yvonne who, in addition to her help, had to tolerate the household in considerable disarray as completion approached.

Birmingham, September 1987   MALCOLM KEELEY

The Transport Inheritance

MCW-bodied Fleetline 6436 of Cleveland Road garage, Wolverhampton, climbs Laurel Road, Dudley, in July 1986. The 581 was created by the combination of former Midland Red and Wolverhampton Corporation routes. M.R. Keeley

The West Midlands Passenger Transport Executive was created in 1969 but, before studying the reasons for its formation, it is appropriate to review what public transport existed before.

The PTE was originally produced by the amalgamation of the municipal bus undertakings of Birmingham, Walsall, West Bromwich and Wolverhampton, under the terms of the 1968 Transport Act. As the tide of West Midlands PTE blue and cream paint and its practices gradually overtook these individual undertakings, it became harder to appreciate their separate and quite distinctive evolutions. Joint operations were not widespread, certainly not by the standards of Greater Manchester. This was because many of the interurban operations were in the hands of the Midland Red company. The PTE needed to gain control of these Midland Red services so

that it could make strides with the integration brief demanded by the 1968 Act. Although only part of Midland Red was absorbed into the WMPTE, it is important to understand the relationship of its West Midland services and those of the private tramway companies which had preceded it many years before.

Local government reorganisation in 1974 saw the creation of the West Midlands County Council, and the PTE boundaries were adjusted to coincide. Out went several logical transport destinations and in came Coventry – a needless loss of a separate and highly regarded municipal bus undertaking.

Finally there were the rail services which, since nationalisation in 1948, had all been under the aegis of British Railways. Local railway services also became the responsibility of the West Midlands PTE although actual operation continued with British Rail.

MIDLAND RED

For seventy years the proper name of Midland Red was 'The Birmingham & Midland Motor Omnibus Company Limited', usually shortened to the initials BMMO. In 1904, when the Company was formed, the British Electric Traction group had a near monopoly of Birmingham's road public transport through the tramway and horse-bus services of its subsidiaries, and the new Company soon became part of the BET empire.

By 1912 control of Birmingham's transport had changed considerably. Nearly all the leases held by BET on tramways within the City had expired and operation taken over by Birmingham Corporation Tramways. The City authorities would also not allow omnibus services to compete with its tramways and, as the tramway network vigorously expanded, BMMO was obliged to withdraw parallel facilities. The Birmingham Corporation Act of 1914 granted full omnibus operating powers without restriction to that undertaking and it was then obvious that conflict with BMMO would be inevitable. Therefore the two undertakings entered into the classic agreement whereby the Company continued to operate services between Birmingham and places outside the City boundary but agreed to leave the operation of city services entirely to the Corporation. For its own part, Birmingham Corporation agreed to restrict its future activities to operations within the boundary and not to compete with the Company outside the boundary. The effect of the agreement was that the BCT purchased from the Company all routes operating solely within the city.

The Agreement was very successful and long-lasting, resulting in happy relations between the two operators right up to PTE days. However, in 1914 it meant that BMMO had to find new sources of revenue and began a network of 'country' services radiating from Birmingham, as well as local services in neighbouring boroughs. The Company went from strength to strength, eventually building up a huge operating territory. The Corporations of Walsall and Wolverhampton were also early operators of motorbuses, thus the Company entered into operating area agreements with the two Corporations in 1919 and 1920 respectively. The dearth, until 1973, of Midland Red services to the north of these towns was a result of these agreements. A similar agreement was drawn up with Coventry in 1920.

In the southern half of the Black Country, the absence of towns large enough to operate their own municipal transport provided the right conditions for the spread of BET company-operated tramways. In the mid-1920s, these tramways came under severe pressure from small operators and BET brought in their Midland Red buses to respond to the competition. It was then a logical step for those buses to replace the tramways of Midland Red's sister companies. The substitutions meant the formulation of agreements with interested local authorities. The last of the tramway routes, that between Birmingham and Dudley via Oldbury, was not abandoned until 1939, having been operated by Birmingham Corporation tramcars for the last few years. Operating agreements were entered into with the local authorities of Dudley in 1929; West Bromwich in 1930; and Smethwick, Oldbury, Rowley Regis and Tipton in 1939.

Thus the situation encountered by the new PTE in 1969 was established by 1930, with Midland Red having operating agreements with all five bus-owning municipalities and all too often possessing firm 'wedges' of territory between them.

Midland Red had recognised a threat to its existence as early as 1966 when 'Conurbation Transport Authorities' were first mooted. The Company's apprehension was understandable. It would not have been beyond the wit of politicians, not always noted for their understanding of the bus industry, to hive off the lucrative Black Country services into a Conurbation Transport Authority, leaving the Company without access to the Birmingham market, and allowing the country services (these were the days before rural bus grants) to wither away.

In November 1967, when there were fears that the Labour Government then in power intended to nationalise the bus industry with little or no compensation, the British Electric Traction decided that its interests in the ailing British bus industry would be better invested elsewhere, and voluntarily sold out these interests to the State in March 1968. Midland Red was thus now totally state-owned and in due course found itself part of the National Bus Company, formed under the 1968 Transport Act on 1st January 1969. In this respect the situation was marginally eased in that future negotiations would be between two public agencies set up by the Act (the NBC and the imminent PTE) rather than between one private and one public body. Grant aid was now available for socially desirable rural services, enabling the sale of the Birmingham and Black Country network to be at least considered.

Midland Red built the majority of its buses itself between 1923 and 1970, although bodies for most of the period were constructed by outside builders to Midland Red design. Prewar vehicles were known by the initials SOS (believed to stand for Shire's Omnibus Specification — Mr Shire being the then Chief Engineer) and post-war production by the Company's BMMO initials. Service 221 from Bearwood to West Bromwich via Warley was jointly worked by Midland Red and West Bromwich Corporation. 1938 Brush-bodied SOS FEDD 2126 loads at Bearwood Bus Station. G.H. Stone

A typical Black Country scene with BMMO S15 4626 in Titford Road, Langley, in October 1962. Alan D. Broughall

Metro-Cammell bodied BMMO S6 3059 in West Bromwich on the jointly worked 252 service to Cape Hill. This required single deckers due to the weakness of Galton Bridge. R.A. Mills

9

AEC 504 and ADC 507 buses of Birmingham Corporation undergoing overhaul at Tyburn Road works in 1930. In the background stand three new Guy Conquest single deckers intended for the first tram to bus conversion on the Bolton Road service. The photograph was taken to show the use of a 'Whipple' engine starter, demonstrated by the gentleman on the right WMPTE Archive

BIRMINGHAM CITY TRANSPORT

Many bus operators are well known because of their size. Others are known because they are or were amongst the best. Birmingham City Transport fitted into both categories. It was the largest municipal bus operator in Britain, and was acknowledged to be amongst the best in terms of service, rolling stock quality and maintenance.

Birmingham Corporation, like many municipalities, decided to operate its own tramways upon expiry of the various leases granted to private companies. The necessary powers to operate and electrify its own tramways were obtained under the Birmingham Corporation Act of 1903. The tramways were, at this time, operated by companies controlled mostly by British Electric Traction. Despite the 'electric' element in the BET name, most of the routes were still worked by steam trams.

The Birmingham Corporation Tramways Department began business in January 1904 when twenty tramcars took over on a newly electrified line between Steelhouse Lane and Aston Brook Street, the boundary with the then separate authority of Aston Manor. The transport system was revolutionised over the next few years as route after route came under Corporation control and electrified, together with the introduction of new routes. It is impossible to imagine today the impact that hundreds of new electric tramcars must have made compared to the steam trams and horse buses that preceded them.

The first Birmingham Corporation motorbuses commenced operation in 1913 and the classic agreement with Midland Red in 1914 has already been referred to. Development was stifled by the 1914–1918 War, but the early post-war years saw the Department concentrating on expanding and improving the tramway network. The Corporation, however, did experiment with early trolleybuses, replacing trams on the short Nechells route in 1922.

Ten Daimler motorbuses with preselective gearboxes purchased in 1933 proved ideal for intensive city work, and diesel versions with Gardner engines were supplied the following year. This Daimler-Gardner combination was to suit Birmingham, together with the municipalities of West Bromwich and Wolverhampton, and followed in post-war years by Walsall and Coventry, through to the replacing PTE, until the late 1970s.

The first big tramway conversion took place in January 1934 when the Coventry Road service was replaced, not by motorbuses but by new Leyland trolleybuses. These vehicles were successful but, with road schemes and one-way systems threatening in the city centre, vehicles bound by expensive overhead wires were seen as a potential difficulty. Subsequent tramway conversions were therefore to the benefit of the motorbus fleet, the changeover programme beginning in January 1937 with the Stratford Road and Warwick Road group of routes.

The first post-war vehicles were delivered in 1947 and the entire fleet was replaced by some 1,750 new buses by the end of 1954. The replacement programme overtook the inferior wartime buses in 1949/50, the Coventry Road trolleybuses in July 1951, whilst the demise of the tramways was undertaken in several stages, the last running in July 1953. Pre-war motorbuses also disappeared from service, but 41 stored Daimlers staged a comeback in 1957/8 when certain services were taken over from Midland Red. The motorbus fleet of 1947–54 was notably well constructed, and some of the vehicles lasted with the PTE, without major rebuilding, until 1977.

Replacement of the early post-war fleet began in 1961. Experimental Leyland Atlanteans and Daimler Fleetlines led to extremely large orders for the latter. By the time of the WMPTE takeover, on 1st October 1969, over 600 Fleetlines were in operation whilst around 700 'Standards' remained, almost entirely Guys and Daimlers built between 1950 and 1954. Some of the Fleetlines were, by now, one-man operated; Birmingham being the first *city* to run double deckers so equipped. The quality and life-long good maintenance of the 'Standards', coupled with the suitability of the existing rear-engined fleet for single-manning, meant that the PTE's future South Division (comprising the ex-BCT operations) would consistently fail to receive its fair share of PTE new bus deliveries.

Left **From 1928 Birmingham Corporation tramcars took over from BET subsidiary company cars on the Dudley Road (via Smethwick and Oldbury) route, thus bringing Birmingham cars into Dudley by a second route. This view of Smethwick High Street shows the junction with St Pauls Road, terminus of tram route 80 upon which Birmingham car 197 is loading for Birmingham in July 1938. No.192 approaches on service 85 which ran as far as Spon Lane, West Smethwick. Each tram route short working had a separate service number — both these could be regarded as 'shorts' of the 87 (Birmingham to Dudley).** W.A. Camwell

Centre Left **A fascinating 1940s scene in Carrs Lane, Birmingham, showing Corporation tramcar 444, trolleybus 48, tram 441 and trolleybus 35. This part of Carrs Lane has disappeared beneath Moor Street Queensway.** R.T. Wilson

Below Left **The tram services from Birmingham to Bearwood, Soho, and Dudley via Smethwick and Oldbury were replaced by motorbuses in October 1939. The various local authorities beyond the Birmingham boundary had purchased the tramways in their areas and, not being bus operators themselves, had agreed with Midland Red that its buses should replace the tramways on their behalves. The Dudley Road group of replacing bus services became jointly operated, although in practice they reverted to the pre-1928 pattern with Birmingham Corporation vehicles generally working the Bearwood and Soho journeys, and Company vehicles running to Dudley via Smethwick and Oldbury. In this late-fifties scene, BCT 1936 Daimler COG5 No. 814, fitted following war damage with an English Electric body intended for Manchester Corporation, works service B80 from the Birmingham boundary at Grove Lane. Midland Red BMMO D7 4421 follows it on service B87 from Dudley. The B prefix indicates a Midland Red Birmingham local service.** Robert F. Mack

This Birmingham City Transport Park Royal-bodied Leyland Titan PD2 was taken out of service on the last day before vesting in the PTE, 30th September 1969. Bus 2211 thus passed to the PTE as a withdrawn vehicle, leaving only 2229 of the type still operational. Most of these particular Leylands spent nearly all their long lives on the B-prefix Dudley Road services, nominally jointly operated with Midland Red. No.2211 is seen in Margaret Street on the B83 to Soho, in practice totally a BCT operation. M.R. Keeley

WEST BROMWICH CORPORATION

The West Bromwich Corporation Act of 1900 gave the Corporation powers to operate tramcars but this right was never exercised. The tramways within the borough instead were purchased by West Bromwich Corporation in 1902, electrified, and then leased back to the South Staffordshire Tramways and the Birmingham & Midland Tramways. The SST lease expired in 1924 and an agreement reached with Birmingham Corporation Tramways for their tramcars to work the mileage in lieu.

The West Bromwich Corporation Act of 1913 gave powers to operate trolley vehicles (again not taken up) and motorbuses. The first Corporation buses were four Albions which provided two services for less than seven weeks when the chassis were commandeered in October 1914 for war work! The bodies were retained, however, and reappeared in 1915 on Edison battery-electric chassis.

The Corporation's first joint route was to Walsall, operated from 1926 by the motorbuses of both towns. Subsequent joint operations included to Aldridge and Streetly with Walsall Corporation; to Wolverhampton with the transport department of that town; and a group of services into Smethwick jointly worked with Midland Red.

The Spon Lane and Bromford Lane tramways, for so long the preserve of BMT tramways, were replaced by West Bromwich motorbuses in November 1929. The April 1939 replacement of the tramways from Birmingham, through the borough to Wednesbury and Dudley, by the buses of Birmingham and West Bromwich Corporations, completed the situation that a third of the annual mileage of West Bromwich was outside the borough boundaries into eleven other local authority areas.

By the 1960s the Oak Lane garage, in addition to well over 100 buses, was responsible for the borough's lorries, vans, cars, ambulances and refuse collection vehicles, a total vehicle stock of over 200. This efficient arrangement had to end with the coming of the PTE. The Corporation's buses are remembered for their complex and beautiful livery of two shades of blue, relieved by cream, lined out in black and gold and accompanied by shaded lettering. A new livery of a bland off-white, relieved only by a somewhat insipid blue, was applied to the first rear-engined double deckers (Daimler Fleetlines) which were of special low-height construction to negotiate a bridge on a busy route. This livery was later applied also to underfloor engined single deckers. The attractive traditional livery survived, however, on the front-engined double deckers right up to the time of the PTE takeover. Cheap fares were also a memorable feature of West Bromwich buses and a special scale had to be maintained in the borough for some years after the creation of the PTE.

An early post-war scene in West Bromwich with Corporation wartime Duple 'austerity' bodied Daimler CWA6 No. 119. Behind, Walsall's then new Guy Arab III/Park Royal 5 (MDH 303) prepares to return to its home town on the joint service. Roy Marshall

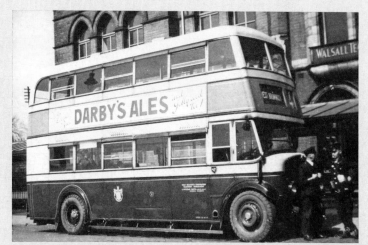

The West Bromwich-Walsall route, commenced in 1926, was the first joint operation for the municipal operators in those towns. West Bromwich 1934 Dennis Lance II/Metro-Cammell No.50 loads in Bradford Place, Walsall, in the 1930s. R.T. Wilson

The largest single batch of West Bromwich buses comprised the 31 Metro-Cammell bodied Daimler COG6 double deckers received for the 1939 tram conversion. Four more similar COG6s were delivered the following year, including No.104 seen on the joint Birmingham-West Bromwich-Dudley 74 service. Roy Marshall

WALSALL CORPORATION

Walsall Corporation purchased the tramways, all operated by South Staffordshire Tramways, within its borough with effect from 1st January 1901. These tramways were already electrified, the earliest conversion in 1893 being only the second overhead-wire installation in the country. Preparations to take over the running of the tramways, including extensions, were made over the next three years and, on 1st January 1904, twenty-eight municipal tramcars marked the entry of Walsall as a public transport operator in its own right.

The Walsall Corporation Act of 1914 gave powers to operate motorbuses, including specified routes outside the borough boundaries. The first service, from Bloxwich to Cannock and Hednesford, eventually got going in May 1915. Dennis H vehicles were employed on the first tramway conversion in 1928, replacing the tramcars to Walsall Wood, the service being joined with the existing motorbus service from Walsall Wood to Brownhills at the same time.

Further tramway conversions followed including, in 1929, the service to Willenhall. The Corporations of Wolverhampton and Walsall, meeting at Willenhall, had wished to operate a through service for some time, and this was permitted by the conversion to motorbuses. Wolverhampton, however, was already running single-deck trolleybuses to Willenhall, while Walsall introduced its first trolleybuses in 1931 to Willenhall. Through trolleybus operation was not immediately possible due to a low bridge in Wolverhampton preventing the use of double deckers. The offending bridge was soon dealt with, however, and one of the few joint operations of trolleybuses in Britain began.

The last company tramways in the Black Country, the South Staffs cars operating in the Walsall – Pleck – Wednesbury – Darlaston – Pleck – Walsall 'triangle', were temporarily superseded by Walsall tramcars from 1st October 1930, prior to replacement by Walsall buses in March 1931. The last Walsall tramcars, to Bloxwich, were replaced on 1st October 1933, the decision to use trolleybuses being eased by the existence of wiring along much of the route for the Wolverhampton service trolleybuses to reach Birchills depot.

A half-dozen rural routes of A. P. Sanders, Chasetown, were acquired in July 1936. This keen interest in serving areas outside the town's boundaries was a notable feature of Walsall's operations which, in some respects, resembled those of a company rather than a municipal undertaking.

The joint motorbus service with West Bromwich to that town was followed post-war by more joint services, including from Bloxwich to Wolverhampton with that town's undertaking. Most interesting, however, was a joint service between Dudley and Walsall, worked with Midland Red, which was extended in 1949 to Stafford. This was inherited by WMPTE but the Stafford participation ceased as part of the 1973 deal with Midland Red (q.v.).

One of the best-known transport managers, Mr R. Edgley Cox, was appointed to Walsall in 1952. Mr Edgley Cox favoured the retention of trolleybuses in Walsall and, in 1955, replaced motorbuses on the busy Blakenall service. The increase in the trolleybus fleet was met by a fleet of new Sunbeams which, being thirty feet long on only two axles, had to have special

dispensation. Their successful operation no doubt encouraged the increase in length to thirty feet for two-axle double deckers, permitted nationally from the following year.

Wolverhampton Corporation decided to replace all its trolleybuses with motorbuses; this and the promise of major dislocation caused by motorway construction, led to the conversion of the joint Walsall – Wolverhampton service in 1965. No other conversions took place before the entry into West Midlands PTE in 1969; the new organisation thus becoming the only PTE to operate trolleybuses in service.

WMPTE acquired from Walsall a highly idiosyncratic fleet of buses and trolleybuses, each painted in the distinctive mid-blue livery, relieved by thin yellow lining, favoured in latter years.

All Walsall's half-cab Guys were withdrawn from passenger service before the takeover, but 143 (MDH310) survived as a trainer. The bus, built in 1948, gave the PTE around a year's service in this capacity. The Park Royal bodywork makes an interesting comparison with the preceding Birmingham bus; the quality of finish is markedly higher on 2211. M.R. Keeley

The Northern Coachbuilders body of this 1950 former Grimsby-Cleethorpes BUT9611T was lengthened by Walsall to 30 feet and converted to forward entrance, one of a number of similar rebuilds of different models. Three of the four Grimsby-Cleethorpes BUTs were rebuilt in this way and the whole quartet came with the undertaking to WMPTE Maurice Collignon

WOLVERHAMPTON CORPORATION

Horse trams, which first appeared in the town in 1878, were brought under municipal control in 1900. The Corporation chose to electrify these by the unusual Lorain surface-contact system rather than overhead wire. Disadvantages with the Lorain system, and the fact that it was worn out before the tracks and cars, caused the Corporation to convert the tramways to overhead wire in 1921.

A batch of Tilling-Stevens single-deck trolleybuses was introduced in 1923 to replace the single-deck tramcars on the Wednesfield route. The Corporation became an enthusiastic user of trolleybuses and by 1928 had not only replaced its own tramways, but also purchased company lines for immediate trolleybus substitution.

Motorbus services were also developing in an interesting fashion, the Corporation adopting a number of relatively long routes in the 1920s. Many were taken over from Midland Red with whom an agreement was reached in 1920, whilst a Bridgnorth service came from the Great Western Railway in 1923.

Wolverhampton was the home of the much respected vehicle manufacturer, Guy Motors. Guy buses and trolleybuses began to be included in Corporation orders from 1925. The expansion of the trolleybus fleet continued in the early 1930s when the electric vehicles replaced motorbuses on some routes.

Guy was chosen by the Ministry of Supply to build buses during the war, and its products entered many fleets including that of its home town. It is worth noting that, for a time during the war, the country's entire production of full-size buses was concentrated in Wolverhampton. Not only were Guy buses, Karrier and Sunbeam trolleybuses built in Wolverhampton but so were the buses of Daimler, bombed out of its Coventry factory.

The first conversion to motorbuses took place in January 1961 when the Oxbarn Avenue trolleybuses were replaced with the

assistance of loaned Birmingham City Transport Daimlers. The conversion programme began in earnest in June 1963 and history repeated itself in October 1964 when Birmingham Daimlers were again loaned (and subsequently purchased) for a premature conversion caused by a railway bridge rebuilding. The last Wolverhampton trolleybuses ran in March 1967 when the long route to Dudley was converted.

The Corporation handed to the PTE four garages (Cleveland Road and the adjacent Bilston Street premises, Park Lane and Bilston) and around 300 buses. Over 200 of these were modern Guy Arab double deckers, purchased largely for the trolleybus conver-

sions, and new saloons. The remainder, however, were elderly double deckers retained beyond their expected lives whilst the trolleybuses were scrapped. The post-1957 double deckers and the new saloons were painted in a livery of green with a solitary yellow band. The remaining stock included a greater amount of yellow in their livery and, as a result, looked much more cheerful. The fleet plied an interesting network including jointly-operated routes with Walsall and West Bromwich Corporations. There were also the long routes, extending well outside the borough, to such places as Albrighton, Brewood, Bridgnorth, Cannock, Dudley and Wombourn.

Above **Early evening in St James Square, Wolverhampton, in October 1965. Corporation trolleybus 449, a 1948 Sunbeam W rebodied by Roe in 1961, is about to commence a Willenhall short working of the joint service 29 to Walsall. An ex-Hastings Sunbeam/ Weymann of Walsall Corporation waits behind to return to its home town. St James Square has been obliterated by redevelopment and the ring road scheme.**
Maurice Collignon

Left **A fleet of Birmingham City Transport 1949 Daimler CVD6 motorbuses loaned to Wolverhampton from 1964 was subsequently purchased by the latter undertaking. No.2023 passes Wolverhampton's Bilston depot in Mount Pleasant. The stonework on the nearest building is inscribed Midland Electric Power Co. Ltd whilst the depot carries the initials WDET, for Wolverhampton District Electric Tramways.**
W.A. Camwell

COVENTRY CORPORATION TRANSPORT

Municipal passenger transport in Coventry began in January 1912 when the Corporation purchased the Coventry Electric Tramways Co. Powers were soon obtained to operate motorbuses. Tramways remained a part of the Coventry scene until November 1940 when the city was devastated by enemy bombers, rendering the system unworkable.

One of the passenger transport industry's most respected General Managers was appointed to Coventry in 1933. He was Mr R. A. Fearnley who soon laid his distinctive stamp on the fleet. Lettering and numerals were brought up-to-date and standardisation began on locally-built Daimlers with preselective gearboxes. Mr Fearnley retired in 1962 and, shortly afterwards, the undertaking switched to rear-engined buses. The first batch were Leyland Atlanteans, causing a furore in Coventry; subsequent double deckers were all Daimler Fleetlines. Over a hundred front-engined Daimlers, representing around a third of the fleet, still survived upon the absorption of Coventry Corporation Transport into WMPTE on 1st April 1974.

Most of the vehicles passed to the Executive wore a bright, rich red and ivory livery although a few survived in earlier colours of maroon and off-white, superseded in 1970.

Above **Wartime losses in Coventry brought many non-standard Guy Arabs into its fleet as replacements. This 1943 example is one of four received by Coventry with MCW group bodies originally intended for Manchester Corporation.** Guy Motors

A considerable proportion of Coventry's operations were works services. Awaiting such duties are these Daimlers at Pool Meadow in 1959. CVA6/Metro-Cammell No.32 of 1948 is flanked by two wartime CWA6 models; 373 with 1951 Roe bodywork and 356 with rebuilt Northern Counties 'austerity' bodywork. T.W. Moore

The National Picture in the Fifties & Sixties

Bus usage had reached its peak at the beginning of the nineteen-fifties. The public, released from years of war, was hungry for travel yet unable to afford motor cars which, in any case, were difficult to obtain and restricted by petrol rationing. Bus operators struggled to secure sufficient vehicles to meet the demand and still replace worn-out stock. Staff recruitment was a worry too. However, despite such problems, these were golden years for the bus industry and few could have foreseen that the situation was soon to change.

The country continued to recover from the setbacks of war as the decade progressed but, as the population became affluent, public transport entered a period of decline. People now stayed at home to watch television and the cinema industry went into an almost fatal decline. With the loss of the cinemas went the public transport journeys to and from those establishments, alleviated only slightly by the conversion of some of them into bingo halls. But the real curse was the private car, now no longer restricted by petrol rationing and becoming within the financial means of an increasing number of families. The private car was taking more and more passengers from public transport at all times of the day. It was not often possible to react by trimming facilities, itself a primary discouragement, so the operator was forced to increase fares to counteract the reduced usage and inflation (although the latter was negligible compared to the high-inflation of the 1970s). Other forces were also at work, such as reduced reliability due to staff shortages, and these factors combined to discourage more and more passengers, who turned to private transport.

It took to the end of the decade before planners realised that the motor car threatened to strangle our cities. Their initial answer was to construct super-highways which severed communities and dehumanised city centres. Public transport received no support from the planners; indeed, at one time, it seemed that the nearest Birmingham buses would get to the city centre was a circuit of the Inner Ring Road, then under construction. More years of decline were to pass before the value and necessity of public transport was to be considered.

The Buchanan study of 1961 indicated that, in all but the smallest towns, public transport was going to continue to be an essential feature. However, social habits, land use and employment patterns were all changing, often to the detriment of public transport. Moreover, even though the railways were the most efficient movers of large numbers of people, that method of travel was reeling under the effects of the Beeching axe, having shown difficulty in competing with either bus or car. Land-use/transportation studies became the order of the day.

The West Midlands Transport Study was set up in 1963, under the sponsorship of local authorities in the West Midlands conurbation and the Ministers of Transport and of Housing and Local Government. Its terms of reference were broadly to survey all forms of transport in the conurbation, to analyse the relationship of transport to land use and produce forecasts giving guidance on the desirable pattern of highway and public transport development. The need for a radical new approach to public transport was all too obvious. Indeed, the evidence of social decay in the United States, following the decline of public transport and de-humanisation of city centres, was beginning to cross the Atlantic. The new approach was thought to be the integration of all bus and rail services within a conurbation to make the maximum use of available assets and create an efficient and acceptable public transport system. However, the confines of local government boundaries effectively prevented the creation of large transport authorities capable of the investment necessary if new techniques were to be employed. It was extremely unlikely that the existing authorities would accept unification voluntarily so a solution imposed by central government had to be devised.

A Government White Paper, published in July 1966, set out major ideas for the organisation, management and financing of transport. The major new proposal for conurbations was the establishment of Conurbation Transport Authorities (CTAs). These were to plan all transportation, including highways, traffic management and car parking, and operate and market all public transport, embracing local municipal bus services, company bus services and local rail services. However, subsequent discussions led to the publication of revised thinking in a further White Paper which reduced the CTA concept to that of Passenger Transport Authorities (PTAs). The new authorities lacked the wider transportation powers proposed, responsibility only extending to public transport planning, operation and marketing. Municipal buses would be vested in the new authorities but company buses, which depended on urban routes to cross-subsidise weak rural services, were protected. The PTAs were required to make agreements with company bus undertakings, unlike the automatic takeover under the CTA concept. This, however, left difficult problems of integration unresolved.

It was decided at Government level that, in the first instance, Passenger Transport Authorities would be set up in four major conurbations, namely: the West Midlands, Greater Manchester, Merseyside and Tyneside.

In April 1968, the Ministry of Transport circulated to all county and district councils in the areas concerned a list of the local authorities whose inclusion in a PTA might be advantageous. The list for each area was divided into two parts. List A comprised those areas where inclusion was considered favourable and it was not unreasonable to assume that they would definitely become part of the PTA area. List B comprised fringe areas where there were considerable movements into the conurbation but not enough to support a definite case for inclusion. The purpose of this exercise was to give the authorities concerned the opportunity to air their views on the desirability or otherwise of inclusion. It was evident that there was much more flexibility regarding those authorities in list B. Informal discussions were followed by a set of proposals and formal consultations between the Minister and the local authorities. For those familiar with the later West Midlands PTE area, it is interesting to note that Coventry did not feature in either list A or B.

The Transport Act, 1968, received the Royal Assent on October 29th of that year. This far-reaching Act was to change the face of the whole transport industry, whether inside or outside a PTA area. However, of principal concern here, the Minister of Transport could now set up the four Passenger Transport Authorities.

The main criterion for settling which areas should be included in the PTA was the 'travel to work' data provided by the 1966 Census. Those areas with a substantial volume of workers travelling into the conurbation were included. Where differences of opinion arose over inclusion, the Minister in most cases excluded the area concerned as it would be easier to extend subsequently a PTA area rather than contract it.

In early consultations it was suggested that two PTAs should be set up in the West Midlands, one based on Birmingham and Solihull and the other on Dudley, Walsall, Warley, West Bromwich and Wolverhampton (basically the Black Country). Whilst it was true that Birmingham/Solihull and the Black Country were, to a major extent, quite separate even in custom and culture, there was still a significant movement of traffic between the two areas. Thus the Minister was unable to accept the suggestions, unfortunately for the bus enthusiast, stating that it would be a negation of proper transport planning to draw a boundary across this heavy volume of traffic.

It was decided that various outlying towns and dormitory areas were largely self-contained so far as passenger transport was concerned. A notable inclusion within the PTA area, however, was Redditch, where an intake of 33,000 people was expected by the mid-seventies. These would largely come from Birmingham and it was anticipated that they would continue to look towards the conurbation.

Facing Page Top **Midland Red feels the threat in September 1967 and advertises the fact on the side of 1962 BMMO D9 5003, parked opposite Sheepcote Street garage. The garage, but not this bus, passed to the PTE in December 1973.** Maurice Collignon

THE PTA AND PTE ARE FORMED

The Minister made the Orders designating the four passenger transport areas at the beginning of 1969. The role of the Passenger Transport Authorities, to be set up on 1st April 1969, was clear. The PTA was to consist of elected representatives from the local authorities in the designated areas. The Transport Act, 1968, required them to promote and create a properly integrated and efficient system of public transport in and around the conurbation. This was to be achieved through a team of professional transport men, known as the Passenger Transport Executive, who would carry out the policies and decisions of the Authority.

The Minister was concerned that the Executive should be appointed as quickly as possible to minimise uncertainties, particularly within the municipal bus undertakings to be

absorbed, about what would happen when the Authority and Executive assumed full control. In the West Midlands, the municipal bus undertakings to be vested in the new body were those of Birmingham, Walsall, West Bromwich and Wolverhampton.

The first Chairman of the West Midlands Passenger Transport Authority was Alderman Francis Griffin, leader of the Conservatives then controlling Birmingham City Council. He said, in an April 1969 interview, that Birmingham would not adopt a 'Big Brother' attitude over the other local authorities. He hoped for co-operation from local authorities in the provision of bus lanes but did not anticipate any restrictions on the use of private cars. The members of the PTA were generally convinced that transport should be able to support itself financially and would avoid charging its losses to the rates. He consi-

dered railways, however, to be the only effective answer to the mass movement of people and that a decision would have to be made whether rail services would be subsidised by the local community when the central Government subsidy was transferred to the PTA in due course. The alternative was to spend 'untold millions of pounds on a fantastic system of road construction'. Regarding co-operation with Midland Red, Alderman Griffin said that discussions were necessary but he believed that an element of competition was always to the advantage of the public – a curious statement in view of the integration brief.

The Director General of the Passenger Transport Executive was appointed early in 1969, he was Mr F. J. Lloyd, formerly Chief Commercial and Planning Officer of the London Transport Board. The appointment of the rest of the Executive team was, of course, one of the first preoccupations. The Executive, in fact, took up its duties on 2nd September 1969.

The livery for the buses of the new undertaking was announced on 3rd September. The basic layout would be that of Birmingham City Transport, the largest contributor, with cream upperworks and blue lower panels. However, the latter would be a somewhat lighter blue, a British Standard colour, compared to the near black favoured by BCT. It seemed likely that the hardwearing BCT khaki roof would be adopted too. New buses would be delivered in the new colours but obviously it would take time to repaint existing stock. More urgent, it was stated, would be the removal of existing names and coats of arms, to be replaced by PTE insignia.

Meanwhile, a competition was being held for the new emblem, with a 20-guinea (vintage currency, this!) first prize, eventually won by Miss Christine Vaughan of Solihull Technical College. The new emblem, chosen from 44 entries, was unveiled on 22nd September but evidently had not met with the full approval of the PTA. One Alderman suggested more time to make a choice, considering 'a ten-second inspection from a distance' inadequate. He added that 'with the arrows pointing in two different directions we might find ourselves split asunder'. Another councillor also objected to the arrows exclaiming 'one of them could be pointing to Hell or somewhere else'. An urgent decision was required, however, as new buses were on the way. Thus Miss Vaughan's creation, only slightly modified, was adopted in lieu of the former municipal coats of arms and survives to the present day.

Thus all was ready for 1st October 1969 when the vehicles of the four municipalities would be transferred.

Boldly venturing outside the confines of Birmingham, fairly new Corporation two-door Daimler Fleetline/Park Royal 3817 on driver tuition duties passes the Oldbury garage of Midland Red on the Wolverhampton Road in August 1969. M.R. Keeley

The Early Months of the PTE

The staff and vehicles of the four municipal bus undertakings were transferred to the PTE on 1st October 1969. That is the date the old bus undertakings ceased to exist and the PTE era began. The West Midlands was, in fact, the first PTE to come into operation, the other three following at monthly intervals.

The new organisation was responsible for public transport in an area of approximately 450 square miles, from Cannock in the north to Redditch in the south, from Stourbridge in the west to Meriden in the east. It involved a population of about 2.75 million and all or parts of twenty local authority areas.

Birmingham generated strong corridor flows from its suburbs although, of course, other flows existed between suburbs and elsewhere which were not so easily catered for by public transport. In the Black Country, the predominant flows were within or between the towns in the area, with smaller flows to and from Birmingham. The strong identification of the area with the motor industry, and its high wage levels, implied comparatively modest use of public transport. In fact, no conurbation in Britain had so high a proportion of car commuters as the West Midlands. The 1966 Census Workplace Transport tables claimed the car took 59% of work journeys, compared to 25% bus, 5% rail, and 11% by other means. The West Midlands Transport Study had given the rail share as only 2%. Obviously, these proportions would vary in different parts of the PTA area and depended to an extent on the quality of public transport from homes to the workplaces. The centres of the four cities or towns whose buses had been absorbed were, of course, linked to the suburbs within their boroughs so, for example, bus was able to achieve 51% of work journeys made entirely within the Birmingham boundary.

THE MUNICIPAL LEGACY

The new organisation inherited around 8,500 employees and around 2,100 buses, including 47 Walsall trolleybuses. Fleet numbers of the acquired buses, not surprisingly, overlapped and this source of possible confusion had to be eliminated. The fleet numbers of the ex-Birmingham buses remained unaltered whilst a simple approach was adopted for the remainder. The last letter of the contributing town was added to the fleet number, eg West Bromwich 247 became 247H, Walsall 401 became 401L, and Wolverhampton 72 became 72N. The general manager of Birmingham City Transport, Mr W. G.-Copestake, became Director of Operations in the new PTE. Mr R. H. Addlesee, general manager of Wolverhampton Corporation Transport, became Director of Labour and Staff Relations. The remaining director was responsible for Finance, and was originally Mr J. M. Hill,

formerly management accountant, Eastern Region of British Railways. Mr R. Edgley Cox, the general manager of Walsall Corporation Transport, became Chief Engineer of the PTE, appropriate in view of his innovative capabilities. Mr S. Jobling, general manager of West Bromwich Corporation Transport, became Operations Manager of the North Division but soon became Chief Planning Officer. His counterpart in the South Division was Mr C. Nurse, deputy general manager of Birmingham City Transport. The South Division corresponded to the former Birmingham City Transport area, whilst the North Division amalgamated the three other areas and became based on Walsall.

PROBLEMS OF INTEGRATION

The four municipal undertakings had few points of contact, most of the intermediate territory and the connecting services being in the hands of Midland Red. The latter also provided all or most of the services in certain of the other towns, including Dudley, Stourbridge, Solihull, Sutton Coldfield and Redditch. All of the municipal bus undertakings had made operating agreements with Midland Red and this obviously restricted service development and integration. At worst this meant that PTE buses terminated at municipal boundaries, once amongst green fields, but now overtaken by housing development way beyond those boundaries. The latter would be served by Midland Red, probably involving a protective fare arrangement within the municipal boundary to discourage local riders from overcrowding long distance passengers. Thus Midland Red services overlapped those of the PTE and, of course, passengers for 'town' would see partly empty 'Red' buses sweep past them. Integration was thus

desirable, although in practice the system worked quite well as the Midland Red with less stops, was able to make better time in and out of 'town' and was regarded as an express facility. It was clear, nevertheless, that the PTE could not function properly without control of the Midland Red services in its area and discussions with the NBC subsidiary would have to be an early priority. Midland Red, however, had to bear in mind that its ability to serve rural areas depended on its paying routes, many of which fell into the PTE area.

The other major problem in providing an integrated network was the role of the local railway services. These were eligible for grant aid which was to be transferred from central Government to the PTE, on a tapered scale, over a seven-year period. The PTE was eventually to bear the whole cost of these services not met by receipts within its area and then share with the Ministry the cost of commuter routes extending up to 25 miles outside the PTE boundaries. The ability of the railways to carry large numbers of people, and thus reduce traffic congestion, was undeniable but this potential was not indicated by then current usage. It was possible that certain lines would lose passenger facilities, the alternative being to pass on to the ratepayers the cost of the subsidies. The attitude of ratepayers who were not geographically well placed to take advantage of the trains they were subsidising could easily be imagined. However, as the PTE was 'paying the piper', it could also call the tune and decide the train frequency and fare structure. Therefore, a further available alternative was to realise that potential by developing rail services and modifying bus services as appropriate. The population of the West Midlands was notoriously non-train minded and few in 1969 would have predicted the rail revival that resulted from the discussions about to begin between the PTE and BR.

Turning to the human side, negotiations had to commence immediately on the standardisation of staff conditions and pay scales. Each undertaking had various conditions not enjoyed by the others and naturally these would not be surrendered easily. It was to be expected that staff would demand the best of all four worlds and this could have had an adverse effect on the operating costs of the PTE. In some instances it became desirable to maintain 'local' agreements for the time being.

A loan which spanned the transition to WMPTE was the fleet of Birmingham 1950 Leyland PS2 Tigers operated by Potteries Motor Traction in 1969-70. No.2234 is seen in June 1969; these buses were rather older than the PMT single deckers they were required to relieve. Maurice Collignon

BUS FLEET DEVELOPMENTS

The various municipal operators all had buses on order at the time of takeover. Birmingham City Transport was expecting 100 Daimler Fleetlines with Park Royal bodies to a new length of 33 feet. Wolverhampton also had Park Royal-bodied Fleetlines on order, which would have become the Corporation's first rear-engined double deckers. The specification of this batch of 25 was altered to become identical with the Birmingham hundred and delivery was to follow on. West Bromwich also had 33-feet long Fleetlines on order, seven in number but the bodies were to be by Northern Counties, a builder new to them. Walsall had long favoured Northern Counties-bodied Fleetlines but to an eccentric, short length of 28 feet 6 inches. Fifteen more Fleetline/Northern Counties were on order but these were to arrive to a more orthodox length of 30 feet. All these buses were to be of the front-entrance, centre-exit layout, then very popular. West Bromwich also had an option on a further seven Fleetlines.

New buses carried their first passengers on the very first day. They were 33-feet long Park Royal-bodied Daimler Fleetlines, intended for Birmingham City Transport. Fleet numbers followed on from the last BCT deliveries, indeed 3881–95 were in BCT colours and 3881–2 actually carried Birmingham coats-of-arms. However, the West Midlands Passenger Transport Executive legal lettering in cream, in place of the dignified gold leaf of BCT, was just one sign of the new regime. Even more obvious, however, were 3896 onwards which were delivered in the new PTE blue. The brighter shade contrasted with the sombre dark blue favoured by BCT and naturally caused comment. Some thought the new shade much too garish whilst others considered the dark blue overdue for replacement, the lighter shade being more eyecatching in an era when buses needed to draw attention to themselves. BCT blue certainly tended to look very dull when the shine wore off, although the operator enjoyed a high reputation for vehicle appearance. The substitution of lighter blue on 3896 onwards revealed a barely detectable subtlety in the BCT livery. This was the black line separating the blue and the cream below the lower saloon windows. The two thin lines between decks were also black, not dark blue as many thought. This became obvious when the lighter shade was applied and the buses looked very attractive with the black lining complementing the blue. Unfortunately, this extravagance did not find favour with the new brooms and 3935 onwards appeared in a much simpler livery of blue lower panels and the remainder of the vehicle cream, except for the khaki roof. The only black lining retained was that between the cream and the khaki.

3881–903 were put into service from Yardley Wood garage for service 18, whilst 3904 onwards were allocated to Selly Oak for the Bristol Road services. The Bristol Road group had been the first major radial Birmingham services to be converted to one-man operation, the changeover having taken place on Sunday 20th July 1969, the day man first landed on the moon although the two events were not connected. The former had been achieved using most of the previous batch of two-door Fleetlines, built to the shorter length of 30 feet. The intention had been to use the new 33-footers on the Inner Circle 8 service but, being the first delivered to the bus grant

New Fleetline/Park Royal 3899, in BCT style livery including black lining-out but with the PTE shade of blue, enters Colmore Row, Birmingham, in October 1969 prior to the application of PTE fleetnames.
Maurice Collignon

standards, they were not only longer and wider but also higher than existing stock. A trial run with one of the new buses revealed very little clearance under Icknield Street bridge and thus their regular operation on the Inner Circle was ruled out. It was decided to send the 'Jumbos', as the new giants quickly became known, to Selly Oak displacing their existing 38xx two-door buses onto the Inner Circle. This meant that Selly Oak's double-deck fleet was virtually restocked for the third year running as the 38xx one-manners had replaced double-crew single-door 37xx Fleetlines, acquired when the Bristol Road services were converted to large capacity buses, mostly with new stock, early in 1968.

Accordingly, 3904–66 were all delivered to Selly Oak by January 1970, displacing 3813–61 to Hockley and Liverpool Street to convert the Inner Circle to large capacity buses, and 3862–78 to other Birmingham garages for one-man services. However, the 38xxs were destined to have an even shorter career on the Inner Circle than on the Bristol Road.

The arrival of the first two-door buses, 3781–3880, to Birmingham City Transport had been fraught with problems of passengers attempting to board by the centre door over which the driver had only limited visibility. The centre door had been added as a means of speeding loading and unloading. Signs stressing which door was the entrance and which was the exit were added to ease the problem. However, within months an elderly lady, attempting to board by the centre exit and trapped by the closing doors, had been killed as the bus moved away. The buses were soon declared unsafe and a series of modifications was put in hand. Principal amongst these was the introduction of a time-lag device which meant that a gear could not be engaged until some seconds after the closure of the centre doors.

The Inner Circle is one of the busiest Birmingham services with large numbers of short distance riders. It was to be expected that the extra door would be a boon under such circumstances. However, it immediately became clear that the reverse was applying, the time-lag device on the centre exit increasing significantly the time spent at stops. Thus the Executive soon came to the conclusion that single-entrance buses were more suitable and this was not forgotten when the specification for future buses was drawn up; the PTE being just one of many operators to become similarly disenchanted with two-door buses.

More immediate, however, was the problem of the Inner Circle. The South Division of the PTE quickly looked for a suitable home for the centre-exit buses and, in January 1970, fifty of them (3807–56) at Perry Barr, Hockley and Liverpool Street were exchanged for 3681–3730, these fifty being the entire allocation of Cotteridge garage. The two-door buses thus became a familiar sight on the Pershore Road services (41, 45, 47) and were worked with conductors until those routes were converted to one-man operation in September 1972. The Inner Circle was, in the meantime, operated by 3687–730 (3681–6 had gone to Perry Barr in exchange for 3807–12) until displaced by KOV-registered Fleetlines in June 1971. The KOV buses, although more elderly, had been one-man equipped and enabled the service to be converted the next month.

WM EMBLEM APPEARS

To revert to 1969, all of the earliest new deliveries lacked a PTE fleetname, although they carried PTE legal lettering. However, on the 17th October, No. 3916 was shown to the PTA and the media carrying the new emblem. The bus was displayed outside the Council House, Birmingham, but to those enthusiasts present the event was enlivened by the coincidental passing alongside of 2229, Birmingham City Transport's sole surviving operational Leyland Titan PD2, on training duties.

The emblem on 3916 was not a transfer directly applied to the sides of the vehicle, such transfers not appearing for several months. Instead, the emblem was on a rectangle of self-adhesive plastic, the background colour approximating to the PTE blue. Huge quantities of these stickers were ordered, with a variety of background colours, for application to existing stock over the next few weeks. In many cases the new fleetname was applied over the old coats-of-arms but where the positions did not coincide, the old insignia was painted out. In some cases the painting-out procedure was adopted anyway, prior to the application of the sticker, particularly at Wolverhampton. Notable vehicles which did not receive PTE fleetnames were the Walsall trolleybuses, which merely had their municipal insignia painted out, except for 345 and 856 which remarkably retained their coats-of-arms and fleetnames. Interesting buses to receive the new fleetnames were six ex-Birmingham City Transport Leyland Tiger PS2s, 2249/52/6–9, which had been on loan to Potteries Motor Traction since August 1969 and operated for them until June 1970. A seventh Tiger, 2247, joined them between February and May 1970.

Two-door Fleetline/Park Royal 3860 passes beneath the bridge in Icknield Street, Hockley, that prevented the 'Jumbos' from working the Inner Circle. The two-door buses did not stay long, however, and a substituting single-door Fleetline passes by in the opposite direction in January 1970. The old Hockley railway station deteriorates above the bridge. M.R. Keeley

Ex-Birmingham City Transport 1964 Fleetline/Park Royal 3423 at Five Ways on 19th October 1969, repainted in BCT blue but without black lining except between the cream and the khaki roof. This arrangement was standard for repainted BCT rear-engined buses for the first few months of the PTE. Alan D. Broughall

Fleetline 3947 was amongst those delivered to the PTE in the simplified scheme but in the new blue. The unbroken cream looks uninteresting. The 'Jumbo' Park Royal bodies provided trouble from the outset, 3947 was one of two which soon lost the front hopper ventilators in an attempt to stiffen the front dome, as shown in this October 1970 Navigation Street view — 3914 was the other. M.R. Keeley

FIRST REPAINTS

The first repaints of existing stock into PTE colours appeared fairly quickly. Early examples, of course, were treated at the acquired operators paintshops, each applying its own interpretation of the new livery and drawing from its existing stock of transfers except, of course, for the new fleetname and legal lettering.

The policy in Birmingham was very interesting. One existing Fleetline, 3629, was painted in October in new blue without bands, like 3935 onwards. Then all repaints of rear-engined buses until March 1970 were in BCT blue but without bands! BCT (now South Division) buses at this time received a full overhaul every five years with an intermediate repaint between. Rear-entrance buses, by and large, were not undergoing full overhauls but were receiving intermediate repaints in the form of repainted blue panels and attention to the cream, followed by a coat of varnish. This touch-up and varnish procedure was good enough to give the impression of a fully repainted vehicle. From the end of October 1969, starting with Daimler 3151, the blue was changed to the new shade and the livery simplified by the deletion of the black lining framing the cream-painted belt rail below the lower deck windows. Thus, by March 1970, there were considerable numbers of old-type buses in the new colours but virtually no Fleetlines, except for new stock! A further variation appeared on some of the few rear-entrance buses being fully overhauled. These were elderly Guy Arabs of 1950–1 vintage, originally to have been withdrawn and retained to cover an anticipated fleet shortage, particularly upon the demise of the Walsall trolleybuses. Seven treated in November and early December 1969, buses 2577/86/9, 2600/12–4, were repainted in the simplified livery but in BCT blue. Subsequent overhauls, from the end of December, received the new blue.

The oldest motorbuses acquired by the PTE were Brush-bodied Daimler CVG6 vehicles of Wolverhampton Corporation, some dating back to 1948. 515N, with deleted municipal coats-of-arms, unloads ladies visiting New Cross Hospital in December 1969. M.R. Keeley

FIRST INTER-DIVISIONAL TRANSFERS

Whilst the one-way trip to the breakers was staved off for most of the Guys, withdrawal of the next batch of Birmingham buses, CVD6 Daimlers 2626–2775, continued as the 'Jumbo' Fleetlines arrived. Ten of these Daimlers also gained a reprieve, however, by becoming the first buses to be transferred from one division to another. The Executive was a mere five weeks old when, on 4th November 1969, 2626/30/2/40/1/3–5/7/9 left Birmingham for new duties at Wolverhampton. No. 2645 was one of a number of Birmingham 'Standards' that had been fitted some years earlier with offside illuminated advertisement panels. It soon gained a display appropriate to its new Wolverhampton surroundings and thus began a short chain of suitably equipped Birmingham buses in the town to satisfy the contract, but 2645's reprieve was shortened by accident damage and it was replaced by 2762 in September 1970; No. 2762 was in turn replaced by Guy 3056 in July 1971. This invasion enabled a few of the most geriatric of the former Wolverhampton Corporation fleet to be retired – FJW registered Daimlers and Guys.

One further inter-divisional transfer took place in 1969 when Birmingham Leyland Tiger PS2 2260 was added to Walsall's allocation with effect from 1st December. Like its companions still on loan in the Potteries, 2260 was rather an anachronism, the old-fashioned half-cab layout not having been seen on single deckers in the town for many years.

Birmingham is the home of the well-known bus and railway rolling stock builder, Metro-Cammell Weymann. The bus side of the business had some experience of building integral vehicles, notably for Leyland, but was primarily known as a bodybuilder, particularly double deckers. MCW was alarmed by Leyland's near monopoly of chassis production in the markets where the bodybuilder was strong. The Leyland empire itself included three bodybuilders, Park Royal Vehicles, Charles H. Roe, and Eastern Coach Works, and had announced that a new integral single decker would be built at a new factory in Workington. MCW's defence to these threats to its future was to attack. It thus entered into an agreement with the Swedish vehicle builder, Scania-Vabis, the first fruit of which was an integral single decker built by MCW using Scania running units. The new vehicle was known as the Metro-Scania and a demonstration prototype, VWD 452H, was operated by the PTE between 19th December 1969 and 29th January 1970, returning later in the year. MCW was rewarded by an order for one such machine but the PTE was not very interested in single deckers now that one-man operated double deckers were permissible. Leyland made the same market misjudgement with the National single decker. MCW subsequently produced a double-deck Metro-Scania (the Metropolitan) but this too failed to impress the West Midlands PTE, which favoured Gardner engines, and it was not until the end of the decade that the Birmingham builder produced the formula to satisfy its local PTE.

1970

Ten Birmingham Daimler CVD6 buses had been transferred to Wolverhampton in November 1969; some of these appeared at Walsall after a sojourn at West Bromwich, and 2649 is on an ex-trolleybus route in the Bus Station; these particular Daimlers had replaced Birmingham's Coventry Road trolleybuses in 1951. M.R. Keeley

The year opened with the allocation of new 'Jumbos' 3967–79 to Acocks Green for service 36 (Stechford – Sparkbrook), displacing older Fleetlines. The ensuing switch-around of older buses following the arrival of 3881–3979 enabled the conversion of the Inner and Outer Circles (services 8 and 11) to large capacity buses at the beginning of March – the problems involving the re-equipping of the Inner Circle having been described already.

A total of thirty recently overhauled Guys were transferred as planned to the North Division in January and March 1970. These were 2564–80/2–4/6–93/5–6, the first seventeen being the entire stock of the model at Liverpool Street garage. Some were in BCT colours, being amongst the last to be overhauled before takeover, their places in the South Division being taken by the overhauling of 2597–8, 2601–2 and 2606–9, which had been scheduled for withdrawal. Similar buses 2599–600 and 2612–25 were also overhauled around this time, meaning that a total of 92 of this remarkable batch of 100 Guys had been treated in the past two years or so.

The thirty transferred Guys were intended for service at Walsall but in fact a few spent some time at Wolverhampton, joining some mechanically similar Arabs from the 'home' fleet, as well as the ex-Birmingham Daimlers. The Guys at Walsall enabled the first stage of the trolleybus replacement programme to take effect from 16th February. No reduction in trolleybus route mileage was made but a number of runnings were taken over by the Guys. The ex-Hastings and all but one of the ex-Ipswich trolleybuses were withdrawn at this stage. The Guys were fitted with a motley collection of destination blinds, some of them rumoured to have started life many years earlier in the long withdrawn ADH-registered trolleybuses, but a distinct improvement on the row of light bulbs exhibited by their blindless colleagues at Wolverhampton.

It rapidly became clear that standards of vehicle appearance at Walsall were not the same as Birmingham. The Guys soon collected scuffed and dented panelling, almost unheard of on Birmingham City Transport vehicles, whilst the white interior ceilings became grey with dirt sucked in through the open rear platform and not washed off. Birmingham enthusiasts wondered why Walsall had been blessed with newly overhauled buses when other vehicles could have been sent.

Bus 3980 should have completed Birmingham City Transport's last order for 100 Fleetlines. The original 3980, however, was destined for a more interesting career. Following a request from Daimler, it was not received and was exported instead to South Africa for service with Johannesburg Municipal Transport. Wolverhampton's order for 25 'Jumbo' Fleetlines became 3981 to 4004, plus a further bus numbered 3980. In due course the 125th bus, 4005, was supplied but was tacked onto the West Bromwich order for seven Fleetlines and arrived with a Northern Counties body.

Although ordered by Wolverhampton, 3980–4004 were identical to the Birmingham deliveries, including the BCT destination layout. They entered service in March and April 1970 and were allocated to Park Lane. Their presence at Wolverhampton was much needed and permitted the withdrawal of more FJW registered Guys and Daimlers. Some of the ex-Birmingham Daimlers moved on to the

Above **The initial stage of the trolleybus replacement, in February 1970, eliminated the ex-Hastings trolleybuses. These Sunbeams dated from 1947, and had Weymann bodies. No.306 exhibits the Walsall predilection for white window rubbers.** M.R. Keeley

Above Right **Also withdrawn in February 1970 was 874, the only one of four ex-Grimsby-Cleethorpes BUT trolleybuses not to have been rebuilt to 30-feet long front-entrance vehicles. The Northern Coachbuilders bodies on these 1950 vehicles bore a considerable resemblance to contemporary Eastern Coach Works products.** M.R. Keeley

Right **The bus originally intended to be 3980 seen in the maroon and cream livery of Johannesburg Municipal Transport, South Africa, in 1976.** Stewart J. Brown

Below **The finalised original livery of WMPTE modelled by new Fleetline 3983. The cream is now relieved by a thin blue band but the line separating the cream from the khaki roof has disappeared. No.3983, seen in Wolverhampton in October 1970, was delivered with Birmingham style fleet numbers.** T.W. Moore

ex-West Bromwich garage, Oak Lane, and in due course passed to Walsall. The ex-Birmingham Guys at Wolverhampton also arrived at Walsall in time for the final trolleybus conversion later in the year.

Some of the new Fleetlines at Wolverhampton carried a revised style of fleet number, much larger than the Birmingham size applied hitherto. The three undertakings forming the North Division had all favoured large fleet numbers. The new size appeared in March on some of the overhauled Guys mentioned earlier and also on Fleetline 3701. This was the first Birmingham Fleetline to be painted in the finalised livery of PTE blue and

cream with one blue band at between decks level, plus khaki roof. It will be recalled that until now all Birmingham Fleetlines, apart from one, had continued to be painted in BCT colours to a simplified style.

The fleet thus began to exhibit a commonality of management with a standardised livery and lettering style. One class of vehicles which caused problems, however, were the ex-Walsall Fleetlines. The majority of the panels on these vehicles were pre-coloured glass reinforced plastic to minimise the degree of repainting. It proved very difficult to disguise effectively these Walsall blue panels with cream paint, and several coats were needed.

Not surprisingly, progress in repainting the Walsall Fleetlines was slow.

The West Bromwich order for seven Fleetlines, now increased to eight following the despatch of the original 3980 to South Africa, arrived in the spring. The Northern Counties bodies were similar to the Park Royals in being of 33 feet length, incorporating two doors. They featured the West Bromwich/Walsall style destination layout, however, and also the unusual opening nearside windscreen arrangement favoured by West Bromwich. The eight vehicles were numbered 4005–12 and were all allocated to Oak Lane.

Outside the PTE, Midland Red had recently improved weekday reliability by instituting a Monday to Friday working week, with Saturday and Sunday work covered by voluntary overtime. Part-timers were to be taken on when sufficient volunteers could not be found. This method of improving reliability to protect the most valuable customers, the weekday commuters, was most significant. It became very popular with the Midland Red crews who were no longer compelled to work at weekends and this set them apart from their PTE colleagues. When the Midland Red Black Country services (and crews) passed to the PTE, this method of working became a major stumbling block in the ensuing integration of conditions.

Mr W. G. Copestake retired in June 1970, being the first of the former general managers to leave the service of the Executive.

Most of the bus orders placed by the former operators had now been delivered and only West Bromwich had agreed an option to purchase more. This further batch of seven buses would hardly meet the requirements of the whole Executive. The PTE had placed orders for 200 further Daimler Fleetlines, with the body contract equally split between Metro-

Above The finalised livery applied to West Bromwich 199H, a 1958 Metro-Cammell bodied Daimler CVG6, receiving a steam clean at Oak Lane. The fleet number transfers, however, are still West Bromwich style and in that undertaking's traditional locations. WMPTE Archive

Another repainted West Bromwich CVG6, a 1957 example with Willowbrook body, loads in the town centre in October 1970. This bus, 190H, was one of the first to receive PTE fleet number transfers. This style of bus stop plate was adopted by West Bromwich towards the end of its separate existence. T.W. Moore

Cammell and Park Royal. However, it had to wait in the queue for new vehicles and thus there was to be a hiatus in vehicle deliveries. In mid-summer South Division began a programme of overhauling and recertifying Daimler CVG6 buses in the 2776–96 range, which no doubt would have been withdrawn otherwise. They were not the only BCT 'Standards' to be receiving PTE livery at this time as South Division continued the Birmingham principle of applying an intermediate repaint approximately 2½ years after an overhaul.

Another bus repainted at this time was 3830, the first of its batch to be so treated. This was prior to it being exhibited in Frankfurt, West Germany, in July. Birmingham is twinned with Frankfurt.

A further development in July was the arrival of a mysterious Ford R226 demonstrator with Willowbrook 53-seat two-door body, HVW 798H. This carried PTE livery and fleet number 4028, causing some confusion with a similar vehicle observed elsewhere with the more logical registration TOC 28H. It transpired that both buses were the same vehicle, ordered by Wolverhampton Corporation but to a different mechanical specification. It therefore became a Ford demonstrator instead and worked for the PTE from Selly Oak garage until returning to Ford in February 1971.

The flared panels and ornate West Bromwich livery gave the 1952 Weymann-bodied CVG6 Daimlers a vintage appearance as seen on 175H in October 1970. None of these buses received WMPTE livery. M.R. Keeley

Above **Walsall added cream paint to the fronts of ex-Corporation Fleetlines fitted for one-man operation, as demonstrated by 107L in July 1970. The Walsall livery, of course, was on the way out and so the modification was quickly abandoned.** Maurice Collignon

Above Left **Northern Counties-bodied 'Jumbo' Fleetline 4006, ordered by West Bromwich, crosses Dartmouth Square in the centre of that town in October 1970.** M.R. Keeley

Left **The mysterious 4028, alias Ford demonstrator HVW 798H, in August 1970 picks its way through what appears to be a building site, actually the chaos caused by the construction of Suffolk Street Queensway, Birmingham.** Maurice Collignon

THE END OF WALSALL'S TROLLEYBUSES

Walsall's final order for 15 Daimler Fleetlines entered service between August and October 1970. Unlike previous batches of Walsall Fleetlines these were not special short jobs but built to a standard length of 30 feet. The Northern Counties bodies were to two-door specification but, again, were more orthodox than previous Walsall buses. Overall they resembled shorter editions of 4005–12 and carried fleet numbers 4013–27. Their arrival, coupled with the collection at Walsall of all thirty Guys transferred to the North Division, enabled the complete withdrawal of trolleybuses in October.

The Executive described the retention of the trolleybuses as uneconomic. It is interesting to ponder why this should be so as, only twelve months previously, they were a valuable part of the Walsall operations. Certainly there had not been any rumours that the former municipal undertaking was planning to replace the system. The general manager, Mr Edgley-Cox, had been a great supporter of the trolleybus and had kept the system up-to-date. The maintenance of the overhead was notably good, although the condition of the trolleybuses themselves was more questionable despite the youthfulness (by trolleybus standards) of many of them. It may be that Walsall would have snapped up some Bournemouth vehicles upon closure of that system, which would have solved the rolling stock problem for some years to come. However the long-term availability of trolleybus material seemed doubtful and the PTE no doubt considered that the difficulties of keeping a distinctly non-standard breed of under fifty vehicles not worth the effort amongst a fleet of two thousand.

The last day of normal trolleybus operation was Friday 2nd October 1970. As described earlier, some of the runnings, but not route mileage, had been operated by motorbuses since February. This feature, plus deleted workings due to staff shortage, meant that only three trolleybuses remained in service after the evening peak, although interworking amongst the services meant thorough coverage of the mileage.

Riders on that last night were treated, or perhaps subjected, to some spirited driving with the trolleybuses renowned acceleration and speed being amply demonstrated by at least one of the drivers, evidently determined to fetch down the doomed wiring himself! Enthusiasts were treated to Black Country vignettes such as the following exchange amongst scandal-mongering housewives returning from bingo –

"Ere, Oi con'ear evry werd you'm saying" said one.

"Not from tonight yo won't!" replied another amidst laughter, highlighting the silent servant's finest feature.

Top **1951 Brush-bodied Sunbeam F4 340 survived in remarkably original condition to the end. There were originally ten of these trolleybuses and it is unfortunate that the one to be secured for preservation, 342, had been extensively rebuilt.** M.R. Keeley

Left **The trolleybus abandonment brought an end to this kind of embarrassment. The driver of de-wired 1954 Sunbeam/Willowbrook 'Goldfish Bowl' 853 goes fishing to return his steed to the power supply at the Bus Station in February 1970.** M.R. Keeley

New Northern Counties-bodied Fleetline 4023, ordered by Walsall, beneath the redundant trolleybus wires. T.W. Moore

The last trolleybus in normal service to return to depot was 866. This vehicle had been converted to front entrance to become the last variation of Walsall trolleybus. It was thus appropriate that 866 should work the final genuine service journey.

The following day, Saturday 3rd October, Walsall was taken over by trolleybus enthusiasts from all over the country. Cameras and flashguns were much in evidence to capture the final operations; even tape recorders were observed recording the near silence.

Four trolleybuses operated a shuttle service between Walsall and Bloxwich from 11.30 am to 6 pm. A special flat fare of one shilling (5p) was charged and special Bell Punch tickets were issued. A group of conductors had to be specially trained on the old Bell Punch machines! The four trolleybuses, 342, 353, 859 and 875, were all different types, adding to the interest.

The PTE produced an excellent brochure containing much information about the system. A further venture marking the closure was the preparation of special envelopes and a special postmark by Dr E. R. Clark,

one of the driving forces behind the Black Country Museum, then little more than a proposal. These were much in demand and many Walsall townspeople had to be content with the special stamp on an ordinary plain envelope.

The last service journeys operated at 6 pm, by which time attention was turning to the depot in Bloxwich Road, Birchills. A special party, comprising PTE officials, former employees and other civic dignitaries, were preparing to ride on three trolleybuses for a ceremonial last journey. The three vehicles were 862, 864 and 872 and worked from the depot to Bloxwich, then to Walsall and back to the depot; 872 was the last new trolleybus received by Walsall Corporation and appropriately carried the message 'Walsall's Last Trolleybus' illuminated on each side. Mr Edgley-Cox himself drove 872 for part of this final journey and as it passed through the mesh gates of Birchills depot, Walsall was again without trolleybuses after 39 years. It also meant the end of the only trolleybus system to be operated by a PTE and left only Bradford and Teesside running such vehicles

in the United Kingdom.

An obvious economy upon the demise of the trolleybuses was the operation of certain journeys out of service, and thus faster, against the traffic flow. This was not possible before because of the trolleybuses' inability to overtake their companions.

History will confirm or disprove the correctness of the demise of the British trolleybus; certainly fashion played its unwelcome part in the abandonment of some systems. The demise of the Walsall system was particularly unfortunate, not only because it may have survived had the PTE not been formed, but also because diminishing fuel resources became a major talking point only two years later. The value of retaining a less efficient operating mode for many years just in case it eventually becomes the cheapest is, however, questionable. At the time, despite their minimal maintenance requirements, materials for the Walsall trolleybuses had apparently become too expensive and the only arguments revolved around their environmental aspects — fume-free operation versus unsightly wiring.

The October 1970 works dispute brought Birmingham 'Standards' back to routes which had not seen them in quantity for many a year. The soft riding qualities of the Guy Arab catches the driver out as 3025 corners by Moor Street Station. The 60 service had been the preserve of Fleetlines since 1963. M.R. Keeley

Both the PTE and Midland Red were, by this time, reporting serious difficulties in obtaining spare parts, notably gearboxes which rear-engined buses were getting through at a distressing rate. The PTE's problems were temporarily increased considerably early in October 1970 when a dispute at Tyburn Road works prevented the issue of parts from the stores. Fortunately for the general public, inconvenience was minimal as the PTE still possessed a considerable number of withdrawn Daimler CVD6 buses with unexpired certificates of fitness. These buses returned to the roads in force and, for a short period, it was usual to see numbers of backloaders in all-day service from normally entirely Fleetline establishments like Cotteridge and Coventry Road. It was particularly pleasant to travel again on CVD6 Daimlers along Coventry Road and Bordesley Green, for many years regular haunts of these mellow sounding buses.

The Birmingham 'Standards' may have won some kudos as they helped out the Fleetline operations. However this good favour was well and truly obliterated in mid-October. The union agreement on BCT buses provided for standing on the 'Standards'; eight passengers were permitted to stand during peak periods, and five in the off-peak. Standing passengers were, however, not allowed on Birmingham's rear-engined buses which, being larger, required the conductor to get more fares in. The North Division made no such distinction, standing being allowed on its rear-engined buses.

In an attempt to dispose of this anomaly, a condition attached to the 1970 pay rise was that standing would be allowed in all buses, at the conductor's discretion. Unfortunately, in practice, the conductor's discretion meant that usually no-one stood on Birmingham buses, whether Fleetlines or 'Standards'. This effectively reduced the peak period capacity of the 'Standards' from 62/63 to 54/55, a critical loss. Queues built up as conductors, using their discretion, argued with would-be passengers ordered off because a seat was not available. Worse still were the conductors who preferred not to argue and, to ensure that not one person stood, rang the bell without checking to see if all the seats were filled. This habit, which was regrettably all too commonplace, reduced the available capacity still further. It should be said, in fairness, that some conductors, albeit a minority, acted in the spirit of the agreement.

The Birmingham operations received a monumental bad press. Crews attempted to justify their action by explaining that passengers deserved a seat after paying their fare and drew attention to the lack of grabrails on Fleetlines. The Transport and General Workers' Union made it clear that the matter was not one they sought to discuss. The management never resolved the problem, it largely faded away with the 'Standards'. Suffice to say, the backloaders' capacity, and thus the efficiency of their crews, was effectively reduced by about one-eighth from now on.

THE CLOSING MONTHS OF 1970

It could have been reasonably expected that the rest of the year would be an anti-climax after the excitement of the trolleybus closure. Other events towards the end of 1970, however, were not without interest. Walsall continued to maintain vehicular variety, collecting in November six ex-Wolverhampton Mark V Guys, 72-7N. These were exchanged for short Fleetlines 109–14L, required at Wolverhampton in the push for further one-man operation.

From 5th October, some buses between Wolverhampton and Sedgley were routed via Northway, serving the new estate. The normal stock was the front entrance Guy Arabs much beloved by Wolverhampton Corporation. These buses, which possessed semi-automatic gearboxes, made very impressive noises and seemed to nip along at a terrific rate of knots. They were, in fact, not very powerful, with Gardner 6LW engines being required to pull thirty feet of bus and 72 seated passengers. Unfortunately, Northway possessed a short but punishing hill. Guy drivers would race to the foot of the hill and then swiftly work their way down through the gearbox as the incline bit. The Guy would eventually stagger to the summit in first gear and then sparkle back to life as level ground returned. However, should the Guy's ascent be impaired in any way (even rain could sufficiently reduce traction), then the bus would grind to a halt. The procedure was then to partly unload the bus and re-start the climb. Not such an unusual event in earlier times, perhaps, but an unexpected part of 1970s bus operation.

1950 Leyland Tiger PS2/Weymann 2249 suitably adorned for a Christmas 1970 park-and-ride service. The veteran was only intended as a relief vehicle for the single-deck Fleetlines normally used. Maurice Collignon

This October 1970 scene records the impact of the new PTE on buses in Wolverhampton. Dominating Darlington Street is recently transferred ex-Birmingham Daimler CVD6 2762. A new Fleetline proceeds the other way towards Chapel Ash whilst ex-Wolverhampton Guy Arab IV 36N is an early repaint into blue and cream. The transfer of 2762 is explained by its offside illuminated advertisement panel. It had replaced similarly equipped 2645 the previous month on an advertising contract and was itself succeeded by Guy Arab 3056 in mid-1971. T.W. Moore

FIRST ANNUAL REPORT

The first Annual Report of the West Midlands Passenger Transport Executive covered the fifteen months up to 31st December 1970. The then Chairman, Alderman Sir Francis Griffin, drew attention in the foreword to two difficulties left behind by the 1968 Transport Act.

Sir Francis considered that all power and executive authority rested with the officers of the Executive (ie the professional transport men). The elected representatives, that is the Authority, whilst being responsible for broad policy, merely had the right to pass or withhold the annual accounts. Unless and until the Executive became the transport section of a local authority, the public could not regard the Passenger Transport Authority as being able to bring about reforms demanded by the public. Sir Francis was glad to state that the matter was likely to be rationalised under proposals for the reform of local government.

Secondly, Sir Francis commented that the 1968 Transport Act, having created the Passenger Transport Authority and Executive as virtually two separate units, then created the quite separate National Bus Company which included Midland Red. At the same time the Act, recognising the railways' continuing

financial crisis, gave them £2 million subsidy for the West Midland region alone. Sir Francis described this arrangement as 'Having created this chaos in public transport, the Act at the same time issued an instruction that the Passenger Transport Authority and Executive should integrate with all forms of public transport'. He considered that it was impossible to integrate with the Railway because it was happy to receive the subsidy and would make no arrangment which did not guarantee it as a good sum as it got at that time from the Government. Furthermore, Sir Francis commented that it was equally impossible to negotiate with the NBC because they were charged to run their affairs at a profit. Any suggestion of integration involving a reduction in the numbers of NBC buses competing with those of the PTE would only be considered if the profits were guaranteed to the NBC by the PTA.

The Transport Act was the result of a genuine desire by a Socialist central government to improve public transport through integration. A huge transport undertaking had been created to fulfil this desire. Yet the Conservative Chairman of this empire, instead of being excited by the new era it offered, was describing its role as 'impossible'.

Moreover, its professional officers were apparently largely beyond the control of the elected representatives. A Conservative scoring political points off Socialist doctrine? A local government man protesting at a new structure imposed by central government? A politician grieving over lost power? Nevertheless, the professional transport men of the Executive, apparently so loosely guided by the Authority, were to achieve the 'impossible' with both NBC and BR before control tightened through local government reform.

It was obviously hoped at this time that buses would continue to pay their way without recourse to precepts. However the responsibility for railway losses continued to cause concern, especially because many parts of the PTE area did not benefit from rail facilities. A section of the Annual Report hinted at this dilemma. It considered that, if an item of expenditure occurred which had a particular value to a locality only and is of no interest to the remainder of the PTE area, then the Authority felt that it should be able to exclude from a precept those areas not directly concerned. This point of view was communicated to the Department of the Environment and an amendment of Section 13 of the Act was suggested (unsuccessfully).

1971

The year started with the full overhaul of more ex-Birmingham 'Standards', continuing with Daimler CVG6 buses in the range 2776–96 and extending to Guys 2901–8 which were of the same age (1952). A later CVG6, 3115, had also been completed towards the end of December 1970.

Staff recruitment and the tuition of conductorate to drivers was assisted by the new Perry Barr training centre which was formally opened by Mr Eldon Griffiths MP, Parliamentary Secretary to the Department of the Environment, on 15th February 1971. The school was fruition of a scheme initiated by the former Birmingham City Transport committee and could hold up to 125 trainees at a time. The oval half mile driving circuit included a hill, reversing area, layby, turning circle and a pedestrian crossing. After initial training on this driving course, an assessment of a person's ability to become a driver was apparent at an early stage.

Currency decimalisation was one of the most traumatic shocks to the British way of life and the PTE was required to convert to the new money on the 21st February. Changeover problems were minimised by a fares increase on 3rd January when the fares values were designed to convert easily to decimal currency. This was followed by a comprehensive training scheme for staff and this, coupled with extensive publicity both to staff and passengers, enabled decimalisation to come into operation very smoothly. Conductors immediately noticed one benefit – the new money was much lighter and smaller, thus taking some weight off their shoulders, although the tiny ½p coin had a tendency to hide in the murkier corners of the cashbag.

THOUGHTS ON MIDLAND RED
Towards the end of February, it was revealed that the PTE had proposed the acquisition of Midland Red's operations within the PTA area. Control of these services was necessary to ensure an integrated transport network as required by Section 24 of the 1968 Transport Act. Midland Red employees replied rather more vociferously than they did ten years later when the whole company was threatened with total extinction. In February 1971, 'keep the buses red' petitions were being signed at the Midland Red garages within the PTA area. 'Keep Midland Red' car stickers were made available. However the decision rested with the NBC who, on this occasion, did reject the approach. As an alternative, joint consideration was given to the possibility of entering into an operating agreement. Detailed examination of this proposition at local level, however, revealed considerable difficulties regarding finance and operations, and 1971 was not to see any form of arrangement between the two parties.

The PTE did advance over Midland Red ground, however, in February 1971. The Company's Sutton Coldfield local services S67 and S76 were withdrawn and, as part replacement, the PTE extended service 42 from New Oscott along Court Lane to Six Ways, Erdington. Service 42 was itself a service acquired from Midland Red by Birmingham City Transport in September 1958 when short workings within the Birmingham boundary on services 107 and 113 were handed over.

MAJOR ROUTE REVISIONS
Important service changes regarding the PTE's own network were also taking place, with effect from Sunday 28th February.

Two of the Birmingham cross-City services, the 5 (Portland Road to Perry Common) and 7 (Perry Common to Portland Road); and the 90 (Baldwins Lane to Pheasey Estate) and 91 (Pheasey Estate to Baldwins Lane), were not balanced as half of each service had to turn in the City centre. From 28th February, an appropriate radial service was added to both services so that two Y-shaped groups were formed, ie 6 (Perry Common to Sandon Road) and 92 (Pheasey Estate to Hall Green boundary, Stratford Road) taking over from radial services 6 and 37. The need for buses to turn in the City centre was virtually eliminated, all buses continuing some way to the other side before dividing to their appropriate terminus. A further cross-City service, the 29 (Kingstanding Circle to Highfield Road, Hall Green) and 30 (Highfield Road to Kingstanding Circle) was severely curtailed to become a feeder service within Hall Green only and eventually died away completely. The revisions to the 90/91/92 were reckoned to have achieved a mileage saving of over 300,000 miles per annum.

The new arrangements worked well but subsequent necessary revisions to the Sandon Road and Stratford Road services meant that the new links created in 1971 were severed, thus largely causing a return to the pre-1971 situation (but without the 29/30) with some buses turning again in the City centre.

Arguably the most important innovation on 28th February 1971, however, was the creation of the 79 service (Birmingham – West Bromwich – Wednesbury – Darlaston – Wolverhampton). The 79 superseded a number of overlapping services and introduced Birmingham and Wolverhampton buses to each other's towns for the first time – although Brum buses were not entirely unfamiliar in Wulfrun due to earlier loans, including some eventually purchased by Wolverhampton Corporation. Passengers in Soho Road, Birmingham, further benefited as the Birmingham City terminus was moved from the traditional Snow Hill vicinity to New Street station, giving better penetration.

The 37 service was absorbed into the new 90 (northbound), 92 (southbound) service. Similarly its all-night equivalent, the NS37, became NS92. The all-night service was operated by Fleetlines apart from one round journey, worked by a bus from the daytime/evening runnings. The daytime service was still worked by Daimler CVG6 buses, hence this view of 3173 working the 2300 hours NS37 from the City boundary in Stratford Road, Hall Green, on 25.2.1971. This bus was one of the first into PTE livery, having been repainted in January 1970. M.R. Keeley

Wolverhampton used large capacity buses from the outset in the form of 30-feet long Mark V Guy Arabs, some still in green. Birmingham and West Bromwich continued to use shorter length double deckers, however. The 79 service was immediately popular, particularly the new Birmingham terminus, so all three garages had to use large-capacity buses on all-day runnings from May 1971.

On Sunday 23rd May 1971, a new bus station for West Bromwich was opened as part of the Sandwell Centre. All bus services in West Bromwich used the new facility except the main through routes from Birmingham to Dudley and Wolverhampton (ie the 74/75 and the new 79). Passengers in the County Borough of West Bromwich did well in 1971 for a further bus station. All bus services in the centre of Wednesbury, was brought into use on Sunday 17th October. The new bus station catered for both Midland Red and PTE services including, this time, the 79!

On the vehicle front, the hundredth ex-Birmingham City Transport single door Daimler Fleetline was made suitable for one-man operation in April. The non-appearance of new buses caused the full overhaul of more Daimler CVG6s during the late winter and spring (2859–60/7/9–74/81–2) followed by more Guy Arabs in the summer (2979–80, 3004–18/29/31/3/5/7/40–1).

Above **Big West Bromwich 1959 Daimler CVG6-30 224H pulls away in Lichfield Street, Wolverhampton, during July 1971, ahead of 80N on the Albrighton service.** Maurice Norton

The 79 was basically created by linking journeys of the overlapping 75 (Birmingham — West Bromwich — Wednesbury) and 90 (West Bromwich — Wednesbury — Wolverhampton) services. This 1949 view at the White Horse, Wednesbury, where buses met of all four original constituent municipalities of the PTE, shows Birmingham Leyland PD2/Leyland 2151 and West Bromwich Daimler CVG6/Metro-Cammell 150 on services 75 and 90 respectively. Both buses were new in 1949. R.A. Mills

A new sound in Birmingham brought by the 79 was that of the semi-automatic Guy Arab, taken in considerable numbers by Wolverhampton Corporation. 1965 Metro-Cammell bodied Arab V 160N climbs up from Hockley Brook in July 1971; this was an early repaint bearing Wolverhampton's initial interpretation of the PTE livery with cream domes and khaki restricted to the centre roof panels. Alan D. Broughall

This standard PTE Daimler Fleetline was the last Park Royal-bodied example to be delivered with a khaki roof. Inclusion of 'Please Pay on Entry' in the destination display betrays 4099 as a West Bromwich bus; the vehicle stands at Dudley Bus Station in December 1973 with the town's castle as a backdrop. Alan D. Broughall

FIRST PTE STANDARD BUSES

The need to overhaul BCT 'Standard' buses evaporated upon the arrival of what can be described as the first PTE 'Standard' vehicles. These were the 200 Daimler Fleetlines with Park Royal and Metro-Cammell bodies (100 each). The first to arrive were 4036–60 with Park Royal bodies, being licensed in July 1971 and receiving J-suffix registrations. The remainder were to receive K suffixes.

Following dissatisfaction with the mechanical reliability of 33 feet long Fleetlines, and with centre exits, the new vehicles reverted to the shorter length of around 30 feet and single front entrance/exit. The general shape of the buses, apart from the length, resembled the earlier 'Jumbos' 3881–4004. The buses were clearly spotted, however, by their new PTE destination layouts. The destination boxes were much larger than existing displays in Birmingham and Wolverhampton, and took a little getting used to.

4036–50 were allocated to Wolverhampton and caused a slaughter of the FJW and KJW registered buses from the old Corporation. The new buses were intended for service 79. Hockley and Oak Lane (West Bromwich) were also due for injections of new stock as the whole of the 74/75/79 group was scheduled for one-manning.

4051–81 went to Harborne, however, to allow the conversion of the 21/22 Weoley Castle services to Fleetline and one-man operation in August. Drivers on these services were instructed to show 'City' on inbound journeys in future. This was the first real break with the BCT tradition of showing the outward destination whichever way the bus was travelling – a change which was quite stunning at first! (It should be pointed out that a BCT bus stop usually stated whether it was an inbound or outbound loading point whilst BCT Fleetlines had a small destination box confirming the direction of travel – 'To City' or 'From City'). The arrival of these new buses in the South Division permitted the withdrawal

to begin at last of ex-BCT 'new look' Daimler CVG6 and Guy Arab buses. Included were four of the six crash gearbox Guys, 2997–3000. The remaining pair, 2995–6, were added in August to the variety at Walsall, where the indigenous fleet included crashbox Guys of somewhat different appearance.

The supply of new buses for the 74/75/79 conversion continued into the autumn, with 4082–98 going to Hockley and 4099–4108, 4136–57 to Oak Lane, West Bromwich. The 74/75/79 group accounted for quite a large proportion of the work at Oak Lane and the rapid influx of 32 new buses was comparable to the 31 Daimler COG6 double deckers which arrived in 1939 when the same road was converted from trams.

The new fleet at Oak Lane was not without

interest. Nos 4136–57 began the batch with Metro-Cammell bodies, thus ending speculation as to their appearance. MCW had virtually ceased producing double-deck bodies for the provincial market in 1968, having received a very large order from London Transport for single-deck bodies to be mounted on AEC Merlin chassis. Provincial customers were cast aside to make way for the London contract – a near fatal move for MCW when LT subsequently switched allegiances. Enthusiasts speculated whether Metro-Cammell would revive its 1968 design or move into the square-edge styling of the 'seventies. In the event, 4136 onwards looked so much like the Park Royal design that it was difficult to tell them apart at first, although recognition points were soon identified.

The Metro-Cammell Fleetlines were very similar in appearance; 4140 is seen leaving the new West Bromwich Bus Station in August 1971. The bus is on former West Bromwich 2T service — the unusual T suffix stood for Tipton (Princes End). John Carroll

Of the 'genuine' Park Royals allocated to Oak Lane, 4101 onwards were despatched from the factory with cream, rather than khaki, roofs. It is believed that 4100 was the last Park Royal to be turned out with a khaki roof but, unfortunately, the bus sustained roof damage whilst on delivery. It thus appeared in service a little later than its companions, having received a cream roof during repairs. Metro-Cammell deliveries continued to arrive with khaki roofs into 1972.

However it became clear that cream roofs were to become standard when 3620 and 244H were repainted during the autumn with this feature. Vehicles initially looked brighter, although rather plain, without the khaki paint. However, sure enough, the cream tops acquired a grubbiness after a few months, emphasising why BCT had retained the khaki roof for so long. The writer has always considered the demise of the khaki a regrettable livery simplification but sought solace in the fact that, after the initial lapse with 3620, Tyburn Road paintshops continued to re-apply khaki to buses already with the feature – this novelty may be connected with difficulties in covering the khaki with cream. Thus the only subsequent ex-BCT buses to receive cream roofs were either repainted elsewhere in the Executive empire or resuming PTE colours after spells in all-over advertisement liveries.

The large influx of new Fleetlines into Oak Lane meant that a number of ex-West Bromwich CVG6 buses were rendered surplus there. A total of 27, comprising all those delivered between 1960 and 1964 (228–32/4–49/53–8H), were transferred to Walsall by the end of the year, all in WMPTE colours – a repainting programme which accelerated the demise of the distinctive West Bromwich livery. These buses were largely put to work on the former trolleybus services, displacing the ex-Birmingham Guys which replaced elderly ex-Walsall buses on peak extras, thus increasing considerably the variety of destinations visited by these splendid old machines. Many of these ex-Birmingham Guys at Walsall were to be withdrawn themselves however at the beginning of 1972. The West Bromwich buses did not have the ex-trolleybus routes to themselves, being joined by increasing numbers of ex-Wolverhampton Arab Vs, some of which had been received following a further exchange with ex-Walsall Fleetlines.

Further arrivals at Walsall, entering service in October 1971, were 4029–35, the seven Fleetlines which were an option order placed by West Bromwich. These were thus the last buses ordered by one of the original constituent undertakings to enter service with the PTE. The bodies were by Northern Counties, of similar outline to 4005–27 but incorporating a number of PTE features, notably the destination layout and single entrance/exit.

Buses withdrawn at Walsall included most of the ODH-registered Leylands and Guys, whose cheap and nasty bodies had only achieved twenty years life following extensive rebuilds and a high degree of tolerance by Walsall passengers! Withdrawal of these buses was completed at the beginning of 1972. A number of the rather better Roe-bodied Leylands (RDH registrations) was also taken out of service, together with oddity 400L. · Surprisingly, three of these old Leylands (815/6/8L) and several Walsall oddities (821/3/4/

Five ex-Birmingham Daimlers and Guys, retired from normal service, became full-time tuition vehicles in the second half of 1971 and were renumbered 94-8 in the service fleet. Daimler CVG6 2884 became 97 and its driver is seen practising reversing around corners in June 1972 at the training school opened behind Perry Barr garage, Birmingham. Paul Gray

Leyland Tiger 2257 failed to become a tuition bus but survived as a towing vehicle at Perry Barr for many years. It is seen at the National Exhibition Centre in October 1978, immaculately repainted in PTE colours. M.R. Keeley

41L) were repainted into PTE colours, over the winter of 1971–2, despite the excellent stock being withdrawn in Birmingham. Mr Edgley-Cox, the Walsall Manager until PTE days, was still Chief Engineer at this time.

Sales of withdrawn stock included many of the ex-Birmingham Leyland PS2 Tigers. These had been stored in case the single-deck Fleetlines were rebodied as double deckers, an idea which was finally abandoned at this time. One PS2 to escape sale, however, was the former 2257. This had been earmarked as a training bus, numbered 93. This plan did not reach fruition and the bus was eagerly seized upon by Perry Barr engineers for use as a towing vehicle. It thus began a long second career and was repainted into PTE colours by the garage staff themselves.

Earlier batches of Walsall short Fleetlines lacked an entrance ahead of the front axle and thus could not be converted easily for one-man operation. With a re-modelling of the front

end, there was sufficient room to fit a narrow entrance in similar fashion to the later examples. This work began towards the end of 1971 and continued into 1972. Lex Garages (Stour Valley) Ltd actually carried out many of the conversions. Whilst producing some useful one-man stock, it was unfortunate that the rebuilding transformed quite attractive vehicles into arguably the most hideous Fleetlines to be found anywhere. The first Walsall Fleetline, 1L, had no front overhang and could not be converted. This bus remained in largely original condition, and conductor-operated, until withdrawal.

An interesting little depot closed on 12th November 1971. This was the former Wolverhampton Corporation building at Mount Pleasant, Bilston. Trolleybuses had been operated from here for many years and the yard included a turntable, similar to the rather more publicised one on the Bournemouth system.

A solitary vehicle from the former Wolverhampton fleet was 721N, a 12-seat Ford Transit new in 1967. Alan D. Broughall

The last of the 1950 Park Royal-bodied Guy Arab IIIs inherited from Wolverhampton were withdrawn in 1971; the demise of 541N in September eliminating the type. No.558N is seen in St James Square, Wolverhampton, in March; these vehicles had pre-selective gearboxes. M.R. Keeley

Also withdrawn in September were the last KJW-registered buses which were Guy Arab IVs dating from 1953-4. 572N was a Roe-bodied example but its elegant front upper deck was damaged in a mishap and a Strachan fibreglass front dome substituted in lieu. It became the only 5xx vehicle to receive PTE colours. Maurice Norton

The Government bus grant towards the cost of new vehicles was increased from 25% to 50% from 12th November. No new buses had been licensed therefore on 1st November so the first of the next month signalled the entry into traffic of many more Fleetlines. All the Park Royal series (4036–4135) were in service by the end of 1971, whilst the Metro-Cammells had reached 4170. Of the latest arrivals, 4109–35 were allocated to Quinton and 4158–70 to Miller Street in readiness for further conversions to large-capacity buses and eventual one-manning.

An interesting event towards the end of the year was the entry into service of the PTE's first all-over advertisement bus. The chosen vehicle, 3430, a 1964 Park Royal-bodied Fleetline, appeared in mid-December and attracted considerable comment, mostly favourable. All-over advertisement buses are now such a regular sight that it is important to recall the impact created by 3430, which promoted Barclaycard. Similarly adorned buses were soon to follow – Fleetlines of the same generation as 3430 were the usual choice because of the large amount of panel area available.

The special Park & Ride services operated in Birmingham over the Christmas shopping period were performed in 1971 by Fords 3652–4/6–7. Their places on the 'Rubery

Express' service 99 were taken by new Fleetlines 4109–12/20. This was the first large-scale use of double deckers on Birmingham's two limited stop services (the other being service 98 to Kingstanding). Their operation foreshadowed the permanent double-decking of service 99 in June 1972 when displaced Fords opened a third limited stop route in the City, service 97 to Castle Vale, taking advantage of the newly-opened Aston Expressway which was to motorway standard.

CONSOLIDATION

Further moves towards standardisation of rates of pay and conditions of employees doing like work throughout the Executive had continued during the year. An engineering agreement in February had followed a traffic agreement in October 1970, thus virtually achieving standardisation for manual employees in the four districts. Discussions between all four PTEs and the office staff trade union NALGO regarding future negotiating machinery had led to broad outline agreement by the end of 1971 with formal signing following in January 1972.

The engineering activities had also been reorganised during the year. This included a concentration of major engineering and overhaul work for the whole fleet at the Tyburn

Road works, Birmingham. However, owing to lack of capacity, certain body work continued to be performed at the Birchills garage, Walsall, where a sub-works was established.

Despite the rationalisation expected when the PTE was formed, inflation and the continuing loss of passengers to private cars meant that the anticipated financial surpluses were threatening to turn into a loss. In November the PTE had proposed that some contribution to loss-making routes should be obtained by precept. However the suggestion caused considerable controversy and the Chairman of the PTA, Sir Francis Griffin, threatened to resign if the proposal succeeded. The politician's view was that poor services should be axed or cross-subsidised by good routes, presumably even if such action threatened the health of the latter. The 'social bus network' still seemed an unthinkable concept in 1971!

In the event, 1972 was to see a doubling of one-man operation, bringing that mode into the majority. These economies, and the accompanying increase in reliability as staff shortage lessened, helped to bring another year of profit. Sir Francis Griffin did resign as Chairman and as a member of the Authority on 5th January 1972, to be succeeded by Councillor D. Gilroy Bevan.

Variety at Walsall

Below Left The newest buses at Walsall were the seven Fleetlines originally an option order placed by West Bromwich Corporation. The Northern Counties bodies were modified to resemble the PTE standard but were, nevertheless, quite distinctive.

Below Right Preceding the intake of ex-Birmingham City Transport double deckers to Walsall had been this 1950 Leyland Tiger PS2 which was transferred at the beginning of December 1969 and remained until January 1972. No.2260 (with L suffix erroneously applied) loads for Streetly Works on the 106 service via Barr Beacon in March 1970.
M.R. Keeley

Unexpected purchases of Walsall Corporation had been five London Transport RTL class double deckers, declared redundant in the capital in 1959. These powerful Leylands, with pre-selective gearboxes and Park Royal bodies, were arguably amongst the best vehicles to enter the Walsall fleet. Three operated for the PTE — in this view 201L is prominent (note the nearside headlamp mounting), whilst 203L pulls out from behind Fleetline/Northern Counties 18L in Bradford Place, Walsall. T.W. Moore

Above **Following the big influx of Birmingham Guys in 1969-70 came two more in August 1971. This pair, 2995-6, had constant-mesh gearboxes, however, which were no doubt more familiar to Walsall drivers than those in Birmingham — Walsall having operated large numbers of such Guys. No.2996 is seen at Walsall Bus Station in September. The pair were withdrawn in 1972.** M.R. Keeley

Above Right **West Bromwich Daimlers joined the Walsall allocation in force towards the end of 1971. 1960 short-length example 230H is seen at Beaudesert, Staffordshire, in September 1972, about to depart for Hednesford via Hazel Slade.** M.R. Keeley

Above **The oldest ex-Walsall buses were the surviving Guys and Leylands delivered in 1951 with Park Royal bodies. The bodywork of Leyland Titan PD2 126L at Bradford Place in March 1971 shows clear evidence of rebuilding.** M.R. Keeley

Right **An early repaint into WMPTE colours was Leyland-bodied Royal Tiger 801L of 1952, seen in February 1970.** M.R. Keeley

Widely acknowledged as the best vehicles purchased new by Walsall were the ten Leyland PD2 Titans with Roe bodies delivered in 1953. 815L was one of three repainted into PTE livery, being so treated in December 1971 and thus an early example with a cream roof. Service 118 (Birmingham — Walsall), operated jointly with Midland Red, was not generally host to elderly stock but 815L penetrated central Birmingham in August 1972, being pursued along Navigation Street by 3709.
M.R. Keeley

Three of these buses had suffered surgery, 811-3 having been converted in 1959-60 by Willowbrook to thirty-feet long, front entrance vehicles. 811L stands at Walsall Bus Station in September 1970; none of the trio received WMPTE colours.
Alan D. Broughall

Below Left A selection of buses was purchased by Walsall in 1954, including this Daimler CVG5 with Northern Counties bodywork. It was withdrawn by the PTE in September 1971; this view dates from February 1970. M.R. Keeley

Below 821L was a similar vehicle, but eight feet wide. This fared rather better, being repainted in December 1971, and survived until 1973. It is seen in the Alumwell Road estate in March 1972. M.R. Keeley

Another Walsall experimental vehicle to receive PTE colours was 823L, a 1954 Leyland Titan PD2 with semi-automatic gearbox and lightweight Metro-Cammell body. It is seen at Wednesbury in October 1970 before repainting and ran until 1973. Maurice Norton

The 1956 intake included 15 Daimler CVG6 buses with Willowbrook bodies built to the lowest height possible whilst retaining highbridge layout. No.833L provides vintage transport on the 901 limited stop Walsall to Rugeley service in October 1973. The earliest Walsall repaints had front bulkheads painted entirely blue. M.R. Keeley

A further Willowbrook-bodied Daimler CVG6 was exhibited at the 1956 Commercial Motor Show but was built to the newly permitted length of 30 feet for double deckers. The bus is seen as WMPTE 824L in New Street, Birmingham, in August 1972. It was withdrawn the following year.
M.R. Keeley

Right **Another 1956 Commercial Motor Show** exhibit was this low-height AEC Bridgemaster with Crossley bodywork, badged as a Crossley at the show. It was withdrawn in 1971; a similar bus was disposed of by Birmingham City Transport immediately before the PTE takeover. Alan D. Broughall

Below Right **Walsall Corporation** received a very early example of the first rear-engined model to enter production, the Leyland Atlantean. No.841L was built in 1959 and, being suitable for one-man operation, was retained for some years by the PTE. It is seen entering Birchills garage in May 1973. Alan D. Broughall

Below **Walsall** purchased 30 feet long, forward-entrance buses in 1960-1 but continued to favour front-engined chassis, taking Dennis Loline, Daimler CVG6 and AEC Regent V vehicles in small numbers. The Corporation had also converted a number of existing buses and trolleybuses to the new configuration so the purchase in 1963 of 15 Daimler CVG6 vehicles to the earlier length of 27 feet was surprising. The bodies were by Metro-Cammell. No.73L is seen at Walsall Bus Station in October 1973. M.R. Keeley

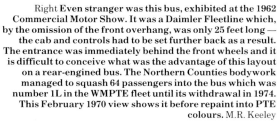

Right **Even stranger** was this bus, exhibited at the 1962 Commercial Motor Show. It was a Daimler Fleetline which, by the omission of the front overhang, was only 25 feet long — the cab and controls had to be set further back as a result. The entrance was immediately behind the front wheels and it is difficult to conceive what was the advantage of this layout on a rear-engined bus. The Northern Counties bodywork managed to squash 64 passengers into the bus which was number 1L in the WMPTE fleet until its withdrawal in 1974. This February 1970 view shows it before repaint into PTE colours. M.R. Keeley

Top Left **The prototype was followed by a succession of short Fleetlines, although there was a small front overhang on the subsequent examples. The 1963-5 examples were mostly of this appearance, No.29L at the Bus Station in October 1971 revealing the red and white striped used ticket bin favoured by Walsall Corporation.** M.R. Keeley

Top Right **No.30L was of this appearance, incorporating standard Northern Counties front panels but taking account of the minimal front overhang. It proved possible to introduce a small entrance ahead of the front axle, allowing the bus to be operated without a conductor from 1972.** Alan D. Broughall

Above Left **The remaining Fleetlines, delivered between 1965 and 1969, were of a modified design with a narrow entrance ahead of the front axle from new. No.32L leaves Chase Terrace, Staffordshire, in March 1972.** M.R. Keeley

Above Right **Two early Fleetlines, 17 and 24, were rebuilt to the two-door layout by Northern Counties before the PTE takeover. No.17L, new in 1964, is seen at the 158 terminus in Union Street, Birmingham, during February 1971. This was one of the first thoroughfares to be involved in Birmingham pedestrianisation schemes and the buildings behind, originally earmarked for redevelopment, were saved.** M.R. Keeley

Left **This Fleetline, 76L, had been an exhibit at the 1966 Commercial Motor Show and featured modified side windows. It is seen in the company of AEC Regent V 894L in the Bus Station during October 1971.** M.R. Keeley

Above **The need for single manning caused entrances ahead of the axle to be fitted in 1971-2 to the remaining early round-fronted Fleetlines, except 1L. The resultant grim proportions are illustrated by 22L, sent to Wolverhampton to assist in the drive for single-manning there. It is pursued up Broad Street, Wolverhampton, by 137N, a Park Royal-bodied Guy Arab V which, like 22L, dated from 1964.** T.W. Moore

The Walsall bus displayed at the Commercial Motor Show was, in 1968, this 36-feet long Daimler CRC6-36 which, of course, followed the purchase for several years of specially shortened Daimler Fleetlines! The power unit was a Cummins V6-200 and, despite two doors and staircases, it originally seated 86 passengers. It became 56L in the WMPTE fleet. T.W. Moore

1972

Two ex-Wolverhampton 1967 AEC Swifts, with Strachans bodies, were sold to Northampton in April 1972, Nos.708N and 711N becoming 21 and 22 in that fleet. The former 711N collects Northampton shoppers in September 1977. T.W. Moore

1972 commenced with a flurry of activity. A considerable number of services were scheduled for one-manning but had been delayed by difficulties with the trade union. However, these services were changed over in January.

As mentioned under the 1971 notes, the remaining ODH buses and a number of ex-Birmingham Guys at Walsall were withdrawn in January. Quite surprising withdrawals at Wolverhampton were most of the SUK-registered Guys. These dated from 1957 but many of the batch were non-standard in possessing Meadows 6DC rather than Gardner engines. A number of ex-Birmingham MOF-registered Guys were temporarily loaned to Wolverhampton in January.

Two hundred new buses were ordered in February. It was not possible to obtain Daimler Fleetline chassis in sufficient quantities so half the order was for Bristol VRT vehicles. The Daimlers were to receive Park Royal bodies whilst the Bristols were to be bodied by Metro-Cammell. Concern over the age of some of the existing stock, together with the single-manning drive, soon led to these orders being doubled.

The supply of Metro-Cammell bodied Fleetlines resumed, after a pause, with the entry into service of 4171–4 on 1st February at Washwood Heath for service 26 (Alum Rock – Bromford Bridge). Deliveries continued well into the year, the last five entering service in July. Nos. 4175–82/91–4210 settled down at Yardley Wood, 4183–90, 4211–30 at Liverpool Street, and 4231–5 at Perry Barr; 4175 was the last bus to be delivered with a khaki roof, the remainder featuring cream.

Moseley Road garage was closed for operation on 5th March when service 50 (City – Maypole) was transferred to Liverpool Street garage. Other services had been transferred to Yardley Wood garage a couple of weeks earlier.

The first buses delivered to the PTE, the 'Jumbo' Fleetlines (3881 onwards), began to be repainted in the spring. Most were treated at Tyburn Road, returning, of course, with khaki roofs. However, a small number were repainted at Walsall and these were clearly identifiable by their cream roofs. During the summer, repainted rear-engined buses began to appear from works with the WM motif applied to the front panels.

Interesting buses withdrawn during June were two experimental lightweights bought by Birmingham City Transport, Guy Arab 3001 and Daimler CLG5 3002. These two buses had Gardner 5LW engines; the demise of 3002 was prompted by accident damage.

Conversions of existing stock for single-manning had been greatly assisted in the South Division by the fact that Birmingham had standardised on Fleetlines for many years. The situation was different in the North but an attempt to use front-engined vehicles was made in July when Guy Arab V 176N was experimentally fitted out for one-man operation. An interesting vehicle converted for single manning later in the year (October) was 841L, the solitary ex-Walsall Leyland Atlantean, an early example of the model dating from 1959.

This Swift stayed at home. 712N with West Midlands fleetnames applied to the Wolverhampton livery; none of the Wolverhampton Swifts received PTE colours. T.W. Moore

Left **1952 Guy Arab IV 3001**, with Gardner 5LW engine and Saunders-Roe lightweight body, awaits a fresh crew from Acocks Green garage at Olton Boulevard East in May 1972. Right **Companion lightweight 3002, a 1954 Daimler CLG5** with Gardner 5LW engine and Metro-Cammell body plods along Colmore Row the same month. Accident damage prompted withdrawal of this non-standard vehicle. M.R. Keeley

NEW BUSES SORELY NEEDED

The supply of new Daimler Fleetlines had dried up with completion in July of the original contract for two hundred. Things were getting serious by the autumn. South Division began a series of short-term recertifications of MOF Guys and Daimlers that should have been withdrawn. These recertifications generally took the form of repainting the BCT blue panels into the WMPTE shade, attention to the cream being minimal. This work was carried out at garages and a number of variations could be discerned, eg some garages applied PTE style fleet numbers. The garage responsible for 3028 got the message completely wrong by re-applying BCT blue paint! This work was usually sufficient to gain a certificate of fitness for a further two years service, sometimes more. However it has to be said that the repainted blue panels tended to exaggerate the shabbiness of the remainder of the bus. Whilst not deriding the hard work put in by the garage staff to extend the lives of these buses, the need to patch them up in this manner represented the first break with the standards of vehicle appearance maintained by Birmingham City Transport.

Meanwhile, whilst elderly buses were being returned to service in Birmingham, a contrasting situation was arising in the North Division. A number of the ex-Walsall Dennis Lolines with Willowbrook bodies dating from 1960 had been overhauled and repainted into PTE livery (800/42–8L). However the cost of these overhauls was so great that the remainder were withdrawn. A similar situation was occurring with the Strachans-bodied Guy Arab Vs ex-Wolverhampton Corporation. Eight of the 1965 batch were overhauled (147–54N) but the extent of the body repairs was such that the remaining pair were simply withdrawn and, indeed, some of the 1967 batch (187–217N) fell out of use in 1972. Thus a situation arose whereby Guys dating, sometimes, as far back as 1950 were being recertified for further service whilst Guys seventeen years their junior were being scrapped! Yet, on body condition, this policy was totally logical and highlights decisions with inherited stock faced by the PTE engineering staff.

Strachans-bodied Guy Arab V buses 197N and 155N, dating from 1967 and 1965 respectively, lie out of use at Oxford Street yard, Wolverhampton in October 1973. M.R. Keeley

Metro-Scania demonstrator VWD451H works the limited stop service from Colmore Circus, Birmingham, to Castle Vale in August 1972. Maurice Collignon

New buses were on the way, however. The first Bristol VRT, numbered 4343, was exhibited at the Commercial Motor show at Earl's Court, London, in October. The Metro-Cammell Weymann bodywork was generally similar to the previous batch of MCW bodies on Fleetline chassis, apart from the obvious differences dictated by the VRT chassis, notably the front radiator. There were some detail changes, the greatest improvement being white ceilings in place of the dingy yellow favoured on previous deliveries. No. 4343 entered revenue service at Wolverhampton in November.

Above **The buses on the Birmingham Centrebus circular service commenced their journeys from Masshouse Circus car park. Commers 4239 and 4238 wait under the concrete columns of Masshouse Circus before making another circuit of the central streets in April 1973. The Commers were delivered in blue and cream, as shown, but were soon repainted all-over orange. This was intended to increase their prominence but, in fact, the loss of the established bus colours made them look even more like delivery vans. Below The Morrison Electricar demonstrator hums along Colmore Row in December 1972. Its Willowbrook body seated 19 and the vehicle remained with the PTE until early in February 1973.** M.R. Keeley/Alan D. Broughall

CENTREBUS INTRODUCED

A completely new type of bus service was commenced on October 2nd. This was the Centrebus, a joint venture with the Birmingham Public Works Committee. It was linked with the City's decision to introduce a limited pedestrianisation scheme for some of the central shopping streets. The service linked the car park at Masshouse Circus with the shopping area. Special small buses of Commer manufacture were ordered for the service but these did not arrive in time. A number of Fleetline single deckers were thus used for the first few weeks and were to be seen trundling sedately around the newly pedestrianised streets. These included Union Street, until then a terminus for conventional buses.

Centrebus was handed over to the small Commers in mid-November. Six vehicles had been ordered and took the numbers 4236–41. The bodies by Rootes of Maidstone seated nineteen. An unusual feature was the exit doors on *both* sides of the vehicle – there was, of course, no risk in alighting on the offside in the pedestrian areas.

Patronage on the original Centrebus route was very low. Losses were shared equally by Birmingham Corporation and the Executive. When traffic did not significantly improve during the Christmas shopping period, it was evident that the original route was not meeting the needs of shoppers and re-planning was already under consideration. Any alterations had to be agreed with Birmingham Corporation, however, as co-sponsors of Centrebus.

An interesting vehicle operated on the Centrebus service from 20th November was CWO 516K, a demonstration Morrison Electricar battery-electric bus, with 19-seat Willowbrook body and owned by the Department of Trade and Industry. A battery-electric bus had obvious environmental merits in a fume-filled town centre and, of course, it did not waste fuel whilst sitting in traffic jams. CWO 516K had a limited turn of speed so the Centrebus service around the congested central streets and the pedestrian area was the most promising route for it to show its

capabilities. Although Centrebus did not operate, at this time, in the early morning or after the evening peak, even this limited period of operation was too long for CWO's batteries. Thus the Morrison Electricar had to be taken off part way through the day. Nevertheless the environmental advantages were clear and it is a pity that further development of the breed has been so slow. CWO 516K was an interesting machine to ride upon, its electronic whine varying widely depending on the power being called for – rather reminiscent of manic organ playing!

Travelcard, introduced in October 1972, was an immediate success and redundant Birmingham 'Standards' acted as additional sales points and promotional vehicles. A one-week Travelcard became available from 25th August 1973, from which date it became possible to renew your card at a considerable number of selected newsagents. The converted 'Standards' were again brought into use; here the former 2548 is circulating around central Birmingham with staff handing out leaflets whilst 2820 is used as a sales point at the junction of Bull Street and Dale End. No.2548 was simply a promotional vehicle and received only minor physical alterations for its new career. M.R. Keeley

POINTERS TO THE FUTURE

There were a number of developments in 1972 which gradually became important features of bus operation in the West Midlands.

A radio network was brought into use in June 1972. The control room for the North Division was situated at the St Paul's Street divisional headquarters in Walsall, whilst that of the South Division was based at Miller Street garage. By the end of 1972, a total of 97 buses (64 South, 33 North) had been equipped with two-way radio whilst 66 pocket-phone personal two-way radio sets were available for use by inspectors. A number of older buses were fitted with radios and such equipment became standard on new vehicles.

The advantages of radio communication were soon recognised. Drivers or inspectors could report interruptions to services immediately and this cut the time taken in instigating remedial action. All radio buses carried a green identification disc on the windscreens which enabled drivers of non-radio vehicles to recognise their better-equipped brethren and ask for a message to be sent. Radio was also seen as an important deterrent to assaults on

bus crews and the South Division all-night services were very quickly exclusively operated by suitably equipped buses. Another advantage was that passengers' enquiries to drivers could be swiftly answered by the control room.

The value of bus shelters is surprisingly under-estimated in some circles. However, they are greatly appreciated by passengers on wet and windy days and it is a pity that, during the lifetime of the PTE, vandalism has been an increasing problem, reducing the effectiveness of the shelters and providing a down-market introduction to bus travel. August 1972 saw the first introduction of advertising shelters which are erected and maintained free of charge in exchange for the right for them to carry advertisement panels. The use of these shelters was subsequently greatly extended, to the benefit of passengers, and in some cases displaced existing shelters which could be re-sited at high priority stops where advertising was not considered acceptable. There was also an arrangement, useful for such sites, whereby one free non-advertising shelter would be provided for every ten

shelters carrying advertisements.

At the end of October, a four-week season ticket was introduced, known as Travelcard, which allowed the holder to travel for unlimited distances on any of the Executive's bus services (except for Birmingham night services which had a relatively high price flat fare). The original cost was £4 for four weeks travel, or £2 for children under 15.

One of the main objectives behind Travelcard was to speed the loading of one-man buses. However it was important to ensure that a ticket offering such wide freedom to travel was confined to the person to whom it was issued and thus part of the card included a photograph of the purchaser. This part of the card was permanently retained by the passenger who merely renewed the other part. It was foreseen that the initial demand for tickets and photographs would exceed the capacity of the permanent sales outlets so four special sales vehicles, converted from former BCT Daimlers and Guys by Tyburn Road Works, were parked at important points in the Executive's operating area for the first few weeks. A fifth bus acted as a promotion vehicle. The five

The Travelcard sales buses initially received lettering applied to the existing colour scheme. The two Daimler CVG6 vehicles, however, were eventually repainted in a special livery for greater impact. The former 2819 proceeds along Summer Lane, Birmingham, near the PTE headquarters, in June 1978. M.R. Keeley

Other organisations found the sales buses of use. Ex-2820 is the centre of attraction in this Christmas 1979 toy appeal, organised by BRMB, the Birmingham independent local radio station. The bus, located in High Street, was manned by station broadcasters who accepted gifts of toys.
M.R. Keeley

Below **Travelcard all-over advertising buses appeared in the mid-70s, including Daimler CRG6/Park Royal 4083. This bus is seen in Colmore Row, Birmingham, in July 1979 — passing a Barclays bank, providing a family connection with the very first WMPTE advert bus for Barclaycard.**
Alan B. Cross

buses were numbered 194–8 in the service vehicle fleet and were converted from 2607, 2819–20, 2548/55. No. 197 (2548) was the promotion vehicle. Once their initial role of augmenting the sales offices was completed, the converted buses went into store but some would re-appear from time to time as the Executive area widened or Travelcard increased its scope. The buses were also useful for other functions, such as display vehicles for city plans or, each Christmas, as the BRMB independent radio toybus, gathering surplus toys to be re-distributed to needy children.

Public response to the Travelcard scheme exceeded all expectations. Sale of the 10,000th ticket came so quickly that it was not possible to arrange any celebration of the fact. Instead, the Chairman of the PTA presented the 12,000th customer, on only the 12th working day of the scheme, with a complimentary ticket. Around 17,000 Travelcards were in use by the end of the year. The cost of the card was fixed to give a little saving to the five days per week outer suburb to centre passenger who did not travel at other times. Important benefits were eliminating the problems of seeking the correct change for the fare, the ability to transfer from one route to another to complete a journey without extra cost and what could be regarded as the bonus of making extra journeys without charge for shopping and recreational purposes.

Travelcard was a means of pursuing the aim of the Authority and Executive in firstly stopping the drift away from public transport and then reversing the process. The evident success of Travelcard in both satisfying its market and speeding the loading of one-man buses eventually led to variations such as local cards, which brought the advantages of Travelcard to those travelling over shorter distances, and one-week, three-month and annual tickets. Travelcard was eventually valid on Birmingham night services upon payment of a supplementary fare. Following WMPTE's success, Travelcard has been widely imitated elsewhere.

The Transport Act, 1968 required the Executive to produce a plan for the future development of passenger transport in the area. This Transport Development Plan was completed in 1972 and received the approval of the PTA on the 29th November. The plan was based on an extensive study of the present situation and future possibilities and described not only the schemes envisaged over the next five years but also the basic philosophy behind current thinking on public transport. This important document was subsequently published as an 88-page illustrated report.

Negotiations between the PTA and PTE and the British Railways Board on passenger rail services had led to agreement by the end of the year, the formal exchange of documents taking place in January 1973. The basic principle of the agreement was that the Executive

took over responsibility for financial and policy matters on most of the local railway passenger services within, or near to, its area. The PTA and PTE could thus specify the fares, frequency, timings, and types and capacity of the trains to be run. Ownership and operation, however, remained with British Rail. Provision was made for railway land or buildings to be made available to the Executive for transport purposes such as car parks and bus/rail interchanges.

As the year closed, rumours were again circulating about the other series of protracted negotiations, those dealing with the future of Midland Red services within the PTE area. This time the grapevine indicated that the services would be taken over rather than an operating agreement being reached. 1973 was to provide the answer.

1973

Below **1953 Guy Arab 3058, newly repainted at Walsall including a cream roof, sets down passengers in Colmore Row, Birmingham, in March 1973. The continued operation of buses with 20-year old Metro-Cammell bodies caused little difficulty, although the image and interior comforts were less satisfactory to the PTE.**
M.R. Keeley

After visits from Metro-Scania demonstrators, the PTE put its own example on the road in January 1973. The vehicle, numbered 4242, remained a one-off with the PTE and by July 1975 was finding employment on a service to Birmingham Airport. It is seen here in the grounds of the old Airport.
M.R. Keeley

The year began with around 300 ex-BCT 'Standards' still in use. Five received repaints at Walsall Works and were the only such vehicles to receive cream roofs. They were 3028, the Guy which had received dark blue panels upon short-term recertification, and 3058/9, 3130/4. These five were followed by a further quintet at Walsall, but with khaki roofs. Two were Guys 2564 and 2580, ready for return to the South Division after working in Walsall, whilst the other three were Daimlers 3120/1/9. All except 2580 featured a thin blue line below the lower saloon windows and looked very smart – 2580 had lost the line on its previous repaint. The programme of short-term recertifications continued until the flow of new vehicles resumed.

The Executive put a new Metro-Scania single-decker, numbered 4242, into service in January. This vehicle, which featured automatic transmission and air suspension, was initially used on the 97 Birmingham centre – Castle Vale limited stop service. It was joined later in the month by a Leyland National demonstrator, FRM 499K, evaluated on the same service for around a fortnight.

The first pair of the new batch of 100 Park Royal-bodied Daimler Fleetlines, 4243–4342, entered service in February. All hundred were intended for the Birmingham garages but, pending the arrival of the Bristols, 4243–72 were initially operated by the North Division and it was March 1974 before these thirty were all working in the South. 4278–85 were also loaned from new to Wolverhampton but only for one month. The main visual change with these new vehicles was to be seen inside where white ceilings had superseded the rather bilious yellow panels favoured by BCT on its post-1961 buses.

Amongst the vehicles withdrawn at Wolverhampton were all the remaining SUK batch, except 6N, and many of the remaining MDA-E Guys which dated only from 1967. A surprising vehicle at Wolverhampton for several months was ex-West Bromwich CVG6 235H which was returned to Walsall in August. At Walsall, ex-West Bromwich short length Daimlers 228–32H were withdrawn, as were the two surviving Leyland Royal Tigers 808/10L. A single-deck Fleetline was transferred from Birmingham to cover the work formerly carried out by 808L. Most of the ex-Birmingham Guys transferred to Walsall in 1970 had been withdrawn by this time. Of the survivors, 2565/83 were transferred to Wolverhampton in March and 2564/80 to Birmingham in March/April. This left only 2592 at Walsall and this was repainted and returned to Birmingham in September.

Guys in Wolverhampton were having a mixed career in 1973. Strachans-bodied Arab V models dating from 1967 were being withdrawn but earlier examples continued, such as 1964 Park Royal-bodied 134N, loading in Wulfruna Street in March. Ex-Birmingham 1951 Guy 2583 assists on the opposite side of the road yet all but one of Wolverhampton's own Guys of 1957, its oldest remaining, were being scrapped. M.R. Keeley

Below Left New buses temporarily resident at Wolverhampton and other North Division garages were Park Royal-bodied Daimler Fleetlines intended for the South. Nos.4263 and 4280 load in Wulfruna Street in May 1973; note the introduction of the WM motif on the front panel Below Right Single-deck Marshall-bodied Daimler Fleetline 3453, borrowed from Selly Oak (Birmingham) garage, covers the Fridays only services from Lichfield Bus Station in October 1973. M.R. Keeley

1973 withdrawals embraced 1953 Park Royal-bodied Leyland Royal Tiger 808L, whose main role was the Friday-only market day services into Lichfield. The bus is seen in September 1972 at Goosemoor Green, mis-spelt on the destination blind. M.R. Keeley

The other Royal Tiger to survive until 1973 was 810L. Both 808L and this vehicle were regarded as dual-purpose vehicles but 810L won in terms of luxury and featured a coach door and no destination box.
Alan D. Broughall

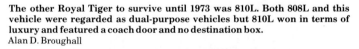

Left **Until new vehicles arrived in quantity in the form of Bristol VRTs, 30 feet long Metro-Cammell bodied buses inherited from the municipalities that made up the North Division were considered suitable for overhaul upon expiry of certificates of fitness at the age of 12 years. Overhauled 1961 Daimler CVG6-30 No.888L stands at Walsall Bus Station in August 1973; the offices in the background were the headquarters of the North Division until 1986.** Right **The overhaul of Willowbrook-bodied vehicles was sporadic. 1961 AEC Regent V 896L was selected and is a fine testimony to the excellent quality of a Walsall bodyshop overhaul. An October 1973 view in St Pauls Street, Walsall.** M.R. Keeley

Other interesting developments in the vehicle fleet were the overhauling of two batches of AEC double deckers, the ex-Wolverhampton Renowns 182–6N and ex-Walsall Regent Vs 891–7L. The degree of repairs required by the latter was quite heavy so 898–900L were never dealt with and were withdrawn by January 1974. Birmingham's original deliveries of rear-engined buses, comprising both Leyland Atlanteans and Daimler Fleetlines, could not be converted for one-man operation without some difficulty because the front destination displays could only be worked from the upper deck. Early in 1973 the Atlanteans, 3230–40, were fitted with revised destination displays and converted for one-man operation. Unfortunately it was not possible to rebuild similarly the Fleetlines, 3241–50, which remained double-crew buses until their withdrawal.

One of the Commer vehicles used on the Centrebus service, 4241, was repainted orange early in 1973. It was felt that this livery would render it more distinctive than the standard fleet colours but, in fact, 4241 looked rather similar to the Commer vans operated by Douglas the contractors. Nevertheless the other five, 4236–40, were similarly repainted in the autumn.

The night services worked from Miller Street, the NS 51/64/67, were the first to be converted to one-man operation, with effect from 1st April. References to one-man operation now become inappropriate because in March, following agreement with the trade union, the first two conductresses successfully passed the PSV driver's test following tuition at the Perry Barr training centre. The PTE employed a large number of conductresses and this development provided a future for them in the industry as single-manning, or one-person operation, continued to spread.

Ex-Birmingham 1961 Metro-Cammell bodied Leyland Atlantean 3233 as rebuilt for driver-only operation. It is seen in Colmore Circus, Birmingham, in its sixteenth year. M.R. Keeley

The five 1966 AEC Renowns purchased by Wolverhampton Corporation were also overhauled in 1973 upon expiry after seven years of their initial certificates of fitness. They joined their AEC Regent V compatriots at Walsall; newly transferred 183N being seen on a former trolleybus service in May 1973. The bodies were true representatives of the MCW bodybuilding partnership, being completed by Metro-Cammell on Weymann frames after closure of the latter's factory at Addlestone. All five were withdrawn by July 1975. Alan D. Broughall

49

One of Walsall's new Metro-Cammell bodied Bristol VRT vehicles, 4360, carried a wraparound advertisement as shown in this October 1973 St Pauls Street view. M.R. Keeley

NEW VEHICLES IN QUANTITY

Metro-Cammell bodied Bristol VR 4344 entered service at Wolverhampton in May, some six months after the prototype. Bristol VRs then began to arrive in force, all being allocated to the Wolverhampton garages (4343-6, 4379-4414, 4425-42) or Walsall (4347-78, 4415-24). Amongst vehicles displaced at Wolverhampton were the five AEC Renowns, which were transferred to Walsall, and two survivors of pairs, 71N (Guy Wulfrunian) and 252H (one of two ex-London Transport Guy GS class 26-seaters purchased by West Bromwich). The arrival of VRs and Renowns at Walsall caused the demise of an assortment of ex-Walsall buses, eg 800/15/6/8/ 21/3/4/42-8L, eliminating Leyland Titans, Daimler CVG5 and Dennis Lolines from the operational fleet. Some of the Lolines were subsequently to re-appear at ex-Midland Red garages, however, whilst Titan 815L found a new career replacing a Bedford SB as the canteen vehicle at Bradford Place, Walsall. Also in the North Division, the last of the 199-210H batch of ex-West Bromwich CVG6s were eliminated.

By July South Division was receiving its new Park Royal-bodied Daimler Fleetlines, commencing with 4273-90 for Acocks Green which enabled the conversion of the Gospel Lane Loop services (31/32) to one-man operation. The influx of the hundred Fleetlines allowed withdrawal of the ex-BCT 'Standards' to recommence in earnest. An early Guy, 2559, had been overhauled in April whilst isolated examples continued to be repainted. The most interesting was 3131, apparently dealt with as a short-term recert by West Bromwich, which re-appeared in May with cream fleet numbers on the blue panels instead of the usual arrangement. Its home garage, Perry Barr, soon eliminated this distinction, unfortunately. A number of 'Standards' with long certificates of fitness were repainted in the summer and autumn, commencing in June with 3115. This bus was followed by 2592 (the last ex-Birmingham Guy at Walsall returning to the South Division), 2780-1, 2872/81, 2903/6/79-80 and 3005/31. Finally, towards the end of the year, Hockley's 2600 received the same treatment as 3131 at West Bromwich, the cream fleet numbers on the blue panels again lasting for only a short time.

All of 4243-4342 were in service by November and short-term recerts were then resumed on 'Standards'. West Bromwich was also not expected to receive any new buses in the near future so Daimlers 181/4/6H were amongst stock similarly treated there.

Amongst vehicles replaced by new Bristols at Wolverhampton was the surviving Guy Wulfrunian, 71N. The Wulfrunian was designed for an entrance ahead of the front axle but 71N was unusual in not taking advantage of this. The engine was in the same position as an Ailsa but the size and weight of the Gardner employed caused space and front axle loading problems. The bus dated from 1962 and carried East Lancs 71-seat bodywork. It is seen in March 1973, two months before its withdrawal from service. Maurice Norton

Withdrawn in May was the surviving ex-London Transport Guy 26-seater, one of two purchased by West Bromwich Corporation, but latterly based at Wolverhampton. No.252H is seen in October in Oxford Street yard, awaiting a buyer — the new owner would secure it for preservation. The Eastern Coach Works bodied bus dated from 1953. Alan D. Broughall

THE BIG ANNOUNCEMENT

Years of speculation ended on 27th June 1973 when it was announced at last what would become of the Midland Red services. Agreement had now been reached for the Executive to take over the NBC subsidiary's stage carriage operations within the future West Midlands county (to be formed on 1st April 1974 following the 1972 Local Government Act) for the sum of £3,600,000. This included the services, staff, vehicles and garages. The basic principle behind the selection of routes for transfer was that those which operated entirely within the West Midlands county would be operated by the Executive whilst those that crossed the boundary would be retained by Midland Red. A total of 76 cross-boundary services were identified and these would become subject to the control of the Executive within the county and regulated by a Cross-Boundary Agreement. The Executive would fix the fare scale for the parts of the routes within the county.

The date set for the transfer was not immediately announced but was to be 3rd December 1973. Thus there were five months to wait for the big changeover, during which time an immense amount of detailed organisation would be worked out. The transfer would involve detaching from Midland Red a section as big as many other complete bus companies and setting up an organisation to run it as part of the Executive.

AN ERA OF CHANGE

Even as preparations for the takeover of its West Midlands services were going ahead, Midland Red was looking at ways of making up for what was to be lost. Enthusiasts received a double blow when two major independent bus operators were taken over by Midland Red. Firstly Green Bus of Rugeley succumbed in November 1973 after years of trying to make a living in what had become a very thin area for bus operators. Green Bus routes could hardly be considered to have been in the same league as those of the Black Country. Then in September 1974 came the loss of Harper Brothers of Heath Hayes. This operator was rather more fortunately placed and ironically gave Midland Red some useful work inside West Midlands County. Whether Midland Red would have taken over these operators without the cash injection from WMPTE is arguable and thus it seems that the PTE takeover of Midland Red services indirectly led to the demise of one or both of these independents.

Times were certainly changing. After years of trying to break even on the bus services irrespective of political party, February 1973 had seen a radical change of thought. The Labour-controlled Authority adopted a fares freeze, initially for six months but subsequently extended. This held bus fares at the levels introduced on 1st January 1972, despite price inflation reaching 9% (little was it realised that inflation was to get even worse). The shortfall was to be made up by rate precept which had only been levied previously for local railway services. In addition, a local railway fare increase planned for June 1973 was not introduced within the PTA area. By the end of 1973 it was already possible to note that the tide of passenger loss, then running at around 3% per annum, had begun to turn and the Executive was almost able to break even on the year's operations.

Another new feature of the times seemed to be the bus manufacturer who did not want orders. Leyland had managed to obtain a virtual monopoly of the market and was distinctly unhelpful when West Midlands PTE attempted in November 1973 to order 600 further Daimler Fleetlines (350 to be MCW bodied, 250 Park Royal). In the upshot, WMPTE was only able to place orders for 420 such vehicles (270 MCW, 150 Park Royal), to which could be added contracts and options for 80 placed by Coventry Transport. It was also becoming difficult to obtain spare parts for vehicles built by manufacturers now within the Leyland empire. It was not surprising, with this general air of dissatisfaction with the major manufacturer, that the PTE showed sufficient interest in the newly announced Volvo Ailsa double-deck design to order three vehicles, complete with Alexander bodies. This commitment to an Anglo-Swedish design caused howls from the local bus manufacturer, Metro-Cammell, whose own Anglo-Swedish double decker, the Metropolitan, had been ordered by every PTE except the West Midlands!

Recruiting of conductors resumed during the latter part of 1973, after a gap of over a year, to ensure adequate cover of services. Platform staff had traditionally been recruited as conductors and subsequently trained as drivers. Conversion to one-man operation of the majority of routes made an updating of this practice desirable and, with union agreement, the Executive began direct recruitment of drivers.

1951 Guy 2600 with cream fleet numbers in Corporation Street, Birmingham, in early January 1974 — one of those days when the dampness has to be reconciled with the thought that at least it's not snowing. M.R. Keeley

THE MIDLAND RED TRANSFER

The transfer of former Midland Red services, staff, vehicles and garages took place on 3rd December 1973. Since the June announcement, arrangements had been made for the transfer of 1,396 employees and 413 buses. They came mainly from eight Midland Red garages, Digbeth and Sheepcote Street in Birmingham, Bearwood, Dudley, Hartshill, Oldbury, Stourbridge and Sutton Coldfield, and six of these garages also passed to the Executive. However, Bearwood, for so long such an important part of the Company's affairs, was closed and its responsibilities passed to other Midland Red or PTE garages as appropriate. Digbeth was retained by Midland Red for long-distance coach services and, for a time, cross-boundary routes. Midland Red also re-opened its Bromsgrove and Cradley Heath garages to handle workings outside or across the West Midlands county boundary. Also obtained by the Executive from Midland Red was Digbeth's overflow bus park at Adderley Street, conveniently situated opposite the ex-BCT Liverpool Street garage. The local services previously operated by Digbeth became operated by Moseley Road, closed since April 1972, specially re-opened by the PTE for the purpose.

The principle of apportioning routes between Midland Red and the Executive remained as originally announced but some consideration was given to services in border areas so as to minimise unproductive mileage for each operator. A typical example was the Stourbridge – Kinver service which ran into Staffordshire but remained worked by Stourbridge, now with the PTE. Interestingly, certain PTE services which ran to country districts well outside the county boundary to the north-west of Wolverhampton were handed over *to* Midland Red. In exchange, the Executive's Wolverhampton district took over eight Midland Red services to the south-east of the town. This arrangement largely reversed the 1920 agreement made between Midland Red and Wolverhampton Corporation and included were some of the first bus routes to have been operated by the municipality, such as the service to Bridgnorth taken over from the Great Western Railway in July

1923. In contrast the Executive retained its Walsall-operated services beyond the boundary in Cannock where Midland Red then had no garage.

For the time being a separate entity existed to deal with the transferred organisation. This was Midland Red (Metropolitan) Omnibus Co Ltd, a subsidiary company whose sole purpose was to provide a temporary service conditions structure for the transferred staff. The company was renamed West Midlands Passenger Transport Ltd in March 1974 but the term 'Metro' or 'ex-Metro' was widely used within the Executive for all things ex-Midland Red for a number of years.

The operational management of the ex-Midland Red section of the PTE was made the responsibility of the Operations Manager (North), in whose area the majority of the transferred garages were included. Operations in the Birmingham and Solihull areas, which included the Moseley Road, Sheepcote Street and Sutton Coldfield garages, were transferred to the South Division in June 1974.

As Midland Red would continue in existence, it was necessary to prepare extensive advance publicity so that the ownership of services and vehicles would be readily identifiable from transfer day. Comprehensive press advertisements and completely new sets of timetable leaflets and route maps were produced. Legal ownership lettering on buses was changed for the first day of operation and new fleet names were applied within a few days.

It was staggering to realise that centres of Midland Red operation such as Dudley were now entirely PTE. As the vehicles handed over were the configurations required to operate the services, the PTE received a cross-section of the Midland Red fleet. Included were a large number of Midland Red's 'home-made' vehicles, ranging from S16–S23 single deckers to D9 double deckers. Leyland Leopards and Nationals were further types new to the PTE. A large number of Fleetlines were included in the deal but, unfortunately, as Midland Red had begun a policy of standardising on single deckers, all had lost their first flush of youth. Not unnaturally Midland

Red's dual-purpose stock tended to be the newer members of the single-deck fleet and these were retained by the Company for their longer services. Thus the number of new single deckers that passed to the PTE was restricted to the 33 Nationals.

Nevertheless, the oldest buses acquired dated only from 1960, mere babes compared to some of the veterans still running for the PTE. However, years of under-capitalisation and high vehicle utilisation had led to all sorts of problems, not the least of which was maintenance. The Black Country services were undoubtedly arduous and, with little variation between peak and off-peak (the Black Countryman traditionally walked to work which would be situated locally), the buses were in harness for most of the day. When it is realised how few of the front-line stock passed to the PTE, some idea of the problems ahead will be gathered. One would not expect all 413 vehicles to have been in running order upon takeover but the procession of buses towed into Moseley Road on the big day was highly symbolic. It was about this time that the manufacturing side of the bus industry began to prove incapable of supplying vital spares. The great bus famine had started. Predictably ex-BCT 'Standards' were helping out at ex-Midland Red garages within days of the takeover, merely the start of all sorts of vehicle types to be seen plying the acquired routes over the next few years. CVG6 Daimlers 3213 and 3214 were sent to Sutton and then joined 3227 at Dudley. No 3224 settled in for an extended stay at Sheepcote Street. Birmingham Fleetlines also went to Sheepcote Street and Sutton and some operated as one-manners using Setright machines.

Two Midland Red buses were repainted into blue and cream prior to the takeover and were at work on the very first day of PTE ownership; BMMO S17 5762 and Daimler Fleetline 6269 providing a foretaste of what was to come. The repainting had been carried out at the Company's Central Works at Carlyle Road – the Executive was unable to deal with such a large influx of vehicles, many of BMMO manufacture, and entered into a four-year maintenance contract with the Company to cover the ex-Midland Red stock.

Left Midland Red Willowbrook-bodied Leyland Leopard 6440 loads at Priory Estate on Dudley local service D11 in November 1973. This Leopard being a modern dual-purpose vehicle, it was retained by Midland Red for longer distance services and did not pass to the PTE. Right BMMO S22 5902 at the Company's Digbeth garage on 26.11.1973 still with Midland Red fleetname but with WMPTE legal lettering already applied. Vehicles lettered in advance carried 'On hire to Midland Red' windscreen stickers until takeover day. This bus had seating to dual-purpose standard but was no longer a front line vehicle and thus passed to the PTE. Alan D. Broughall/M.R. Keeley

The Midland Red Transfer

Below The Midland Red fleet came in several shades; the recently introduced National Bus Company poppy red, a rather deeper shade imposed a little earlier by NBC, and survivors still with the pleasant rich shade once favoured by Midland Red. The PTE endeavoured to obtain Fablon stickers to match all these shades. This disreputable 1960 BMMO D9 came still wearing the long discontinued livery with traditional 'MIDLAND' fleetname stretched over three panels. The old fleetname has been masked with dark red Fablons with the 'West Midlands' emblem applied over the top on a poppy red Fablon. M.R. Keeley

Left **Certain country services to points outside the future West Midlands County were transferred from the PTE to Midland Red as part of the 1973 deal. The principal link between Wolverhampton and Bridgnorth was the 17 service which became Midland Red 890. Strachans-bodied Daimler Roadliner 714N is seen in Bridgnorth during September 1970; this vehicle was burnt out the following year.** Right **A less frequent link between Wolverhampton and Bridgnorth was the 31 via Pattingham and Ackleton, which became Midland Red 899. Park Royal-bodied AEC Reliance 705N, one of three purchased by Wolverhampton in 1963, waits for passengers with Northgate in Bridgnorth High Town as a backdrop in May 1973.** Maurice Collignon/M.R. Keeley

Left Fourteen BMMO S16 service buses came to the Executive. These buses had crash gearboxes and were not fitted for driver only operation; conductors were thus essential and they tended to be used on busier services that were restricted to single deckers. No.5534, built in 1964 and allocated to Oldbury, loads in the grim bus station of that town in February 1974. Right The same bus station but a different stand and with a vintage timetable case. 1969 Daimler Fleetline 6188, with Alexander body, was one of the Company's D13 class with front entrance and centre exit, although passengers were frequently discouraged by drivers from using the latter. Note the Midland Red lettering cast in metal, hence its survival. M.R. Keeley

Older Alexander-bodied Daimler Fleetlines had a single front entrance/exit, and formed Midland Red classes D11 and D12. A 1968 D12, 6133 allocated to Moseley Road, pulls out of the old Birmingham Airport en route for Coventry in June 1975. This long and interesting route proved very popular with pensioners taking full advantage of their West Midlands free passes, and buses often suffered overcrowding on fine days. The blue and cream livery suited these buses which were mostly repainted at Midland Red's Carlyle Road Works. The omission of the between decks thin blue line, not applied due to the lack of a beading strip, was unfortunate as was the tendency of the cream to turn vaguely pink as the red began to weather through — a problem not encountered on former Midland Red buses painted at PTE establishments. M.R. Keeley

Below Left An early repaint of a BMMO S17 single decker before a more sympathetic treatment of the grille area was adopted. No. 5494 works Sutton Coldfield local service S62 from the Parade in August 1974. Paul Gray

Below Dudley Bus Station in April 1974 with repainted BMMO S22 5908 and D9 4947 still in red. M.R. Keeley

Left Stourbridge local service S56 became the preserve of 1952 Daimlers borrowed from Liverpool Street, introducing the novelty of pre-selector gearboxes to Stourbridge garage and reintroducing open rear platforms after around a decade of totally enclosed Midland Red stock. No.2783 swings out of Stourbridge garage, which doubled as one of the town's bus stations, in August 1974. Right Fleetlines were borrowed to maintain driver-only services. Stourbridge garage made every endeavour that its borrowed buses could present a destination display; other ex-Midland Red garages were content with a bare row of light bulbs or fluorescent tubes. Park Royal-bodied No.3520 in April 1974. Alan D. Broughall/Paul Gray

Left A most bizarre addition to Harthill's stock was the giant Daimler CRC6-36 built for Walsall Corporation in 1968. The operation of such a non-standard machine at Hartshill speaks volumes for the flexibility of ex-Midland Red drivers who seemed prepared to handle anything! No.56L is seen at Dudley Bus Station in April 1974; the bus was withdrawn in May Right Other ex-Walsall buses to be resurrected temporarily from the graveyard were 1960 Willowbrook-bodied Dennis Lolines despatched to Oldbury and Dudley. No.842L, working for Oldbury, precedes 6131. M.R. Keeley

Left Wolverhampton's full-front Guy Arab IVs were more unexpected buses for the entertainment of ex-Midland Red crews. Oldbury, in April 1974, was using 19N, the solitary 1958 example with Burlingham bodywork. Still in green, it is seen here at Dudley Bus Station in the company of BMMO D9 4945 which featured non-standard ventilators. 19N was retired in September 1974. Right The remaining full-front Guys, built in 1960-1, had Metro-Cammell bodies. No.37N assists Dudley garage in July 1974, the 126 service number is displayed in the nearside windscreen. A sunny day at the King's Head, Bearwood. M.R. Keeley/Paul Gray

1974

The delivery of new buses continued to be behind schedule, threatening the conversion of services to one-man operation and causing manning difficulties. In an endeavour to compensate partially for this, conversion by Tyburn Road Works of existing buses for single-manning was stepped up. This delayed other work but, by mid-January 1974, all suitable buses had been equipped and had allowed the route conversions to proceed without serious postponements. The shortage of new buses put additional pressure on the Executive's engineering facilities in other respects. Old buses were being retained in service, sometimes requiring additional repairs and possibly obsolete spare parts. At garages, the unexpected programme of short-term recertifications added to the workload of the maintenance staff. In addition the supply of spare parts continued to cause concern.

The Executive placed an order for 30 Leyland Nationals early in 1974, which was soon increased to 60. This was the first bulk order for full-sized single deckers to be placed by the Executive since its formation. They were intended to replace certain ex-Midland Red vehicles and help to alleviate the general shortage of new buses.

South Division carried out a very interesting exercise with effect from 17th February 1974. It was intended that the last Birmingham service to retain conductors would be the Outer Circle 11 but this service had been converted to large-capacity (ie Fleetline) operation some years previously. Two attempts were made to release the Fleetlines and yet retain large-capacity buses by introducing ex-Wolverhampton full-front Guy Arabs. South Division trade union officials were not impressed and, quite possibly, indirectly condemned the MDA-E batch of half-cabs to an early grave as the full-front Guys soldiered on in the North.

Thus from 17th February, Monday to Friday daytime operation of the Outer Circle reverted to 'Standards', complete with increased frequencies to match their smaller capacity. The released Fleetlines permitted the conversion of services 5/6/7, 9, 25, NS5 and the Quinton garage share of 33/34 to one-man operation. Only the garages working the Outer Circle were involved in this exchange, which minimised the number of buses requiring transfer. The totals of Fleetlines and Standards at the garages needed some adjustment, however, notably at Acocks Green which had been all-Fleetline since the summer of 1973. The end result of the exercise was that the proportion of single crew operation in the South Division had reached 82%.

Meanwhile in the North Division, the extraordinary ex-Walsall 36-feet long Daimler double decker with Cummins rear offside engine, 56L, had become persona non grata in its town of origin. In January 1974 it became a surprising addition to Hartshill's stock. This vehicle was designed for one-man work with the extreme rear exit supervised by a television camera. It was never allowed to be used in this manner and thus it always performed double-crew duties at Walsall, and similarly at Hartshill. It was withdrawn in May. In addition, Dennis Lolines 842–5L were returned to service during February at the ex-Midland Red garages of Oldbury and Dudley. They received little use, particularly the pair at Dudley, and the last one had been withdrawn again by the end of the year. They were replaced by an ever-changing selection of ex-Wolverhampton full-front Arab IVs including, at one time, 19N, the solitary Burlingham example. Purely on the debit side, the last of the Strachans-bodied MDA-E batch of Guys was withdrawn in February, their demise coinciding with the closure of the bodybuilders' factory. Other relatively modern Wolverhampton buses to be eliminated around this time were the AEC Swifts, also Strachans-bodied.

Birmingham's Centrebus service had continued to suffer from low patronage but on 14th January 1974 the route was extensively revised. The new route vacated the pedestrian streets in the very centre to take in points slightly further out such as Moor Street station, Paradise Circus and Great Charles Street. The 2p flat fare and 5-minute frequency were retained but the hours of operation were extended to become 8am to 6pm. Commer 4237, now in orange livery, picks up in Dale End on the re-routed service. Note the special Centrebus stop — each was numbered to assist passengers unfamiliar with the City centre. The revised route was immediately more successful in terms of passengers carried and augmentation of the service soon had to be considered as the small number of Commer 19-seaters, designed for the pedestrian streets, began to fail to cope. On 18th November 1974, the service was converted to single-deck Daimler Fleetlines which, with their short length and adequate power, were ideally suited. The displaced Commers, still in orange, were then used for miscellaneous duties and, due to the vehicle shortage, could turn up in the most unlikely places. The Centrebus service was given the number 101 upon the introduction of the Fleetlines. T.W. Moore

LOCAL GOVERNMENT REORGANISED COVENTRY ABSORBED

The reorganisation of local government, including the creation of the West Midlands County Council took effect from 1st April 1974. On this date the West Midlands Passenger Transport Authority, the body of representatives from various authorities, was dissolved. Its rights and liabilities were transferred to and vested in the new County Council which became the passenger transport authority for the area of the county of West Midlands.

The boundary of the passenger transport authority was altered to become identical with that of the County Council. Areas now officially outside the authority's area were Bromsgrove, Cannock, Redditch and Seisdon, as well as parts of Stratford-upon-Avon and Meriden. The new county, however, included the new Coventry district council area and thus the City of Coventry's transport department was added to the Executive. The significance of these changes cannot be too strongly stressed – the sensible transport basis of the Executive's operational boundary was replaced by one which suited the politicians. The passage of the years may have brought Coventry closer ties with the West Midland conurbation but, even today, it is arguable whether the attachment of the City's transport undertaking was a necessary, or even desirable, step.

The takeover of the Coventry undertaking increased the fleet by slightly over 300 to around 2,600 buses. The Midland Red and Coventry additions had, in fact, swelled the fleet by over 50%. There was immediately a problem at Coventry because the senior management had obtained promotions to posts with undertakings elsewhere. This did provide the Executive, however, with maximum flexibility in creating a new management structure in the East Division (or mystic East) as Coventry became known. In the short term, Mr C. Nurse, due to retire as the Operations Manager South, was persuaded to stay on as Operations Manager East until the end of the year. Mr Nurse had been with Coventry Transport prior to obtaining a senior post with Birmingham City Transport and it was most fortunate that the Executive was able to bring in this tough, experienced man during the transition period. When Mr Nurse finally did retire, the Executive was able to repeat the exercise by promoting Mr J. Stokes into the top East Division job, another man whose career fortuitously linked the two undertakings.

Extensive preparatory work prior to 1st April 1974 ensured that the changeover of responsibility went smoothly. Obvious signs of this were visible from January 1974. From this time all vehicles emerging from the Coventry paintshops carried the Executive's blue and cream livery and so, for a short time, it was possible to see buses so painted bearing 'Coventry Transport' fleetnames on their flanks. In addition, the task of adding the suffix letter Y to Coventry fleet numbers began well before the changeover. The change of fleet name and legal ownership lettering took place largely overnight on the transfer date.

A surprising move by Coventry Transport in its closing months was the advertisement for sale of four of its six Bristol RE single deckers, 516–21. These machines were approaching

seven years old and thus a major overhaul to gain new certificates of fitness. Coventry had next to no requirement for full-size single deckers by this time and their disposal was a logical step. The Executive, however, was rather hard-pressed for single deckers and ensured the retention of the Bristols. The four could not be put into service with the PTE before 1st April but they did go for overhaul prior to the takeover. The former 517/8/20/1 entered service at Wolverhampton in April carrying, rather surprisingly, fleet numbers 4443–6 instead of Y-suffixed Coventry numbers. A fifth Bristol RE was transferred in June, by which time 4447 was in service, so when the bus was repainted the following month it retained its Coventry number 519, *without* the Y suffix.

The Executive's annual report for 1974–5 praised 'the excellent condition of the Coventry Fleet' which 'assisted the Executive in the difficult circumstances arising from late deliveries of new buses and the poor availability of spare parts'. Coventry's stock of Daimler CVG6 vehicles, including two withdrawn examples, was raided to cover shortages elsewhere. Nos. 225Y and 231Y were sent to Oldbury in May, followed by 216Y and 230Y which were returned to service at Sutton Coldfield in June. Coventry was, by this time, receiving a batch of 20 new East Lancs bodied Daimler Fleetlines, ordered by the defunct undertaking and completely to CCT specification. These were numbered 4447–66 by the Executive and made available from July around twenty further CVG6 Daimlers which should have been withdrawn. Instead the CVG6s were despatched to Birmingham's Acocks Green garage, primarily for use on the Outer Circle and enabling more elderly ex-BCT rear-entrance vehicles to be scrapped. The Metro-Cammell 'Orion' bodies on the Coventry Daimlers were rather plain but were considerably lighter than their more elaborate Birmingham brethren, so performance was noticeably livelier. All these refugees entered service in Coventry colours,

three bearing an old maroon shade that had been superseded by a brighter red some years previously. The arrival of the ex-Coventry buses at Acocks Green caused a little difficulty as the Y suffix could be read as a 7 by clerical staff. Their fleet numbers were thus soon increased by 1000 and the Y suffix dropped (ie 211Y became 1211) and the Oldbury and Sutton Coldfield quartet were similarly treated in August. Those remaining at Coventry were not renumbered, however, at this stage. The total of Coventry Daimlers at Acocks Green reached 23 in January 1975.

PAINTING PROGRESS

Midland Red's Central Works continued to repaint the vehicles transferred to the Executive into blue and cream. This output was supplemented to a small extent by repaints within the Executive. In March 1974, Fleetline 5247 was the first of a number to be handled by Walsall paintshops, each distinguishable by the thin blue band at cantrail level – a feature not added on Midland Red repaints because there was no beading strip to work to. In June two D9s were turned out by Walsall, 4866 and 4982, these having cream fleet numbers on the lower panels instead of black numbers above the lower saloon windows. The blue band was not applied due to the positions of the upper saloon drainage holes. At least two further D9s, 4883 and trainee bus 5002, were similarly repainted subsequently.

In addition to the Coventry and Midland Red colours so recently introduced to the fleet, it was still possible to see most of the liveries of operators absorbed in 1969. These survivors were largely a result of the need to retain older vehicles in service on short-term certificates of

Not all ex-Midland Red buses were repainted at Carlyle Road; 1962 D9 4982 was a Walsall repaint featuring cream fleet numbers. It enters Anderson Road, Bearwood, in August 1974.
Paul Gray

Walsall coped with the narrow blue band between decks, despite the lack of a beading strip. 1963 Fleetline/Alexander 5287 was fresh from the paintshop when photographed on the forecourt of Sutton Coldfield garage. Paul Gray

fitness without overhaul or full repaint. The elaborate West Bromwich livery had gone unfortunately but the Walsall blue could still be seen on a handful of Fleetlines (106–11, 113–9L). The last dark blue bus in Brum, No. 2612, had its panels repainted PTE blue in spring 1974. Two veteran Guys, now at Wolverhampton, 2565 and tuition bus 2599, still boasted the old colours, however. This pair plus the other veteran at Wolverhampton, 2583, were taken out of use in December 1974 and January 1975. Most surviving Birmingham 'Standards' had received short-term recertifications over the past two years and, in the autumn of 1974, it was necessary to repeat the process on the same vehicles, starting with 3107. Needless to say, despite the efforts at the garages where this work was carried out, such machines were beginning to look rather tatty. In Wolverhampton full front Guys 20–8N and 31N, all still in green except 23N, received short-term recertifications towards the end of 1974, some receiving partial repaints, although 20–2/4–7N were soon given a coat of blue and cream. A Guy of another batch scheduled for withdrawal, 129N, similarly received a partial repaint in green during January 1975 and 28N, 31N and 129N remained in that livery until their withdrawal in August 1975.

VARIETY IN NEW VEHICLES

Some relief in the form of new vehicles came during the second part of the year upon the arrival of the 60 Leyland Nationals, which were numbered 4467–4526. Later examples carried a smaller, neater roof pod. The manufacturer showed its then-characteristic reluctance to supply what the customer wanted as they arrived in all-cream livery and requiring other modifications before they could enter service. Walsall works therefore added the blue relief, PTE pattern destination indicators, luggage accommodation, Autofare ticket machinery and radio equipment. So desperate was the need for new vehicles that ten Nationals, 4503/5/7/10/1/7/9–21/3, entered service in October without these modifications, the service numbers and destinations having to be stuck to the windscreens. They thus had the standard National layout of 52 seats, the luggage arrangement favoured by WMPTE reducing this capacity to 50. Expectations of their reliability were not raised when, in July, ex-Midland Red National 113 was completely destroyed by fire caused, according to the manufacturer, by a freak mechanical occurrence. Upon completion of modifying 4467–4526, Walsall works began to fit the ex-Midland Red Nationals with PTE style destination boxes.

Delivery of the first 100 Bristol VRTs with Metro-Cammell bodies, 4343–4442, was completed in the autumn. The last examples were immediately followed by the first of the second batch of 100, to be numbered 4630–4729. Also delivered in the autumn were the three prototype Alexander-bodied Volvo Ailsas, 4527–9, of which one was exhibited at the Commercial Motor Show. The three were initially put into service from Perry Barr garage, generally on the now defunct 39 City – Witton service. The Executive was evidently satisfied with the prototypes and promised delivery dates because an order for fifty production examples was quickly forthcoming. The vacant numbers 4530–4629 were reserved for 100 Fleetlines still awaited, of which fifty would add further variety in having Leyland 0680 engines – Gardners being in short supply.

Amongst vehicles withdrawn in the second part of 1974 was the very last Daimler COG5 service vehicle, CVP 122, one of many such machines converted by BCT from buses to lorries.

Throughout the year, services had been prone to interruptions and diversions due to bomb scares, many of which were hoaxes but occasionally there was the genuine article. This culminated in the appalling events of 21st November 1974 when IRA devices exploded in two Birmingham City centre public houses with dreadful loss of life and injuries. Some idea of the force of the devices is registered by the damage sustained by bus 2544 which happened to be passing on service 90 as the bomb placed in the Tavern in the Town, New Street, went off. The side of the bus was literally peppered, the windows disappeared and the crew and some passengers injured, fortunately not seriously. Bearing in mind the damage to the bus, which was written off, one is left to wonder how anyone survived the blasts inside the public houses. The only consolation of these obscene incidents is that, due to the condemnation which followed, the bombing campaign ceased, as did nearly all the hoaxes. Before leaving this grim subject, the uncomplaining performance of the bus crews whose duties were frequently extended and certainly made more harrassing by delays and diversions must be recorded.

The County Council and the PTE were now committed to retaining fares at the January 1972 level and this belief was being rewarded by a clear increase in the numbers of passengers carried. Travelcard, still priced at £4 for four weeks unlimited travel throughout the enlarged area represented by the new county, increased in popularity. However, due to the rapidly increasing rate of inflation, it was becoming obvious that a grant on bus operations would be necessary for the first time.

Some changes to the fares structure were made in December 1974 as a first stage towards standardisation of fares throughout the area. Some fares were increased whilst others decreased, the latter being on former Midland Red and Coventry services. This exercise caused a small net reduction in the Executive's income. The ex-Midland Red platform staff, perhaps more than any others, were used to the upward spiral of charges and there is no doubt that the combination of reduced fares, Travelcard, *and* free travel for pensioners required a considerable mental re-adjustment!

New Leyland National 4473, based at Stourbridge, featured a non-standard enlarged WM above the entrance. The garage forms a backdrop in this July 1975 view of Foster Street. Paul Gray

Left **National 4510**, pressed into service in all-cream livery and without destination blinds. The destination and service number are displayed in the nearside windscreen as 4510 enters Navigation Street, Birmingham, on service 140 in November 1974. Right 4518 received an out-of-sequence registration number. It loads at Dudley Bus Station in August 1976 whilst, at the foot of the hill, a Bristol VRT waits to return to Walsall and Hednesford on the service then still numbered 265. In pre-PTE days, Midland Red buses on that jointly worked service showed 265 but Walsall, many of whose buses only had two-track number blinds, used to display 65. The Dudley-Walsall-Hednesford service became 301 in the 'Walsall' series. Maurice Collignon/M.R. Keeley

Left **Ex-Midland Red Nationals** received modified destination boxes, like 4467-4526, to suit the PTE style of display. No.138 (still in red) and No.139, before conversion, are seen at Dudley Bus Station in May 1974. Right Alexander-bodied Ailsa 4527 stands at the Piers Road, Handsworth, terminus of service 40 in February 1975; the location then being favoured with a BCT Bundy time recording clock. M.R. Keeley/Paul Gray

Left **Some of the ex-Birmingham City Transport Daimler COG5 buses** converted to lorries, of which the last was retired in 1974, had spent around a quarter of a century in their second career. CVP122 was a comparative youngster, having been built as recently as 1937(!) as bus 1022. A recovery crew prepares to tow away a defective 37xx Park Royal-bodied Fleetline in July 1972. Right Desperation indeed as tiny orange-painted Commer 4237, displaced from Centrebus, waits outside Moseley Road garage (re-opened to cover ex-Midland Red routes), ready to give puny assistance on the busy 175 service. Note the offside exit, intended for use in pedestrianised areas, on this 19-seat vehicle. M.R. Keeley/Alan D. Broughall

Coventry's Buses in Pictures

Below **Two-door Bristol RESL6G/ECW 4446, built in 1967 as Coventry 521, during its Wolverhampton career. The request stop plate has a representation of the WM logo and fleetname on the bus side symbol. The 63 (Sedgley — Bilston — Rocket Pool) was the former Midland Red 863 route and a modified successor became 563 under the renumbering of Wolverhampton area services.** T.W. Moore

East Lancs-bodied Fleetline 56Y was one of a handful of vehicles passing to the PTE retaining Coventry's original paint scheme for rear-engined buses. Architecture of the City's post-war reconstruction dominates in this November 1974 view. T.W. Moore

West Midlands fleetnames and Y number suffix applied to ex-Coventry 338, a 1964 Willowbrook-bodied Leyland Atlantean. This particular livery of maroon and ivory was most attractive but a simplified version had been adopted before the PTE takeover. Broadgate in August 1975. M.R. Keeley

Twenty new East Lancs bodied Fleetlines for Coventry were delivered in the summer of 1974. They were built entirely to Coventry specification but carried PTE livery and fleet numbers. They spent their entire lives at the Coventry garages; 4465 is seen here in the attractive village of Berkswell in November 1977. M.R. Keeley

Above **The solitary batch of Park Royal-bodied Fleetlines, delivered to Coventry in 1970, would not look too out of place in the WMPTE fleet once blue and cream was applied, although the destination layout would remain an obvious recognition feature. Allesley village is served by 69Y, still in Coventry colours in June 1975.**

Left **Ex-Coventry 1958 Daimler CVG6/Metro-Cammell 225Y was one of two sent to assist at Oldbury from May 1974. It is seen in August in Summer Row, Birmingham, on an obscure short working of the 87 service to Dudley; the 84 ran as far as St Paul's Road, Smethwick.** M.R. Keeley

Below **Withdrawn Daimlers 216 and 230 were revived in June 1974 and despatched to Sutton Coldfield. Both carried an earlier, less attractive, style of Coventry livery. The former 216, renumbered 1216, proceeds around Colmore Circus, Birmingham, in August 1975.** M.R. Keeley

The main recipient for surplus Coventry Daimlers was Acocks Green garage, Birmingham, to replace veteran 'Standards'. Their main employment was on the Outer Circle but the duties included odd journeys on other routes, including a morning peak trip on the 92 from Hall Green to Birmingham city centre, basically the preserve of Yardley Wood garage. No.235Y, renumbered 1235, climbs the Bull Ring in March 1975. M.R. Keeley

Below Many CVG6 Daimlers, of course, remained in Coventry, including 1961 example 308Y, waiting for time in Broadgate in August 1975. Coventry repaints into PTE livery featured all-blue front bulkheads. The A service number suffix would not suit the PTE numbering system — 'A' was reserved for the anticlockwise direction of circulars. Services 9 and 9A would be renumbered 29 and 39 in due course. M.R. Keeley

1975

Leyland-engined Daimler Fleetline 4574, delivered in 1975 with a Park Royal body, was destined to spend its entire WMPTE career from Yardley Wood garage. It is seen running along Tanworth Lane, Shirley on the 190 service from Solihull to Cheswick Green, introduced in November 1975. Fleetlines 4580 onwards reverted to Gardner engines. South Division allocated mid-summer deliveries 4586-605 to the ex-Midland Red operations at Moseley Road and Sheepcote Street garages; a last gasp modernisation as both garages closed in November. No.4594 passes through picturesque Allesley in August.
M.R. Keeley/T.W. Moore

The orders for 400 double deckers, of which 4530–4729 formed the second two hundred, were due to have been completed in December 1974. As noted earlier, delivery had begun towards the end of 1974 of Bristol VRTs 4630–4729. The first of the final batch of Daimler Fleetlines in this contract, 4530–4629, entered service in January 1975.

Of these Fleetlines, the first fifty had Leyland 0680 engines which gave rise to distinctly Atlantean-like noises. Curiously, they seemed louder on the outside but quieter inside. The Leyland engine undoubtedly produced a smoother machine, mellower and arguably more pleasant to listen to and which was decidedly better in performance. These qualities resulted in higher fuel consumption, however, and the engines never appeared happy in the Fleetline, lacking the legendary reliability associated with the Gardner or the same Leyland unit in the Atlantean AN68. Two garages with a long Leyland tradition were chosen to receive these buses, 4530–57 going to Perry Barr and 4558–79 to Yardley Wood. The latter was also to receive the first of the Gardner-equipped batch, 4580–5.

The Park Royal bodies on 4530–4629 were very similar to the previous batch but, like the Metro-Cammell bodies on 4630–4729, all the nearside windows in the lower saloon featured opening ventilators. Lower saloon ventilation always had been a problem on BCT and PTE Fleetlines during the summer months, as the 'hopper' type seems unable to provide an adequate flow of air, and the increased number of ventilators went a little way to improving matters.

One of the ex-Coventry Daimlers transferred to Acocks Green re-appeared in blue and cream colours during January. This was 1248 which returned carrying its old fleet number 248Y, an error which was soon corrected. The solitary SKV-registered example, 1211, was dealt with in February and was followed by a steady stream of Acocks Green Daimlers. These vehicles were not repainted at Coventry and, by their cream front bulkheads, could be recognised from the Coventry paintshop output on CVG6s still in their home town, which had blue bulkheads.

Whilst on the subject of repaints, a surprising vehicle to receive blue and cream in February was Guy Arab IV 6N, the sole surviving rear platform ex-Wolverhampton bus. This contrasted with the demise of the ex-Wolverhampton Daimler Roadliners, of which the last were withdrawn in January 1975.

Tightening-up at Coventry enabled the transfer to Dudley of five Willowbrook-bodied Daimler Fleetlines. By the time 360–4Y had reached Dudley in January and February they were clad in blue and cream and carried fleet numbers 1360–4. Other vehicles on the move included, in March, 4029–35 which were

transferred from Walsall to West Bromwich to help with increased one-man operation there. It will be recalled that these seven Northern Counties-bodied Fleetlines were originally an option order placed by West Bromwich Corporation but, until now, had always operated from Walsall. Some double-crew buses surplus at West Bromwich were loaned to Wolverhampton, eg 186H and 214–9H, reintroducing open rear platform buses in quantity to the town. Members of the 220–5H batch joined their newer ex-West Bromwich brethren at Walsall.

Local newspapers reported on 7th April that passenger transport chiefs (presumably several operators) had been discussing with an unnamed manufacturer the possibility of setting up a production line in the West Midlands. This would be a rival to British Leyland and the aim would be to meet the continuing shortage of new buses. It would create fresh job opportunities for skilled Midlands workers, filling the vacuum recently created by the transfer of Daimler Fleetline production from Coventry to Leyland's plant in Lancashire.

West Midlands County Council leader, Councillor Stan Yapp, had been highly critical of delays by British Leyland in meeting orders for new buses, which had led to a shortfall of some 200 vehicles. He confirmed that initial talks had been held with other PTEs on the possibility of getting together on bus production and he expressed his desire to see bus manufacturing returning to the Midlands.

ROUTE CHANGES IN THE SOUTH

1975 was a traumatic year for South Division operations with several major service revisions and the demise of a number of Birmingham traditions. The 90/91/92 services, the cross-city group created in its present form in February 1971, were extensively revised on 6th April 1975. The 92 was extended further along the Stratford Road from the Birmingham city boundary through Shirley to the junction with Cranmore Boulevard at Monkspath. At the same time it was separated from the 90/91 which now showed the former number whether travelling to Pheasey Estate or Baldwins Lane, Hall Green. The removal of the 92 from the group also meant the return of all-day short workings between City and Pheasey Estate and these were also numbered 90. This caused confusion so, after a few weeks, these shorts became numbered 91. All other short workings were numbered 90E or, in due course and to the north of the City only, 91E.

Top Buses 4243-4442 had their rear registration numbers behind glass and this was perpetuated on 4630-49. The registrations proved very difficult to read so they were remounted, without glass, early in life. Bristol VRT/Metro-Cammell 4649, in original condition, proceeds along Corporation Street, Birmingham, in July 1977 whilst working service 79. The hard-pressed or lazy driver has not changed the rear blinds. M.R. Keeley

Centre Bristol VRT 4715 in Bilston Street, Willenhall, in September 1978. This shows the extra ventilators provided on the nearside lower deck of 4530 onwards. M.R. Keeley

Right The first Birmingham-based ex-Coventry Daimler to be repainted into PTE colours was 1248, which re-appeared erroneously numbered 248Y, soon corrected. It is seen entering Bristol Road from Chapel Lane, Selly Oak, in February 1975. Road widening has altered this area considerably. Paul Gray

Above Left **A concerted effort over the winter of 1974-5 to rid Wolverhampton of green buses embraced the repainting of 1957 Guy Arab IV 6N which had already survived its sister vehicles by a couple of years. It had also outlived the ex-Wolverhampton Renowns, Swifts, Roadliners and numerous Arab Vs, these vehicles being up to ten years newer! These disparities in length of life were due to the need to keep vehicles running to the very end of their certificates of fitness and the inadequacies of many of the newer buses. Paul Gray**

Above **6N was not the only open-platform veteran plying the streets of Wolverhampton in 1975. Apart from the ever-changing pageant of Birmingham Guys, 1955 West Bromwich Daimler CVG6 186H was also at work, disproving the once held theory that Metro-Cammell 'Orion' lightweight bodies would not last. It proceeds through Queen Square bound for Tettenhall in March. M.R. Keeley**

Left **1958 Daimler CVG6 219H, borrowed from West Bromwich, loads in St James Square in April 1975 on a Wolverhampton to Willenhall short working of service 29 (renumbered 529 in February 1976) to Walsall. In the distance 237H, resident at Walsall since 1971, approaches on a through journey from that town. M.R. Keeley**

These changes were made with the introduction of large capacity buses although, due to the shortage of such vehicles, Daimler CVG6 models continued to be normal on the 92 during daytime for the time being. Conversion to one-man operation on the 90/91 and the NS90 (the Pheasey Estate night service) was achieved on 1st June, and the 92 on 3rd August.

3rd August 1975 was a highly significant day in the history of Birmingham's bus services. Birmingham buses had always shown the outer terminus destination on its radial services, irrespective of whether the vehicle was going into or out of town. Generally, therefore, changes of destination display were only required on cross-town or inter-suburban services. The direction of travel 'To City' or 'From City' was stated clearly on the bus stop which was, after all, the first item of transport furniture encountered by a potential passenger unfamiliar with the system. The tradition was said to cause confusion and, mindful of this, BCT Fleetlines had small supplementary destination blinds which advised passengers of the direction of travel. Whatever the merits or otherwise of the system, BCT, or rather the Executive's Birmingham services, were out of step with the rest of the PTE, if not the world. Out of step that is until 3rd August from which date Birmingham buses actually showed when they were City-bound, a relatively rare destination display hitherto! It will be remembered, however, that the principle of

changing destinations according to direction of travel had been established in August 1971 upon the conversion of the Weoley Castle 21/22 services to one-man operation using exclusively the then new Fleetlines 4051–81 which, with PTE destination layout, were the first in Birmingham without the little 'To City/From City' displays.

Initially buses traversing the City loop (New Street, Corporation Street, Colmore Row) showed 'City Centre' whilst the remaining radial services displayed 'City Terminus'. These displays had replaced in recent years the solitary word 'City'. Destination blinds were subsequently updated so that 'City Terminus' was replaced by 'City', accompanied by the terminating thoroughfare. A fine point of detail was that buses on services from across the City boundary, eg service 92 extended through Shirley, were to show 'Birmingham' on inward journeys.

Birmingham also possessed a somewhat involved system of suffix letters for short workings, commencing with A for the turning point nearest to the City centre and running through the alphabet as one moved further out, reaching L on some services. Some short workings were a regular sight but other turning points were rarely used and seeking out buses showing these rarer displays gave Birmingham bus photographers hours of enjoyment or frustration, depending on one's attitude to life. From 3rd August all these 'short' workings were suffixed with the letter

E, meaning Exception, the arrangement first tried on service 90 earlier in the year. The destination displays remained, of course, but with the demise of the suffix letters, most of the colour went out of 'short' workings! It is arguable whether the travelling public had ever understood the plethora of letters but buses hastily drafted in showing, for example, '58E SERVICE EXTRA' was even more unhelpful than the previous '58C', '58F', etc. Despite this complaint, it is probable that life became simpler for passengers, and certainly for drivers, with just the E suffix.

Another aspect of Birmingham's operations were the three Circle Services (Outer, Inner and City services 11, 8 and 19 respectively). Reports of strangers travelling around three-quarters of the Outer Circle, having boarded a bus going in the wrong direction, were part of BCT folklore. From 3rd August this too changed because the Outer and Inner Circle service numbers were suffixed A or C, depending on whether the bus was travelling anticlockwise or clockwise. Thus the stranger could be informed that he needed an 11A or an 11C and the chances of travelling the wrong way round were considerably reduced. Short workings, previously neither *numbered* nor lettered, now showed 8E, 11E or 19E. The City Circle, by this time, was virtually extinct, basically comprising only short workings of the original circle.

Some ex-Midland Red services had been revised in the Solihull area on 1st June, largely in connection with the creation of a group of cross-borough services from Chelmsley Wood, through Solihull itself to Shirley and beyond. This corridor was immediately successful but was restricted to single deckers due to low bridges en route and the very popularity constantly threatened to cause capacity problems at certain times of the day.

These revisions, however, were minor in nature compared to the upheaval of 16th November. On that date a considerable integration exercise took place involving ex-BCT and former Midland Red services in Birmingham along the Walsall, Warwick and Stratford Roads and the Castle Bromwich route, as well as presenting Solihull with a virtually new public transport network. At the same time, the two garages in Birmingham operating ex-Midland Red services were closed, Moseley Road and Sheepcote Street, and their work transferred to other South Division garages. The vehicles were similarly redistributed and ex-Midland Red stock, a few still painted red, became a regular sight on ex-BCT services. The Alexander-bodied Fleetlines, sometimes in small quantities, were moved into Acocks Green, Coventry Road, Lea Hall and Liverpool Street. BMMO-built single deckers featured at Coventry Road, Lea Hall and Yardley Wood. Nationals were concentrated at Liverpool Street whilst Moseley Road's Leopards passed to the Leyland stronghold of Yardley Wood. A side detail of the changes was that Sutton garage took over the 42 City-New Oscott-Erdington service from Miller Street – this route had been extended to Erdington in 1971 to replace Sutton-worked Midland Red local services along Court Lane, and originally had been commenced by BCT in 1957 to take over journeys purely within the City on the Midland Red College Road group of services (107, 109, 113).

The new Solihull network was of considerable significance as it also introduced the concept of bus/rail interchange, encouraged by more frequent trains and, less subtle, by the withdrawal of certain through bus routes to Birmingham. Adequate interchange facilities existed, and were being improved, at Solihull and Dorridge stations whilst Olton and Shirley interchanges opened in February and March 1976 respectively. Solihull now had a remarkably good public transport network considering the nature of the area and, if the PTE subsequently diluted the facilities, at least it could never be accused of not trying. Not surprisingly there were a few causes for complaint following such a major upheaval – the most justified being the loss of the busy 154 service. Travelling from Solihull to Birmingham via Shirley, the 154 hardly posed a threat to the railway but its demise deprived Widney Lane area residents of their Birmingham service whilst the distance to the nearest station (Solihull) made the replacement rail plus feeder bus combination unattractive. Such are the problems encountered by those who would attempt to change travel habits. The residents of Solihull are not reticent at making known their hurt feelings and the loss of the 154 got a fair amount of press coverage.

One feature of the Solihull scheme was slightly delayed. This was the Dial-a-Bus system, created with the assistance of the Transport and Road Research Laboratory who, with the PTE, would monitor its progress closely. Dial-a-Bus was a fashionable idea of the time, the principle being that passengers would contact a control room, be collected as close as possible to their point of origin, quite probably their front doors, and then be delivered to any practical point on the Dial-a-Bus network. The control room would give an approximate time of collection, often remarkably soon, and then notify an appropriate bus. Regular passengers were pre-booked on a daily basis so it was only casual custom, such as shopping and entertainment traffic, that would have to ring in. Freephones existed at certain points but, nevertheless, high telephone ownership in the area was a prerequisite for a Dial-a-Bus system. The chosen district, that of Knowle and Dorridge, certainly fulfilled this point, being one of the most affluent areas in the West Midlands – the sort of place which had largely deserted the orthodox public transport network already.

It was hoped that Dial-a-Bus would reverse the swing away from public transport in such areas and the WMPTE system, based on Dorridge station, evidently met with some success for it was soon carrying 1,000 passengers per day. To penetrate adequately the housing estates, a fleet of eight new Ford 'A' series midibuses with Alexander (Belfast) bodies was acquired and numbered 4730-7. This octet followed the appearance of a similar vehicle, registered GSA 860N, which had been used on the Centrebus service for four weeks in June and July. It was intended to extend Dial-a-Bus to Solihull from the Knowle and Dorridge direction in due course to displace some through bus services. The eight Fords represented sufficient vehicles for this enlarged system but their reliability record initially proved so poor that Acocks Green garage was often hard-pressed to keep the original smaller network provided for!

The Knowle & Dorridge Dial-a-Buses went into action on 15th December 1975, operating on Mondays to Saturdays only. No ordinary bus services in the area were replaced at this stage. The Dial-a-Bus control room was housed in a former Lincolnshire Bristol SC4LK, parked alongside Dorridge station and provided by the Transport and Road Research Laboratory. This was only a temporary arrangement, pending the extension to Solihull, but interesting low-technology accommodation nevertheless for such a high-technology transport service!

To round off a year when the BCT system experienced its first major dose of integration and had its traditional customs and practices seriously eroded, the Birmingham night services were renumbered from 30th November. The NS prefix was replaced by an N suffix, eg NS14 became 14N, enabling the service number to be correctly displayed in the number box.

SECOND-HAND BUSES
The serious delays in the deliveries of new vehicles, not to mention the difficulties in obtaining spares, continued to threaten the PTE's single-manning programme. However a number of operators who had standardised on rear-engined buses since they first became generally available were now beginning to replace such machines and these could be single-manned unless there was something peculiar about their design.

In 1975, Kingston-upon-Hull Corporation advertised for sale 14 fifteen-year-old Leyland Atlanteans buses which, following an inspection, were considered good enough to be added to the WMPTE fleet. Five had bodies by Metro-Cammell and the remaining nine by Roe. The first of the secondhand purchases arrived at the beginning of the summer, comprising four Metro-Cammells and one Roe. The Metro-Cammells were in quite good condition but the Roe looked distinctly poor. All fourteen were in WMPTE service by November, five at Dudley and the remaining nine initially at Bilston Street, Wolverhampton. They carried fleet numbers 1142–9/ 51–6, an increase of one thousand on their former Hull identifications.

Two of the five Willowbrook-bodied Fleetlines, transferred to Dudley from Coventry in 1975, seen in the Bus Station in August. No.1361, with Dudley Castle apparently sitting prettily on the roof, is working the D5 local service to Cradley Heath via Darby End and Dudley Wood, renumbered 275 the following month. M.R. Keeley

As the newcomers arrived, a number of types disappeared, notably Wolverhampton Corporation's tenuous links with the manufacturer AEC. The last Reliance, 707N, was withdrawn in May; July saw the demise of 183/5N, the last two of the five AEC Renowns, and October the withdrawal of 114/6N, the final pair of ten AEC-engined Guy Arab Vs (an exceedingly rare combination that gave rise to splendid aural effects). The Renowns were not particularly old, having entered service in 1966, and had finished their careers at Walsall. The Reliance had also been at Walsall since January, being short enough for use on the tortuous market day (Friday) routes into Lichfield.

By mid-summer the delivery rate of new Fleetlines and Bristols had increased considerably but the mass withdrawal of real veterans was prevented by difficulties in obtaining spare parts for certain existing types. By June, a significant number of JOJ Guys rendered surplus at Hockley by the conversion of service 90 to Fleetlines were in use at Wolverhampton covering for Guys off the road in that town. Ex-BCT Daimler CVG6s were again a familiar sight at former Midland Red garages. Then in July, the Executive took advantage of reduced summer schedules at Coventry to draft a number of VWK-registered Daimlers into Hartshill to become a familiar sight on the 245/246 (Stourbridge – Dudley – Wednesbury).

Left **Veteran Daimler CVG6 buses were also prominent at Dudley Bus Station in August 1975. Dudley-based 3155, built for Birmingham in 1953, performs a journey on the D9 service to Cradley Heath whilst 254Y, a 1958 Coventry bus working for Hartshill, loads for Stourbridge on the 246 service.** M.R. Keeley

Above Left **Another duo at Dudley Bus Station, showing two ex-Hull Leyland Atlanteans introduced to the town's garage in 1975.** M.R. Keeley

Below **The oldest bus acquired from Midland Red, the first production BMMO D9 built in 1960, received PTE colours in May 1975. The Oldbury based vehicle, No.4849, is seen in Summer Row, Birmingham, in July.** M.R. Keeley

BUSY DAYS AT COVENTRY

The VWKs transferred to Acocks Green were receiving repaints, as mentioned earlier, but it had become clear that the remainder at Coventry would not be withdrawn either so they were thus prepared for re-certification. This attention included a repaint and those treated in March and April (246/9/53/4/9Y) reappeared in blue and cream. These additional and unexpected repaints evidently caused some difficulty because, to Coventrian enthusiasts' delight, no doubt, the remainder received a fresh coat of maroon and ivory. The reason was that each bus spent less time in the paint shop at Harnall Lane if no colour change was involved and old stocks of paint could also be employed. It was evident that the Coventry colours were still going to be around for quite some time. The recertification of elderly stock was not restricted to Coventry, however – rather older buses in Birmingham continued to receive short-term recertifications. The most astonishing repaint of the lot appeared at the end of the year when 25-year-old Guy Arab 2533 emerged in pristine state from Tyburn Road works. This bus was back at Hockley having been returned, like many of its brethren, from service in Wolverhampton where it had become rather shabby.

Other work that had occupied Coventry, in this case the body shop at Sandy Lane, was the conversion of two-door Fleetlines to single-door as the vehicles fell due for recertification after seven years' service. By the end of 1975, buses 23–58Y, with ECW or East Lancs bodies, had been dealt with. The Park Royal batch, 59–75Y, was next but only 70Y was ever reconstructed as it was not found possible to meet Construction & Use regulations on gangway widths and staircase clearances without unacceptable loss of lower deck seating capacity. Thus from December 1975 the bodyshop talents were partly diverted to the overhaul and conversion to single-door of thirty-five of the ex-Midland Red D13 class Daimler Fleetlines, this work continuing throughout 1976 and into 1977. Eventually, some way beyond the period currently being reviewed, the final batch of Coventry two-door Fleetlines, 77–94Y, had their East Lancs bodies converted whilst being prepared for recertification.

WOLVERHAMPTON WANDERER

One final vehicle movement in 1975 is worthy of special mention before pressing on with other matters. In 1966–7, Wolverhampton purchased a mixed fleet of Strachans-bodied single deckers, comprising six AEC Swifts, six Daimler Roadliners and a solitary Ford R226. Of this unlucky thirteen, the Swifts and Road-liners had all been withdrawn after short lives as recorded earlier. In contrast, the Ford, probably the cheapest of the lot, continued to give satisfactory service. In October 1975 this bus, always an odd man out at Wolverhampton, was transferred to Birmingham's Perry Barr garage for use on the 998 Kingstanding limited-stop service alongside ex-BCT Fords. It was renumbered from 720N to 1720 at the same time. It did not prove very popular at Perry Barr and, from June 1976, 1720 became a full-time member of the PTE's training fleet, which happened to be based behind the garage, until withdrawal in April 1977.

The 1950 Guy Arab repainted at the end of 1975, bus 2533, was destined to be one of the last 'Standards' in service. It overtakes similar bus 2609 in Colmore Row, Birmingham, whilst working a lunchtime extra in May 1976. M.R. Keeley

One of Coventry's East Lancs-bodied Fleetlines, built in 1969 with a centre exit, after conversion to single entrance/exit. Coventry's one-man operated buses were identified by the 'MONOBUS' sign on the front. A rainswept view of 41Y and Broadgate. T.W. Moore

Having outlived the technically more sophisticated, and no doubt more expensive ex-Wolverhampton AEC Swifts and Daimler Roadliners, the solitary 1966 Ford R226/Strachan 720N was transferred to Birmingham in October. The bus is seen in Lichfield Street, Wolverhampton, in June, prior to transfer. Paul Gray

The 1971 East Lancs-bodied Fleetlines, 77-94Y, remained in original condition until major overhauls began at the end of 1977. The importance of lady passengers to the health of the bus industry is well illustrated by this Broadgate view. T.W. Moore

1975 had seen the PTE 'running on all six cylinders' with solid advances being made in many directions. The ability to integrate was bearing fruit as witnessed under the Solihull scheme where former BCT and Midland Red services had been combined and the advantages of the railways brought into play. The PTE was indeed proceeding with confidence, backed by a Socialist County Council, led by Councillor Stan Yapp, firmly committed to a growing public transport network.

The new bus station in Walsall town centre had opened on 31st August. This was built on the site of the old bus station, outside the St Paul's Street offices, the rebuilding having been encouraged by the loss of one corner for a new traffic layout. Thus, with a new but slightly smaller bus station and a revised traffic scheme, including some pedestrianisation, a re-arrangement of Walsall bus termini took place. The St Paul's Street bus station now handled services to the east of Walsall. A new terminus in Park Street and Station Street catered for services to the north and west, including the ex-trolleybus services, which had previously departed from St Paul's Street and other isolated locations to the north of the town centre. The Bradford Place terminus continued to operate services to the south of Walsall. These three main centres were connected by the pedestrian area.

The year had seen also the first large-scale increases in the PTE's fare levels since January 1972. Firstly fares in Staffordshire, which were being subsidised by West Midlands ratepayers, were increased in May by an average of 45% as a first stage towards breaking even on services operated in the shire counties. Then, in recognition of national inflation which had been running at an unprecedented rate, fares in West Midlands county were raised by an average of 34% from 30th November. Also on a fares note, it had been possible in June to introduce combined bus/rail Travelcards, after considerable discussion with British Rail. This partly met one of the arguments against bus/rail integration schemes whereby through bus services were withdrawn and passengers were obliged to change mode. However, ordinary farepayers still had to pay again on the second mode and would continue to do so.

Many of the Executive's administrative staff had been on the move in 1975 too. A small number of PTE staff had been housed in an office block at 16 Summer Lane, Birmingham, since the middle of 1974. Basically Midlands Electricity Board premises, these were serving also as temporary accommodation for West Midlands County Council staff until they moved to premises in Lancaster Circus early in 1975. The vacated space was taken up by the PTE which transferred both its Executive headquarters staff from 'Pitmaston', a secluded building off Moor Green Lane and remarkably distant from any bus or train service (!), and its South Division staff until then still established in the ex-BCT offices on Congreve Street.

Reference to secluded areas brings to mind the village of Clayhanger, near Brownhills. This was situated some way from existing PTE services and could not be served by a through route due to an extremely humped bridge over a canal to the east of the village. Clayhanger is not particularly large but there was considerable demand for bus facilities which, with a County Council committed to good public transport throughout the West Midlands, had to be met. In December 1975 services between Clayhanger and Brownhills were begun on a licence held by the PTE but operated by a local minibus operator, J. W. Wickson. This cut costs to a minimum but even so losses were to prove considerable. As is all too often the case, actual support did not match the alleged demand but, despite these reservations, there was some real need for a service to Clayhanger.

It was not progress in all directions, however, because it was in 1975 that concern began to be registered about falling standards of vehicle appearance and cleanliness. In earlier years even Birmingham City Transport, one of the smartest operators in the UK, had been criticised over dirty buses at certain times of the year. However, some of the operators absorbed into the PTE were undeniably scruffy and it was arguable whether bad habits were spreading or maintenance standards were levelling out. Of course, maintenance staff were under pressure and having to retain in service tatty vehicles that should have been replaced earlier. It is also possible that the low fares policy was causing a frugality in some departments. Thus it seems likely that the growing volume of complaint over vehicle appearance was not unjustified.

South Division Changes

The April reconstruction of the 90/91/92 group of services gave rise to scenes such as this, photographed in Corporation Street during July. Service 90 has been converted to large capacity buses, represented by Perry Barr's 1966 Fleetline/Metro-Cammell 3609. The 92, no longer cross-city but newly extended through Shirley to Cranmore Boulevard, presses on with Yardley Wood's allocation of veteran CVG6 Daimlers, including 2853 delivered in 1952. Note the new design of blind on the Fleetline, giving greater prominence to the ultimate destination. Paul Gray

The imposition of the suffix E for all short workings brought an end to the selection of letters previously employed in Birmingham. This unusual September 1972 view in Coventry Road, Small Heath, shows three 'Standards' from foreign garages assisting the Fleetlines, used on this road since 1963, with football traffic to the Birmingham City ground. The correct destination is not on the blind, hence the unhelpful 'SERVICE EXTRA', but a proportion of passengers may have been aware of the extent of the 58F short working. Also visible is Midland Red 5638 on service 159 (Birmingham — Coventry) in pre-PTE days. Paul Gray

The sole surviving SKV-registered Coventry Daimler CVG6, built in 1957, was amongst those transferred to Acocks Green for the Outer Circle, suffixed 11A or 11C depending on direction, from August. The bus, carrying fleet number 1211, travels down Linden Road, Bournville, in May 1977. M.R. Keeley

The extensive November revisions brought ex-Midland Red buses and personnel to ex-BCT garages in quantity. Service 60 to Cranes Park survived unchanged, apart from unavoidable minor re-routeing in the city centre, from BCT days. Coventry Road garage, however, received allocations of ex-Midland Red stock with services transferred from closed garages. Included were red BMMO S23s and D13 class Daimler Fleetlines, such as 6261 approaching Moor Street station in March 1976. M.R. Keeley

Below Left BCT buses were, in turn, to be seen on a regular basis working ex-Midland Red services. 1966 Fleetline/Metro-Cammell 3596 of Lea Hall loads at a Midland Red stop plate on Chelmsley Road, Chelmsley Wood in May 1976. The pick-up and set-down restrictions referred to on the destination, designed to protect BCT buses within the City boundary, survived until re-organisation of the Bordesley Green/Chelmsley Wood services in November 1976. M.R. Keeley

Below Washwood Heath's 3318, an older Fleetline/Metro-Cammell of 1963, works a short working of the ex-Midland Red service 168 to Coleshill in July 1976. M.R. Keeley

Sutton Coldfield's S-prefixed local services were renumbered in November. The extensive borrowing of Birmingham Fleetlines for ex-Midland Red services is well illustrated here. Perry Barr's 3245, one of the 1962 trial batch of Fleetlines, loads in South Parade during July on the S71 to Erdington. No. 3973, ordered by BCT and loaned by Acocks Green, stands behind on service 114. Paul Gray

This Alexander-bodied Ford demonstrator, actually Grampian No.60, used on the Centrebus service in mid-summer, foreshadowed the similar buses introduced on the Knowle and Dorridge Dial-a-Bus experiment in December. GSA860N pulls away from the Dale End Centrebus stop in July. M.R. Keeley

Below The Dial-a-Bus experiment commenced in a stronghold of the upwardly mobile or 'yuppies' as they have become known in the 'eighties. To travel to work in a middle-aged Fleetline compared unfavourably with the family Volvo motorcar, but to be picked up at one's doorstep by Dial-a-Bus and delivered to Dorridge station for a fast, relaxed train ride to Town had style. Two ladies embarking on a shopping expedition approach 4732; each Dial-a-Bus on the road carried its radio identification number on the front — the 2 display had no significance for passengers. T.W. Moore

1976

Top **Leyland National 4799 works a shuttle service through the grounds of the new National Exhibition Centre in May 1976** Maurice Collignon

Centre **The 197 was the original link between Solihull and the National Exhibition Centre. No.4793, in Poplar Road, Solihull, is overtaken in March 1976 by ex-Midland Red 1963 Leyland Leopard/ Willowbrook 5175, working from Yardley Wood garage.** M.R. Keeley

Bottom **The special Nationals escaped onto other routes, particularly when there was not a major exhibition in progress. Lea Hall had put No.4796 to work on the 185 service, a frequent beneficiary of the red, white and blue vehicles, in June 1977. This is the northern approach to Solihull's attractive station.** M.R. Keeley

In the late sixties, the Government began planning the construction of a new National Exhibition Centre. This was expected to be in the London area but, in 1969, Birmingham's City Council and Chamber of Commerce, inspired by Sir Francis Griffin, proposed that the new Centre be sited near Birmingham airport, at the hub of the country's motorway network and alongside the (then) recently electrified London – Birmingham railway line. These overtures were successful and, in 1970, a 400-acre site was bought. In the face of opposition, notably from those who believe London to be the centre of the universe, construction proceeded apace and by the turn of 1976 the huge complex was virtually ready for action.

All that remained was to test the ability of the National Exhibition Centre's facilities to cope with large numbers of people. Thus on 3rd and 4th January 1976, the NEC was opened to the general public for the first time, with a free exhibition of all manner of displays by professional and voluntary organisations, including a spread of preserved buses. It was anticipated that Birmingham rate payers, who had contributed so much to its construction, would turn out in force and an estimated attendance of 60,000 over the two days was expected. In fact around a quarter of a million people are said to have turned up!

The new railway station, constructed to serve the NEC and christened Birmingham International, went into action for the first time. However, rail operations had to be on a limited scale because the track turn-round facilities enabling short-working trains were not complete. Thus the January 1976 exhibition, whilst a good test of events to come, was something of a one-off for WMPTE because the extreme burden put on the bus side would not be repeated. Special bus services were operated between the NEC and Birmingham centre, Coventry and Chelmsley Wood, whilst the internal shuttle services to and from the car parks further stretched resources. The intense bus activity drew a wide variety of rolling stock from all over the South Division and the approach roads to the NEC entrance were literally filled with buses travelling to and fro. However, despite the unexpected number of visitors, the PTE ably coped with the pressure.

In service for the first time at the exhibition were the first three of twelve Leyland Nationals specially purchased for NEC operations. The twelve were numbered 4788–99 and carried the NEC colours of red, white and blue, a livery which generated considerable favourable comment. The bodies were constructed to a two-door layout, reducing the seating capacity to 46. The PTE, of course, had rejected the two-door configuration for its standard fleet but it was realised that rapid loading and unloading, without the need to collect fares, would be a feature of the NEC internal shuttle services, for which these low-floor buses were ideal. The twelve Nationals were to be employed not only on the internal shuttles but also on new services linking the NEC with Chelmsley Wood, Solihull and the 'hotel belt' along Hagley Road. The latter service was actually an extension to both ends of the City centre – Birmingham Airport route. The red, white and blue Nationals were also to be found on normal bus services from time to time, particularly when there were no major exhibitions in progress.

A splendid view of Ailsa 4783 in Victoria Square, Birmingham. T.W. Moore

The last five Bristol VRT/Metro-Cammell buses, 4725–9, entered service in January 1976. Metro-Cammell then immediately turned its attention to its next contract for WMPTE, an order for 270 bodies on Daimler Fleetline chassis. It will be recalled that this chassis order had caused considerable ill feeling amongst the politicians and officers guiding WMPTE because of the manufacturer's reluctance to accept an order for 600 chassis. The Fleetline order was subsequently reduced to 420 plus 80 from contracts placed by the former Coventry undertaking. The engine and body split on these 500 Fleetlines should have been as follows:

6301–420: Leyland/Metro-Cammell

6421–570: Gardner/Metro-Cammell

6571–720: Gardner/Park Royal

6721–800: Gardner/East Lancs

Forty East Lancs bodies had been ordered by Coventry Corporation and, in the event, that was the quantity taken by the PTE, 6761–6800 receiving standard Metro-Cammell Weymann bodies. Park Royal was to fall well behind on delivery dates and thirty of its bodies were cancelled, 6691–6720 also

receiving coachwork by Metro-Cammell Weymann who served the PTE extremely well during this difficult period.

Nos. 6301/3–9 entered service in January from Dudley garage and deliveries were to continue at a good rate over ensuing months. The sudden increase in fleet numbers from the 47xx series was to avoid clashing with ex-Midland Red stock – several D9s from the 4849 batch were still in service at this time. Deliveries had reached 6341 by April and, starting with this particular vehicle, subsequent buses had a revised front dash and trafficator arrangement. The new buses had 204 litre (45 gallon) fuel tanks compared with the 159 litre (35 gallon) capacity of earlier PTE Fleetlines.

Also placed in service in January were the first two of the eagerly awaited production batch of 50 Volvo Ailsas. Delivery of these was also maintained at a fine pace, all fifty (numbered 4738–87) being in service by May. To minimise the number of establishments holding Ailsa spares, the fifty were concentrated into two ex-Midland Red garages; an action which it was hoped would cure vehicle maintenance problems at those premises. Nos. 4738–67 were allocated to Oldbury whilst

4768–87 went to Sutton Coldfield, joining the three prototype Ailsas, 4527–9, which had been moved from Perry Barr in July 1975. The 79-seat Alexander bodies were slightly redesigned at the front end, compared with the prototypes, and incorporated the PTE's preference for flat windscreens.

In addition to the Oldbury Ailsas, the first 150 Metro-Cammell Fleetlines (actually 6301–430/4–53 – more of the missing three in due course) were also all intended for North Division garages. Apart from the Sutton Ailsas, South Division was to receive quantities of new buses in due course but in the meantime had to soldier on with its large fleet of ex-BCT Fleetlines (contemporary with the buses being withdrawn in the North), not to mention the ranks of seemingly indestructible rear-entrance buses dating from the early 'fifties. Nos. 6358–62, intended for Stourbridge, did operate in the South for a short time when new, assisting at Yardley Wood to allow the double-decking of service 189 (Solihull to Shirley Station). This caused some amusement to Stourbridge staff who were used to loans in the opposite direction! Subsequently, 6415–9 spent a short time at Hockley before passing to Stourbridge.

One of the most important arteries of the North Division was converted to one-man operation on 15th February. This was the 29 service between Wolverhampton and Walsall, and worked by garages of both those towns. As in other cases, single-manning provided the opportunity to re-number into the PTE system; this service upon conversion becoming 529 in the Wolverhampton series. The 29 was, at one time, a member of that select band of British bus routes operated jointly by trolleybuses of two operators (Walsall and Wolverhampton Corporations).

The injection of thirty Ailsas into Oldbury garage permitted the conversion of its most important route to single-manning. This was 'The Track', a nickname recalling its tramway heritage, and embracing the 87 Birmingham to Dudley service and its short workings, 85 to Spon Lane and 86 to Oldbury. This conversion was achieved on 22nd February.

Walsall also had its own 'Track', referring to the ex-trolleybus services which plied to Bloxwich before fanning out. Recent deliveries to Walsall enabled its 'Track' to be converted on 7th March. Until now, these services had retained the ex-trolleybus numbers 15, 30–3 but upon conversion were restructured into the Walsall series as services 329–35 inclusive.

An insufficient number of Ailsas had been received at Oldbury by 22nd February so three Walsall-based Fleetlines, 4022/5/7, were sent on loan to help out. In exchange Walsall received three Oldbury D9s, 5304/47 and 5401 – of all the miscellaneous stock operated in Walsall by the former Corporation and the PTE, perhaps these three BMMO D9s are the most unlikely! The three Fleetlines were required back at Walsall for the 7th March conversion and so the exchange ceased, by which time more Ailsas were available at Oldbury.

The new arrivals caused the demise of the last survivors of a number of types. The last rear-entrance Wolverhampton Arab IV, 6N, and the last four Walsall AEC Regent Vs were withdrawn in January. March saw the last of the BMMO S16s and also the KEA and PEA Daimlers ex-West Bromwich. Newer ex-West Bromwich CVG6s rendered surplus at West Bromwich and Walsall were transferred to the South Division, appearing at Hockley in March and Liverpool Street in May. They were primarily used on the 15/16 (Hamstead – Yardley, Whittington Oval) services.

Top **The arrival of 30 Ailsas at Oldbury permitted conversion of the Birmingham-Oldbury-Dudley services to driver-only operation. The reign of the BMMO D9 was thus over, ending scenes such as 5326 in July 1975 loading in Freeth Street, Oldbury at a shelter bearing a fading 'MIDLAND' transfer.** Paul Gray

Centre **D9 5347 in Station Street, Walsall, on 27.2.1976 during its sojourn at Walsall garage. The Town's station, alongside, was subsequently redeveloped as part of a shopping centre.** M.R. Keeley

Right **In addition to the Oldbury Ailsas, the large influx of new Metro-Cammell bodied Fleetlines revolutionised the ex-Midland Red Black Country garages in 1976, providing them with their first new double deckers since the D13 Fleetlines of 1969-71. Leyland-engined 6307 of Dudley garage passes through Old Hill on Halesowen Road in September 1979.** M.R. Keeley

The last of the 1955
and 1957 CVG6
Daimlers ex-West
Bromwich were
withdrawn in March
1976. Willowbrook-
bodied 194H is seen
in Tabernacle Street,
Oldbury, in June
1974. M.R. Keeley

Two Metro-Cammell
bodied Daimler
CVG6 buses with
separate histories
meet in Colmore
Row, Birmingham, in
June 1976. No.242H,
new to West
Bromwich in 1962, is
a recent arrival at
Hockley garage,
overtaking Acocks
Green's 1263
ex-Coventry.
M.R. Keeley

The 1937 Daimler COG5 preserved by the 1685 Group leaves the Council House, Birmingham, for the anniversary circuit of the Outer Circle. This fine vehicle resides at the Midland Bus & Transport Museum, Wythall, and occasionally gives rides to visitors. WMPTE 'Fare'

OUTER CIRCLE GOLDEN JUBILEE

The PTE celebrated the 50th anniversary of the introduction of Birmingham's Outer Circle in some style on 7th April. The 1685 Group, as owners of the oldest ex-BCT bus in running condition, were persuaded to run a special circuit of the Outer Circle using preserved 1937 Daimler COG5 1107. The driver was 1685 Group Treasurer Monty Russell whilst the writer acted as conductor and had to undergo a rapid tuition course on a veteran Bell Punch machine. The passengers comprised several civic personalities, PTE personnel, genuine 1926 Outer Circle drivers (all over seventy years of age and very sprightly too!) and a horde of press and local radio men. Prior to the circuit of the Outer Circle, 1107 was given a civic send-off from the Council House by the Lord Mayor and BBC television. A splendid celebration!

SINGLE-DECKER RATIONALISATION

Between March and July, Coventry Road's allocation of BMMO S23s, used on service 186 (Solihull-Olton-Sheldon), passed to Sutton Coldfield, being replaced by Nationals from Sutton and Walsall.

Then between May and August, the Leyland Leopards (BMMO class S18) at Stourbridge were passed to Yardley Wood apart from 5223/43 sent, rather surprisingly, to Oldbury. Except for the pair at Oldbury, the model was now concentrated at Yardley Wood. The latter also received extra double deckers and, as a result of this influx, the BMMO S17 was eliminated from the garage. By coincidence, Yardley Wood received its first Nationals around the same time when a shortage of vehicles was created upon the extension of service 4 to Hawkesley.

Stourbridge received in turn a variety of S21–S23 types and, in June and July, the five Bristol REs (519, 4443–6) from Wolverhampton. As well as displacing the Leopards, Stourbridge's S17s and Nationals were rendered surplus. The sixth Bristol RE, 516Y, had remained at Coventry until this time. Coventry did not have a requirement for a single-deck service bus but a reserve vehicle for its Ford coach, 407Y, was needed. An ill-fated exchange was therefore arranged in May, with 516Y passing to Stourbridge and semicoach S21 5877 travelling in the opposite direction. Unfortunately 5877, formerly the pride and joy of Stourbridge garage, soon suffered a serious mechanical failure and vanished into the withdrawn vehicle park at Harnall Lane. Meanwhile 516Y entered Walsall paintshops to lose its Coventry colours

and become embroiled in an industrial dispute which delayed its return to service for some considerable time. The muddled fleet numbers of the REs were 516Y, 4443–4, 519, 4445–6, but fortunately the six were renumbered into one series as 5516–21 in September.

The ability to transfer Nationals to replace BMMO S17s was due to the increasing use of double deckers and indeed elsewhere further S17s were directly ousted by double deckers. Thus, by the end of summer 1976, the allocation of single decker types to garages had been rationalised and their numbers reduced considerably. This policy meant that many BMMO S17s could be taken off the road.

New Fleetline 6361, intended for Stourbridge but loaned to Yardley Wood garage to permit double-decking of the 189 service, passes Solihull station in July 1976. M.R. Keeley

An ex-Coventry Bristol RESL, transferred to Stourbridge and given fleet number 5517, leaves Bearwood for Woodgate. Mark Alexander

The Executive's solitary luxury coach, 1972 Plaxton-bodied Ford R226 No.407Y, parked at Harnall Lane, Coventry. Roy Marshall

The BMMO S21 sent to Coventry as reserve vehicle for 407Y. No.5877 is seen in July 1977, the month it was withdrawn. The destination box was panelled over in an attempt to give a more coachlike appearance. Mike Greenwood

Daimler CVG6-30 237H, first operated in 1962, was one of many ex-West Bromwich Daimlers transferred to Walsall in 1971. It moved to the South Division in September 1976, firstly to Hockley garage and then, in December, to Sutton Coldfield where it was distinctly an odd-man-out. It works a journey along Priory Queensway, Birmingham, in July 1977. M.R. Keeley

Below Oldbury-based Volvo Ailsa 4738 loads in Halesowen Road, Old Hill, near the start of trans-Sandwell service 415 to West Bromwich. M.R. Keeley

TRANS-SANDWELL ROUTES

One of the stranger areas created by the Local Government Act 1972 was Sandwell Metropolitan District Council. Its northern quadrant comprised the clearly identifiable town of West Bromwich and this was combined with the nebulous housing mass known as Warley, itself a relatively recent creation. A tentacle added to the south-western corner contained the Cradley Heath and Old Hill areas of the Black Country which, at the foot of a ridge, surely had more in common with the new Dudley district. Clearly Sandwell Metropolitan District Council had an identity problem to overcome!

The PTE quickly realised that residents would want to travel across this odd hybrid to the district offices in West Bromwich as well as wishing to sample the shopping facilities of that town. It therefore created two trans-Sandwell services by amalgamating routes inherited from Midland Red and West Bromwich Corporation. Both services travelled from West Bromwich via Oldbury to Blackheath. Service 415 then descended Perry Park Road and Waterfall Lane to terminate in Old Hill. The 417, however, crossed into Dudley District to serve Halesowen and terminate, virtually amidst green fields with views of the Clent Hills, on the County boundary at Hayley Green. The new routes began on 6th June, jointly worked by Oak Lane and

Oldbury garages, and their service numbers were the first use of the Sandwell 4xx series.

Other important services in West Bromwich were revised on 6th June. The 79 Birmingham (New Street Station) to Wolverhampton service included a host of short workings (numbered 71, 72, 73, 75, 77, 78) emanating from either end. Basically these short workings were eliminated and the through service increased. At the same time service 74 (Birmingham–Dudley), which still terminated at the Birmingham end on Snow Hill, was extended to New Street Station. Both these changes benefited longer-distance passengers who often had difficulty in boarding the busy 79s due to short-distance riders.

FLEETLINES IN AND FLEETLINES OUT

The first of the Park Royal batch of Fleetlines, numbered from 6571 upwards, entered service in July. These vehicles were welcome additions to the South Division fleet and, in due course, permitted conversion of the last major Birmingham radial route, the cross-City 15/16 service (Hamstead – Yardley, Whittington Oval), from rear-entrance buses to large-capacity one-man vehicles. This was achieved on 5th December, after which buses showed service number 16 in both directions. Birmingham's surviving rear-entrance buses, comprising ex-BCT Guy Arabs and CVG6 Daimlers from the Birmingham, Coventry and West Bromwich fleets were now concentrated on the Outer Circle. This caused the introduction of ex-West Bromwich Daimlers to Harborne and Quinton garages, including some further examples received directly from Walsall in March 1977. One oddity, however, was 237H which passed to Sutton garage for use alongside D9s on their last double-crew workings (basically on the half-hourly 111 Birmingham – Sutton – Roughley service).

Deliveries of Park Royal-bodied Fleetlines reached 6610 by November, then ceased and did not resume until September 1977. A good rate of delivery was maintained, however, from Metro-Cammell. On the debit side, early examples of ex-Walsall Fleetlines were being taken off the road, requiring attention to their deteriorating Northern Counties bodies. In due course these vehicles were classed as withdrawn and subsequent examples finished their careers upon expiry of their certificates of fitness after twelve years service.

Other Fleetlines in the news were 6210 and 6213. These were the last buses in the fleet carrying Midland Red livery and were repainted into WMPTE colours in September and October respectively. Further ex-Midland Red buses creating interest were S21s 5849/51 and S22 5903, which were drafted into Selly Oak in September to assist on single-deck service 27. They remained there until the early part of 1977.

A surprising vehicle received on extended loan from October was NVP 533M, the Metro-Cammell Weymann Scania-powered 'Metropolitan' double-deck demonstrator. It arrived in WMPTE colours, carried fleet number 6299, and was put to work from Miller Street garage. WMPTE had paid little attention to the thirsty Metropolitan upon its introduction several years earlier and was the only PTE not to purchase any. However MCW was about to announce its new Metrobus, with Gardner engine, and WMPTE was showing distinct interest. The Metrobus, although in many ways a new design, had its roots in the Metropolitan and the arrival of the demonstrator gave the PTE the chance to sample a double decker equipped with air suspension. Certainly 6299 cost its manufacturer a considerable amount of money as it was converted from double to single-door layout, including re-positioning the staircase, before entering service with WMPTE. This conversion, however, was done whilst MCW had a reduced amount of work in hand.

Characterful vehicles to reach the end of their lives in November were the last of the full-width cab Guy Arab IVs inherited from Wolverhampton Corporation.

Whilst every effort was being made to maintain and improve the public transport network within the West Midlands, the atmosphere

Park Royal turned out 40 of its contract for Fleetline bodies in 1976. Included was No.6586, turning from Corporation Street into Upper Well Street, Coventry, in June 1977. The long ex-Midland Red 159 service was usually blessed with the newest buses at Liverpool Street garage which had been responsible for it since November 1975. In the background, working service 7, is 249Y, one of the few VWK Daimlers to remain in Coventry and be repainted into WMPTE colours. T.W. Moore

was rather different outside the county. Cuts were made to services in Staffordshire with effect from 5th September 1976. Amongst the victims were the Friday only Lichfield market day services, 45 to Beaudesert and 46 to Goosemoor Green, whose exceedingly rural and winding roads had forced the allocation of one short-length single decker to Walsall garage.

Whilst South Yorkshire will go down in history as the County Council which most determinedly supported a cheap fares policy, in the mid-seventies the West Midlands Labour-controlled council pursued the idea just as vigorously and virtually halted the swing away from bus travel. Not surprisingly, the escalating rates subsidy came under increasing fire from the Conservative group. The ultimate irony, however, came in November 1976 when the council was forced to increase the fares when the *Labour* central government threatened to withhold certain grants! A fairly hefty increase (23%) was reluctantly applied, although the revenue derived still did not approach commercial viability.

Secondhand Leylands at Cannock Bus Station in November 1976. Walsall-based Roe-bodied Atlantean 1151, ex-Hull, is about to be passed by Midland Red 2223, a Northern Counties-bodied Titan PD3 purchased with the business of Harper Bros. M.R. Keeley

The Stourbridge Scheme

In May 1974, the Executive had created a specialist section, with a particular brief to carry out market research, known as the Field Survey Unit. A number of major area revisions to bus services had taken place but the first to use fully the expertise of the Field Survey Unit was the Stourbridge scheme.

The PTE bus services in Stourbridge were all inherited from Midland Red, who still had a presence in the town on a handful of out-County routes. The PTE bus services comprised three important routes, to Birmingham, Dudley and Kingswinford, a number of weaker services serving some of the smaller population centres that are a feature of the Black Country, plus a range of local services (distinguished under the Midland Red numbering system with the prefix S) which ran the risk of withering away because their short length did not necessarily generate good loads. Stourbridge was thus a typical Midland Red town network with a considerable density of services often running on low frequencies which contrasted with the higher frequency but less dense network pattern encountered elsewhere in the WMPTE area.

Also requiring consideration was the role of the railway in the town. The principal facility was the Birmingham – Kidderminster line which called at Stourbridge Junction, some distance from the centre of the town. The centre was linked by the Junction – Town Station shuttle, a single diesel unit which met each train on the Birmingham line. Development of the Birmingham line was not in doubt, although the effect of any improvement to the rail service on the 130 Stourbridge – Birmingham bus route had to be considered.

The question of whether to retain the Junction – Town rail link or replace it whilst revising the bus network was probably the most important decision to be made in the Stourbridge scheme.

Buses in Stourbridge centre all terminated within a close proximity but were divided into three sites. This was not an ideal arrangement, worsened by the fact that one of them was the PTE garage itself where the need to maintain a good quality environment for the passengers did not equate easily with the efficient operation of a bus garage.

Following the extensive market research exercise, a much altered bus network was introduced to Stourbridge on 5th December 1976. The Town – Junction rail link was retained, as was the 'rival' 130 Stourbridge – Birmingham bus service, which served a different set of intermediate points to the railway. Indeed, most of the bus routes to neighbouring towns survived largely unaltered but the town services were extensively revised. In some cases they were incorporated into services reflecting the increased demand for facilities towards Dudley (now the administrative centre for the district) and Brierley Hill. The S prefix disappeared as the town routes were revised and numbered into the 2xx Black Country series.

The opportunity was taken to increase the proportion of one-man operation at Stourbridge garage. The relatively small garage had complete responsibility for the 130 service, which was still double-crew worked, generally with BMMO D9s. Simply to convert this service to one-man operation would have rendered too many conductors surplus at one

time. Therefore, under the Stourbridge scheme, the 130 was indeed converted but conductors reappeared on other services from Stourbridge. D9s and thus their conductors ousted from the 130 became the mainstay of the new 294 service (Stourbridge – Pedmore Fields – Lye – Brierley Hill – Dudley) and made a surprising entrance on the 'Khyber Pass' 258[1] (Stourbridge – Brierley Hill via Vicarage Road), previously worked by one-man single deckers. D9s also took over from double-crew single deckers on the Pedmore Fields local services, now numbered 298 and 299. As indicated by the previous existence of double-crew saloons, Pedmore Fields had not been blessed with double deckers before December 1976 and a considerable amount of tree pruning was required. The distribution of conductors onto a number of shorter routes would enable the single-manning programme at Stourbridge to proceed less painfully in future.

These changes coincided with the first big influx of new PTE standard buses into Stourbridge garage. Plans were also on the way for a new, single, bus station adjacent to a reconstructed Town station, making ingenious use of the site presented by two of the existing bus termini and the railway station. This new bus station, opened in May 1980, would allow the garage to be used solely for its proper purpose and for the improvement of inspectorate and crew facilities. The rail service to Birmingham was to be improved and park and ride facilities provided at the Junction station were extremely successful. Thus the visitor to Stourbridge ten years after the PTE takeover would recognise very little from Midland Red days – a new bus and railway station, a much altered bus network and a complete change of vehicle stock. Even the town had changed with the completion of the ring road – about the only items that stayed the same were the diesel trains!

[1]Service 258 travelled along Amblecote Bank which was being reclaimed from industrial spoil. Large scale housing development was planned and the continued operation of 258 was largely an act of faith. In the event, however, development was very slow and the 258 could be a very lonely run indeed – along Hillfield Road very little life could be seen on either side – hence the 'Khyber Pass' nickname!

Left **A reminder of the old regime at Stourbridge with Midland Red AEC Regent II double deckers (BMMO AD2 class) 3111 and 3109 providing local services from the Town railway station in the late 'fifties.** Right **Stourbridge Town Station in December 1977. The canopy to shelter waiting passengers has long gone but the faithful diesel railcar prepares to shuttle another load to the Junction Station** Robert F. Mack/M.R. Keeley

The Stourbridge scheme showed the benefits of evolving new bus networks using market research and the majority of subsequent major revisions used this approach. The WMPTE method leaned heavily on household interviews, thus discovering travel patterns currently not met. This differed considerably from the National Bus Company's well-known MAP projects, which were mainly based on on-bus surveys. However, as in all market research exercises, success depends on correct interpretation of the results and resisting the temptation to go beyond the territory for which information has been collected. Services in Wombourne, Kingswinford, Gornal and the Straits estate were also revised on 5th December and, whilst the changes caused remarkably little difficulty, any problems that did occur tended to involve the areas not covered by the market researchers.

The Pedmore Fields circular, numbered S48 (clockwise) and S49 (anticlockwise), was worked by single deckers with conductors until the Stourbridge revisions. BMMO S23 models 5969 and 5929 load at the Vauxhall Road bus station in August 1976. No.5969 is a recent transfer to Stourbridge, unable to display the S prefix, whilst 5929 has the grille from an S17. M.R. Keeley

The ex-Midland Red Leyland Leopards at Stourbridge were transferred elsewhere in 1976 — most moving to Yardley Wood, including Weymann-bodied 5160 seen here in April 1974. Stourbridge to Wolverhampton service 256 was modified in the revisions; some buses now going via Cot Lane into Kingswinford as service 255. M.R. Keeley

The 294 was a new service introduced with the Stourbridge revisions. It exploited the growing demand for Dudley, taking a circuitous but useful route via Pedmore Fields, Lye, Quarry Bank and Brierley Hill. Its usual vehicles were initially BMMO D9s, displaced from the 130 service. No.5342 negotiates the busy High Street in Brierley Hill in September 1977. M.R. Keeley

1977

The beginning of the New Year saw the population of the West Midlands still able to enjoy, or otherwise, the finer points of 66 ex-Birmingham 'Standards' and 34 BMMO D9s. Amongst buses withdrawn in January was 149N, the last of the ill-starred Strachans-bodied Guys.

Metro-Cammell announced its new design, the 'Metrobus', in January and West Midlands PTE immediately ordered five prototypes which would be numbered 6831–5. Also ordered around the same time were 30 Leyland Nationals (6836–65; thirty Nationals were already on order as 6801–30) and 135 Leyland (as they were now called) Fleetlines with Metro-Cammell bodies to be 6866–7000.

1977 saw the country celebrating the silver jubilee of Queen Elizabeth II's accession to the throne and a number of bus operators placed silver-liveried buses on the road. Companies were willing to pay more generously to have their wares advertised on these eyecatchers. WMPTE received three new Fleetlines in January in silver; these were 6431–3 which, like most all-over advertisement buses, spent their first year moving from garage to garage so that they could be seen by the maximum number of people. The trio lost their silver liveries in March 1978. A fourth bus to receive silver was 6299, the Metropolitan demonstrator which carried congratulatory messages from its builder, MCW. Unlike the other three, however, it did not indulge in a grand tour, remaining at Miller Street.

The first of the Fleetlines with East Lancashire bodies modified to WMPTE specification arrived in March. Although bristling with PTE fittings, it was quite clearly distinguishable from the standard product from Metro-Cammell and Park Royal. The East Lancs bodied vehicles were all intended for Coventry, whose municipal undertaking had ordered them. However the single-manning programme had not been proceeding well at Coventry so the first twenty, 6721–40, were diverted to Acocks Green garage for the time being. This South Division garage was developing quite a Coventrian air at this time as it was also home to the exiled CVG6s.

The last front-engined ex-Walsall buses were withdrawn during the spring, with the demise of Daimler CVG6s 67L and 887/9L in March and 70L in April. As recorded earlier it had become necessary to begin withdrawal of the ex-Walsall Daimler Fleetlines, threatening to exacerbate the difference between the average age of vehicles operating in the North and South Divisions. Thus some of these machines were succeeded at Walsall by earlier PTE standard stock transferred from the South Division. April and May 1977 saw the transfer of South's only J-registered Fleetlines, 4051–60, whilst K-registered 4211–20 followed in March 1978. Many of these found their way back to the South eventually, however.

Above Left June of Jubilee year and Metropolitan demonstrator 6299 and Fleetline 6432, in commemorative silver, withstand the English summer at the Yenton, Erdington terminus of service 64. The previous year had seen a serious drought with emergency measures preventing the machine washing of buses. M.R. Keeley

Left Silver Fleetline 6431, working from Perry Barr, rounds the Old Square, Birmingham, in July with an ex-Midland Red D11 Fleetline to the rear. M.R. Keeley

The first numerical ex-Birmingham AEC Swift, 3663, had undergone a pilot overhaul and following this it was decided that it was not worth the expense of repairing the remainder for further service. Thus the Swifts were prime candidates for withdrawal upon arrival of Nationals 6801–30. The first fifteen, 6801–15, which had standard bus seating, entered service in April. Most of these went to Selly Oak, permitting the withdrawal of the unoverhauled short-length Swifts, 3664–74. Two of these Swifts did have a brief extension of life when 3673–4 passed to Oldbury, displacing their two Leopards 5223/43 which, just as surprisingly, surfaced at Dudley. The saga of this strangely allocated quartet of saloons ended upon their withdrawal from service in August and September. Other single-deckers on the move during the summer were the Bristol RESLs which were transferred from Stourbridge to Dudley (5516–8) or Cleveland Road, Wolverhampton (5519–21). The movement of 5516 was probably a paper transfer, due to its continuing involvement in the paintshop dispute; it finally emerged at Dudley in September so it is doubtful that it ever ran at Stourbridge. The withdrawal in June of the last BMMO S17 was the signal to commence inroads into the next class of BMMO single-decker, the S21.

No.6724, one of 20 East Lancs bodied Fleetlines diverted from Coventry to Acocks Green garage, negotiates Victoria Square in August.
M.R. Keeley

The East Lancs bodies were easily recognisable from the PTE standard: a rear view of 6724 in Corporation Street, Birmingham.
M.R. Keeley

The last of the businesslike BMMO S17 buses were withdrawn from West Midlands service in 1977. No.5553 hauls itself up the incline of Dudley Bus Station in February 1977, eventually to descend the precipitous depths to Lodge Farm estate. M.R. Keeley

New Leyland National 6806 awaits the rush of Cadbury's workers at Bournville whilst providing peak strengthening on service 27 (King's Heath to West Heath). Paul Gray

The other fifteen Leyland Nationals, 6816–30, were fitted out to dual-purpose specification with a special livery, capacity reduced to 45 very comfortable seats, and overhead luggage racks. The receipt of dual-purpose buses into the PTE fleet was something of a departure, the only previous vehicles to a higher quality specification were the ex-Midland Red S21s and S22s and the ex-Coventry Ford coach. The Nationals were purchased with a view to increasing the private hire side of the business but they were still required to play their part on stage services during weekday peaks. Indeed it was a bus grant requirement that they should operate at least 50% of their mileage on stage work. Particularly appropriate niches were two of the Birmingham peak-only limited stop services, to Castle Vale and Kingstanding (967 and 998 respectively), upon which they displaced

the uncomfortable ex-BCT Fords 3651–62. These Fords, although primitive, had done very well to last ten years on peak-hour city work bearing in mind their lightweight design.

The last ex-West Bromwich single decker, Leyland Tiger Cub 251H, was withdrawn in August. Its final stint had been on the Asda, Tipton, free bus contract, worked by Dudley garage. It was succeeded by a Bristol RESL. By the end of the year, the ex-Birmingham AEC Swifts were also history – the overhauled example, 3663, finding a ready buyer in the form of Mid-Warwickshire Motors, Balsall Common.

A major new housing development was under construction at Frankley, to the south-west of Birmingham. A minor part of the estate was within the West Midlands County but the majority was actually outside in Here-

ford & Worcestershire. A total of 5,000 people were expected to be living there by the end of 1977, this figure rising to 12,000 upon the planned completion of the estate in 1980.

It had been planned to serve Frankley with a spur of the Cross-City railway line, then under development, but unfortunately this did not come to fruition. Instead the Executive's proposals to meet the initial needs of the estate were two bus services, limited stop facility 949 to Birmingham centre, and local stopping service 149 to Northfield. These had to face rival proposals before the Traffic Commissioners from Midland Red and Everton Coaches of Droitwich. In the event, the PTE proposals and a modified service from Midland Red were granted, the PTE commencing business on 9th July. As Frankley grew and traffic demand became clearer, the PTE revised its Frankley services.

The dual-purpose Nationals were perfectly acceptable for long runs. This expedition for 6821 has taken it to Combe Martin, North Devon. Paul Gray

A greater climatic contrast is hard to imagine as 6819 slithers away from Solihull Station in January 1979. Alan B. Cross

Left **1977 casualties were the AEC Swifts which had provided the backbone of service 27 (Kings Heath to West Heath) since the inception of the PTE. Swifts 3675-80 were 36 feet long, an enlargement of three feet over 3663-74. Traffic from Cadbury's tries to exit into Linden Road, Bournville, in May 1977, including Swift 3678 and new National 6806.** M.R. Keeley

Centre **The peak period limited stop service to Kingstanding is always popular. Ford 3660 provides noisy transport around Colmore Circus in June 1977, new dual-purpose Nationals would soon provide a greatly improved standard of comfort.** M.R. Keeley

Bottom **The last Leyland Tiger Cub was withdrawn in 1977. No.251H, built in 1963 with Roe bodywork, works the Asda contract in Tipton during February** M.R. Keeley

A CHANGE OF POLITICAL COLOUR

Labour had enjoyed control of West Midlands County Council during its first three years of existence. However in the local elections of May 1977, control was gained by the Conservatives. Criticism of the local Labour transport policy had been a main issue in the Tories election campaign but, as is all too often the case in local elections, it was probably a reaction against central government activities that caused the Tory victory – not a protest against subsidised bus fares.

Out went Sir Stan Yapp to be replaced by Councillor David Gilroy Bevan as transport chief – a role he had occupied in pre-County Council (ie PTA) days. Bevan proposed to keep West Midlands the best PTE in the country and, in furtherance of Conservative philosophy, the PTE was immediately required to apply to the Traffic Commissioners for a 30% fares increase (25% on Travelcards), which would still leave the Executive's operations subsidised to some extent.

An impressive line-up of assorted interested parties opposed the application, foreseeing the PTE re-embarking on the downward spiral of fares increases and passenger decline. The Conservative approach was good news to ratepayers who did not use buses, of course, but there was always the risk that the money saved would be used to devastate more areas for the 'road improvements' to counter increased traffic congestion. After a very lengthy hearing, the Traffic Commissioners granted the fares increase, which took effect in August.

As new brooms, the Conservatives intended to sweep exceedingly clean. In July the PTE hit the national daily newspapers when County Council Finance Committee Chairman Anthony Beaumont Dark threatened to sue British Leyland. The motor giant, whose unnatural growth and unhealthy monopoly position had been encouraged politically, had poured millions of pounds into the bottomless pit of its chaotic acquired car divisions. The once splendid commercial vehicle group had been starved of investment as a result. Here was entertainment aplenty for the interested bystander as Mr Beaumont Dark treated the beleaguered manufacturer to the sharp end of his wit.

"We spend millions in public money because the manufacturer is providing us with a bum product. They just lie there at the side of the road. They are not buses, they are traffic hazards".

Above Left **Dial-a-Bus was extended to Solihull in July 1977. The eight Fords received assistance from two Commers displaced from Centrebus. No.4238 picks up at Solihull Station in July 1978; the offside door and, thankfully, the orange livery have gone. Above Right Ford A4733 pulls away from a temporary stop in Station Road, Solihull, in March 1978 — this location received very attractive passenger shelters. Below BMMO S21 5850 squeezes through the bridge in Colebrook Road, Shirley, shortly before the alterations which diverted the route away in July 1977. The once polished grille has received unsympathetic treatment from a blue paintbrush. Bottom The 185 service continued to be single-deck operated, this bridge in The Radleys being a further obstacle to double deckers. An ex-Midland Red Leyland National passes beneath the main Birmingham to London railway line, which also carries the local train service to Coventry, in November 1982.** M.R. Keeley

DIAL-A-BUS EXTENDED

The services in Solihull and Shirley were again revised on 24th July. These changes were quite major in nature but the most significant was the extension of Dial-a-Bus from the existing operations in Knowle and Dorridge along Warwick Road to Solihull. The Dorridge to Solihull link via Widney Manor Road continued to be operated by ordinary buses. A low frequency double-deck service (182) was also retained, duplicating Dial-a-Bus between Knowle and Solihull, but continuing via Warwick Road to maintain a link towards Birmingham as far as Acocks Green. Knowle and Dorridge passengers requiring Tyseley or central Birmingham were expected to use Dial-a-Bus to Solihull or Dorridge stations and then train.

The eight Ford A midibuses, 4730–7, should have been sufficient to work the extended Dial-a-Bus operation. However their reliability record had not been good so two of the Commers originally purchased for Centrebus duties, 4238/41, were converted to 15-seaters for use as relief Dial-a-Buses. Their offside doors were removed during conversion. The Dial-a-Bus controllers were also more comfortably situated by this time. Their temporary housing at Dorridge in the ex-Lincolnshire Bristol SC4LK had been replaced by rather better accommodation in a room attached to the PTE's Solihull enquiry office.

A minor, but significant, detail of the Shirley alterations was the diversion of service 185 (Kings Heath – Chelmsley Wood North) from Colebrook Road to follow companion services 164/5 (Wythall – Chelmsley Wood North) via Shirley Station. Although slightly longer, it improved the chances of a satisfactory rail to bus interchange at the station, and was more in line with the PTE's 'frequent corridor' approach compared to Midland Red's 'serve every road' philosophy. Equally importantly, it removed operation from under one of several single-deck only bridges that beset this long route – in January 1983 this group of services would be divided and total double-deck operation at last made possible on the Shirley side of Solihull.

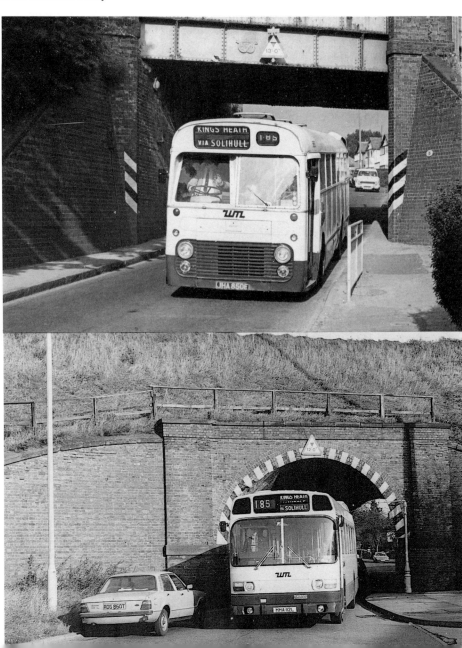

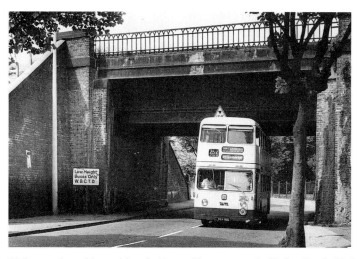

Whilst on the subject of low bridges, this structure in Hydes Road, Wednesbury, prompted West Bromwich Corporation to buy low-height buses. Single-deck route 252 from Smethwick, jointly operated with Midland Red, had been extended in the mid-sixties to cover the single-deck route that previously served Hydes Road. Low-height double deckers were introduced in 1967. Daimler Fleetline/ECW116H, built in 1969, carries the modified livery adopted by WMPTE for low-height buses. Renumbering of West Bromwich services into the 4xx series was completed in 1977. Some of the 1969 low-height Fleetlines found their way to the ex-Midland Red garage at Hartshill in 1977. No.120H stands at Dudley Bus Station as the year draws to a close. T.W. Moore/M.R. Keeley

EXPERIMENTAL FODEN BUS

Amongst the manufacturers encouraged to re-enter PSV production by the inability of British Leyland to meet the needs of the market place was Foden.

The Sandbach builder had built up an enviable reputation for well engineered and solid trucks but its foray into the PSV world during the late forties and fifties was largely forgotten. Nevertheless in 1977 it evolved a rear-engined bus design, of typically beefy Foden construction and powered by a Gardner 6LXB engine. A handful of prototypes was produced and the specification sufficiently interested West Midlands PTE for it to purchase one.

The design was evolved jointly with Wigan bodybuilder Northern Counties and was known as the Foden–NC. The bodywork was in the square idiom then favoured by Northern Counties and produced in large numbers for operators like Greater Manchester PTE. The West Midlands example was numbered 6300 and entered service in August 1977 at Liverpool Street. No. 6300 was destined to spend almost its entire WMPTE career on the 50 route (Birmingham, High Street, to the Maypole) — although for a period it was also the regular performer on the 50N night service. The body was finished to WMPTE specification, complete with standard red seats and blue formica interior, and did not look out of place to the average passenger. The layout was the standard 43 upstairs and 33 down.

For some reason, probably shortage of finance, Foden made no attempt to persevere with the model, despite the costs it must have incurred in designing and producing the prototypes. No. 6300 thus remained unique in the WMPTE fleet and, as Foden production did not even reach double figures, spare parts were to be a continual problem for it.

Above Left **The solitary Foden-NC, 6300, unloads at the busy terminus of service 50 in High Street, Birmingham, during March 1978.** M.R. Keeley

Left **The Foden's rear end treatment showed the greatest departure from the standard PTE design for the Fleetline. The bus passes through King's Heath in November 1978.** Alan B. Cross

PROGRESS IN SERVICE RE-NUMBERING

The renumbering of West Bromwich services into the PTE scheme may have made a slow start but progress in 1977 was so rapid that all services had been renumbered, in some cases revised, by 30th October.

The numbering scheme for PTE services was as follows:

1–99   Birmingham City services (basically ex-Birmingham Corporation).
100–99   Services from Birmingham to points outside the City, plus Sutton and Solihull locals. (Basically ex-Midland Red).
200–99   Dudley MBC services. (Basically ex-Midland Red).
300–99   Walsall services, including Staffordshire.
400–99   West Bromwich services.
500–99   Wolverhampton services.
600–99   North Division works services.
700–99   North Division schools services.
800–51   South Division works services.
852–99   South Division schools services.
900–99   Limited stop, hospital, football, dogtrack, supermarket contract, bingo services.
(800-99 works and schools services subsequently intermixed)

In achieving the above, most ex-Birmingham City Transport and Midland Red services could retain their existing numbers. Some of the acquired Midland Red services in the Wolverhampton area had been in their 8xx series but were renumbered upon takeover. The D or S prefixed ex-Midland Red locals in Dudley, Stourbridge, Sutton and Solihull were swallowed up in area schemes or renumbered when opportune. The ex-Walsall, West Bromwich and Wolverhampton services were frequently the old Corporation numbers with the appropriate hundred figure added, although service revisions overtook many traditional routes before renumbering. Some Walsall services were renumbered twice, a start having been made in the early days of the PTE to put them in the 2xx series later required for ex-Midland Red services. Notable omissions from the above scheme were the Coventry services which were so removed from the rest of the system that they were able to keep their existing numbers. The use of suffix letters for groupings of similar services was frowned upon, however, so routes like 9/9A would be renumbered.

THE LAST BIRMINGHAM 'STANDARDS'

The end of October saw the inconceivable happen – the last Birmingham 'Standards' were withdrawn after service on Friday 28th October. The newest was a mere stripling of 23 years but the oldest, Guy Arab 2533, had seen 27 years continuous service without major rebuilding. During this time it was reckoned to have run nearly 700,000 miles and, bearing in mind inevitable unit changes during its six complete overhauls, found employment for three engines, nine gearboxes, twelve differentials and propeller shafts, and 150 sets of new brake shoes.

Enthusiasts were able to warm themselves with the satisfaction that the surviving 'Standards' had outlasted a few ex-Birmingham Fleetlines, a decade newer, which had fallen by the wayside in recent months. Withdrawal of these Fleetlines, themselves up to fifteen years old, would now become a pre-occupation of the engineers.

In their final months, the 'Standards' had been restricted to workings covered by the Outer Circle 11 crews, the only double-crew service left in Birmingham. Thus they had rare excursions onto other services, ie peak extras scheduled to be covered by Outer Circle crews, but by and large they had not been seen away from the 'Desert' as the Circle is popularly known amongst staff. The 'Desert'

retained its conductors for the time being but was now re-scheduled for large-capacity buses. The ex-Coventry CVG6 Daimlers, although only 60-seaters, had to be regarded as large-capacity for a brief period but were replaced as soon as possible when further Fleetlines became available. Those with a reasonable expectancy of life were, in fact, returned to Coventry where they replaced some of their brethren. They did not revert to their 'Coventry' numbers so it was possible to see 1233 alongside 239Y etc.

As if the loss of the 'Standards' was not bad enough, the same weekend saw the demise of the last BMMO D9s. The 1685 Group marked the double blow with a tour employing Guy Arab 3015 and D9 5342. The D9 ran excellently, of course, and passed into preservation but 3015 was the real eye-opener. Its fine performance did not let down the 24 years of care it had received and its interior, spared the attentions of late evening yobbos for some time, was as immaculate as the outside. Sadly when the writer returned 3015 with pride to its final home, Acocks Green garage, it was never to carry a passenger again. Its next run was to a withdrawn vehicle park where it would await collection by a scrapman and then the torch.

The odd D9 would still be seen in Birmingham on Midland Red services, notably the 110 to Tamworth. However these refreshing visitations gradually diminished, even before their final demise, as the survivors retreated to the Leicester area. The PTE would possess half-cab buses for a little while longer, although many would consider those types to be of a lower calibre than the 'Standards' and D9s. Thus, for many enthusiasts, October 1977 marked the end of their interest in the West Midlands current scene.

There was a spate of vehicles carrying between-decks wrap-round advertisements, as exemplified by 1968 Fleetline/Park Royal 3743 at Five Ways in November 1979. The bus is not far at this point from the brewery of the advertiser.
Alan B. Cross

1978

As the year turned, Director General Mr F. J. Lloyd was looking forward to his retirement from the PTE. Mr J. K. Isaac, for several years the Executive's Director of Operations, was already installed as Director General-designate.

James Isaac was described correctly by a newsman, upon his appointment, as one of those remarkable men who, even as they sit behind a desk, seem always to be on the move. His bus career started as a student in the BET training scheme with Ribble, then becoming assistant to the traffic manager of Aldershot & District. His next appointment was a complete contrast – assistant traffic manager of Jamaica Omnibus Services, giving a fresh view on operating methods. He returned to England in 1964, joining firstly Midland Red and then North Western. He then moved back to Midland Red in 1969 as traffic manager just at that Company's second-bleakest hour (the bleakest was to come in 1981!). He helped pull the Company through but then in August 1973 joined the PTE, an organisation which fully reflected his interest in how transport forms part of the community. He succeeded to the top job just as the political climate changed and he was going to need all his varied skill and experience to steer the PTE through.

Mr Lloyd's last official function before retirement was the official opening on January 18th of the rebuilt Cleveland Road garage in Wolverhampton.

The garage, costing more than £1.5 million, occupied the site of the former Wolverhampton Corporation depot and offices, and was virtually a new structure. The original premises were on two levels, the upper facing Cleveland Road and the lower, some ten feet below, on Bilston Street. A feature of the old Cleveland Road depot, designed for tramcars, were the numerous narrow bays, impossible for the convenient manoeuvring of buses. The new garage, in contrast, had a roof spanning an area of over 6,400 square metres, one of the biggest structures in the Midlands without centre supports. With side supports kept to a minimum, there was easy passage for buses.

The main garage was now in the upper level which included pits and workshop area, and was connected to the lower level by a ramp. The lower level included more of the garage's maintenance facilities. The office staff were now housed in a new two-storey administration block.

The frontage of the old depot included stonework inscribed 'Municipal Tramways Car Depot'. As a pleasant reminder of the garage's history, the stonework was included inside the new premises.

Above Left **The Executive's original Director General, Mr Fred Lloyd, retired at the beginning of 1978. The writer extracts a fare from him for the benefit of photographers on the occasion of the Outer Circle 50th anniversary run in 1976. On the extreme left is Councillor Sir Stan Yapp, then Leader of the West Midlands County Council and Chairman of its Passenger Transport Sub-committee.** WMPTE 'Fare'.

Left **Interior view of the new Cleveland Road garage in Wolverhampton. Plenty of staff have been marshalled for the photograph; vehicles in evidence include Leyland and Gardner-engined Fleetlines, two ex-Hull Atlanteans, a pair of Bristols (VRT models), and a Leyland National.** WMPTE 'Fare'

With the Birmingham 'Standards' gone, the veterans of the fleet in January 1978 were the ex-Coventry CVG6 Daimlers. No.239Y, at Jardine Crescent terminus, Tile Hill, was now in its twentieth year. The conductor of this open platform bus looks frozen and no doubt would find the shelter advertisement ironic — his driver may be faring better with a warm Gardner 6LW at his side T.W. Moore

1963 Weymann-bodied Guy Arab V 99N waits in pale sunshine at the Patshull Avenue terminus of service 502 in January 1978. The introduction of two digits into one of the number boxes was a late reconciliation between the need to renumber services and the restricted displays offered by some of the acquired stock. Also just visible above the destination box is an aerial, 99N being one of comparatively few half-cab buses to have been favoured with two-way radio. The Guy Arab model was eliminated from the fleet by the end of 1978. M.R. Keeley

The low railway bridge in Station Road, Old Hill, that defeated Leyland Nationals. Lowering of the road began in January 1978, bringing a death sentence for BMMO buses such as 5932 passing beneath at the end of the previous year. S23 type 5932 was actually to be one of the last two BMMO-built buses in the fleet, surviving in service until January 1981. M.R. Keeley

METRO-CAMMELL IN TOP GEAR

By the beginning of 1978, Metro-Cammell Weymann had completed its contract of bodies up to bus 6570. Park Royal had fallen seriously behind with deliveries so the PTE had cancelled part of its contract, favouring Metro-Cammell Weymann with an extra 30 bodies. Thus upon completion of 6570, Metro-Cammell then began work on 6691–6720, previously to be bodied by Park Royal, and a number of these entered service in January 1978. Two months later, that batch of thirty was complete and a number of the series 6761–6800, at one time pencilled in for East Lancashire bodies, were also on the road.

At the turn of the year, the Guy Arab V had been reduced to only 18 vehicles. The ex-Coventry Daimler CVG6s were still around in some numbers but only in their home town. The only other CVG6s in passenger service were the final batch supplied to West Bromwich, 259–65H, which were still allocated to that town's garage in Oak Lane. The Arab Vs and Coventry CVG6s were under withdrawal, of course, along with the ex-Midland Red Leopards and ex-Walsall Fleetlines. The spring would see the end of more of these types, all of 259–65H, and representatives of the D11 and D12 classes of Midland Red Fleetline. Most of the Bristol RESLs were also withdrawn whilst, in the BMMO line, the ranks of S21s and S22s were thinned and inroads even made into the relatively youthful S23s.

The ability to withdraw all BMMO stock was at risk because of an extremely low railway bridge in Station Road, Old Hill. Two services worked under the bridge, the 202 (Cradley Heath – Blackheath – Quinton) and 235 (Cradley Heath – Coombs Wood – Halesowen – Hasbury), both operated by Stourbridge garage which, as a result, still had quite a BMMO flavour. It was anticipated that eventually the entire single-deck fleet would be composed of Leyland Nationals which, with their roof-mounted heating pods, would not pass under the bridge. (The 'podless' option was not available at this time). Thus, in January 1978, work commenced on lowering the road beneath the bridge to permit the use of standard Nationals. The road was closed for approximately three months and the 202 and 235 services diverted. It was necessary to introduce a shuttle service, numbered 400, between Old Hill Cross and Blackheath, connecting with other services to maintain links and involving a complete turn as near to Old Hill station as possible. A small bus was essential, so Commers 4236–7 working out of Stourbridge garage were pressed into service for the duration.

The next batch of Nationals began to arrive in April. Of this batch, 6836–50 were to service bus specification whilst 6851–65 were dual-purpose vehicles.

In addition to bodying Fleetlines at a splendid rate, MCW was also pressing on with development of its own design, the Metrobus. The first for West Midlands PTE, 6831, was completed by the end of 1977 but did not enter passenger service until February 1978. No. 6831 was actually the third Metrobus to be built but was the first to enter service with its purchaser – the first two Metrobuses were a test shell and demonstrator TOJ 532S. No. 6831 was conveniently allocated to Washwood Heath garage, virtually opposite the MCW works, where the manufacturer could keep a

Cleveland Road, Wolverhampton, received prototype MCW Metrobus 6834, seen leaving Queen Street in September 1979. The greater area of blue reduced the excessive amount of cream whilst matt black window surrounds may have been intended to end the need to repaint those awkward areas. Matt black skirt panels and the stepped cream band echoed features of trendy 70s cars. The blue applied to Metrobuses was a lighter shade compared to other WMPTE buses. M.R. Keeley

close eye on its performance. Nos. 6832–4 were delivered during the summer and, to fully evaluate the model, were spread throughout the Executive at Harnall Lane (Coventry), Dudley, and Cleveland Road (Wolverhampton) respectively. The fifth WMPTE prototype, 6835, would be a Motor Show exhibit of which more later.

There was one further job for Metro-Cammell. In October 1971, the body of Daimler Fleetline 3531 had been burnt out. The remains of the body were broken up in June 1972 and since then the chassis of 3531 had been used for test purposes. Upon the evolution of the Metrobus, the Fleetline was rapidly becoming past history and so it was

decided to fit the low mileage test chassis with a new body. This was not as easy as might be expected because earlier Fleetline chassis were a shade shorter and narrower. Thus the standard PTE Metro-Cammell body had to be re-designed to fit the earlier chassis, these alterations being discernible to the skilled eye. This hybrid received a higher fleet number, 5531, more appropriate to its appearance although it retained its 1965 registration number. It was placed into service in September from Washwood Heath garage. It looked quite ordinary at first glance but the C-suffix registration on a PTE standard body seemed strange.

Leyland Titan demonstrator FHG592S and prototype Metrobus 6831, both working from Washwood Heath garage, load in Bull Street, Birmingham, on 1st April 1978. WMPTE was to order many new generation Titans but Leyland failed to produce the goods — on whom was the joke this April Fool's Day? T.W. Moore

Above **The former 3531 with its new Metro-Cammell body as bus 5531, loading in Bull Street, Birmingham, during October 1978. The rear view clearly shows the extra width of the body (8ft 2½ inches) compared to the 8 feet wide chassis and engine cover. Vehicles of the same batch were only a couple of years away from the scrapyard.** M.R. Keeley

Right **Even earlier Fleetlines to capture attention in 1978 were 3241/3/4, with Metro-Cammell bodies, which were amongst the first of the model to be built, having entered service with Birmingham City Transport in 1962. The three moved to Coventry in 1978, one seen in Ironmonger Row on the busy Wood End service soon after transfer.** M.R. Keeley

SINGLE-MANNING PROGRESS

Birmingham's Outer Circle 11 service was converted to one-man operation on 18th March. All the ex-BCT garages were now converted, a notable achievement bearing in mind the heavy loads carried by many of the city's routes. The South Division did still possess a few conductor duties at the ex-Midland Red garage in Sutton.

The Outer Circle conversion rendered homeless the survivors of the first ten Birmingham Fleetlines, 3241–50, which, it will be recalled, had to be worked with conductors. Eyebrow raising was accorded to the despatch of 3241/3 to Harnall Lane, Coventry, in June with 3244 following them to the East in November. No. 3241 was the first production Daimler Fleetline and its return, in the autumn of its life, to the city of its manufacture could be viewed as appropriate!

The extension of single-manning at Coventry was now a major priority and, with it, the demise of the still numerous CVG6 Daimlers in the city. The five Willowbrook-bodied Fleetlines which had spent several years at Dudley returned to their original home in the spring of 1978. Nos. 1360–4 lost the thousand prefix upon return but not all received the Y suffix in lieu. Metro-Cammell was still pressing on with Fleetline deliveries and a number of its next batch, commencing with 6866, entered service in June. Twenty of these (6871–90) were to go to Acocks Green displacing its East Lancs-bodied Fleetlines, 6721–40, which joined the rest of the type, now all in service, at Coventry (6741–60). East Division was not to miss out on new deliveries, however, for by the end of the year 6916–35/62–71/84–9 were either in use or, in a couple of cases, awaiting entry into service at the two Coventry garages.

Below **New Metro-Cammell bodied Fleetlines 6887 and 6881 at Acocks Green. Partial redevelopment takes place in the background, threatening the village atmosphere of this shopping centre at the hub of a Birmingham suburb.** Paul Gray

94

ENTER MID-WARWICKSHIRE MOTORS

The PTE was required by its political masters to ensure an adequate transport service throughout the West Midlands county. One area where facilities were not particularly good was the no-man's land between Coventry and Solihull, south of Meriden, the centre of England. Notable settlements in the area are Hampton-in-Arden, Balsall Common and, rather smaller in size, Berkswell but many of the houses belong to those at the richer end of the social scale, depressing the public transport potential even further.

Midland Red provided the best services it could, considering the passenger traffic on offer. The area was also served by the Birmingham – Coventry electric trains stopping at two stations, Hampton-in-Arden and Berkswell (a misnomer, the station is on the outskirts of Balsall Common). WMPTE's presence was restricted to the infrequent ex-Midland Red 158 service between Solihull and Hampton-in-Arden. The PTE also supported the 569 Coventry – Balsall Common service, operated on the Executive's behalf by Midland Red.

Some improvement in facilities occurred from January 1978 when the Coventry to Burton Green or Berkswell services (28/28A/29/29A) were diverted to Balsall Common as services 42–45. This was a logical decision, but it did mean the PTE service to Berkswell was reduced from five journeys per day to a special service (46) operated twice in each direction on Wednesdays and Fridays only!

A more radical solution to the problems of serving the Heart of England was in the pipeline, however. Services from the area to Solihull would involve a considerable amount of empty running to and from garages. It was logical, therefore, to enter into an agreement with a local independent operator, who would have lower overheads as well as being better placed to run the services. This was the cue for Mid-Warwickshire Motors to step in, with effect from 1st April 1978, operating a network of services tailor-made to meet the needs of the the area with financial support from West Midlands. MWM was a relatively new operator but was already operating private hire, works and schools contracts, as well as a stage service acquired from Shirley's of Meriden.

The PTE/MWM agreement worked reasonably well for a time, after some initial teething problems, although relations were never entirely happy. Unfortunately, in due course, Mid-Warwickshire Motors was forced to vacate its premises in Balsall Common and then worked the Heart of England services from a base in Water Orton which, being well out of the area, increased costs considerably. This meant that the PTE could probably run the services just as cheaply itself and have greater control over the journeys operated, so consequently it became increasingly unhappy with the arrangement. Mid-Warwickshire Motors got into severe difficulties in the early part of 1983, of which more later.

Mid-Warwickshire Motors Daimler Fleetline/Willowbrook YAY701J crosses the Birmingham-Coventry-London railway at Berkswell Station whilst on a positioning journey in November 1978. This Fleetline was an astute purchase by MWM, being a low mileage vehicle purchased from the Road Transport Industry Training Board. *T.W. Moore*

Another astute Mid-Warwickshire Motors purchase was KOX663F, the WMPTE AEC Swift overhauled and then sold with the others when it was decided on cost grounds to replace rather than overhaul them. MWM stripped out the unwelcoming standee interior and fitted coach seats to produce a cosy and attractive service bus. It is seen leaving Pool Meadow, Coventry, on MWM service 169. *T.W. Moore*

Mid-Warwickshire Motors at its peak in March 1981 with four modern Plaxton-bodied AEC Reliances, on West Midlands sponsored and other services, filling Poplar Road, Solihull, to the extent that WMPTE 4584 cannot enter the street. *M.R. Keeley*

The former Dial-a-Bus Fords were now normally restricted to Knowle and Dorridge, apart from runs to and from garage, but for a time continued to penetrate Solihull on Sunday only service 184. Ford 4737, with all Dial-a-Bus signwriting obliterated, approaches Solihull Station from Blossomfield Road on 24th September 1978. Alan B. Cross

DIAL-A-BUS ENDS

Despite being such a poor area for public transport operation, Solihull continued to provide much of interest to the enthusiast – this must be due to the desperateness of the services attracting so much managerial thought!

The labour-intensive Dial-a-Bus service ended in September 1978. It was replaced by a fixed route (183) serving Knowle and Dorridge only and traversing the estate roads most popularly specified by Dial-a-Bus passengers. Dial-a-Bus philosophy partly lived on in certain thoroughfares where there were no fixed stops – passengers would be picked up and set down anywhere in those roads on request. The Ford midibuses were used on the 183 service whilst ordinary buses became again entirely responsible for serving the Warwick Road into Solihull on Mondays to Saturdays. On Sundays the network was rationalised. Most of the estates were still served but the route continued via the Warwick Road into Solihull as service 184, dispensing with the 'heavy' bus. The 184 was introduced as a midibus service but, with the section west of Dorridge station not operated on Sundays, there was little reason why ordinary saloons could not run the route and, indeed, Nationals did appear on the 184 in due course.

Knowle and Dorridge thus continued to receive a rather more personal service, feeding into Dorridge station for reasonably quick travel into Birmingham. However the 183/4 was never as popular as Dial-a-Bus and the estate roads still did not generate sufficient passengers for the cheaper form of service provided. Not surprisingly, the 183/4 fell by the wayside in the severe cuts of November 1980. The pattern of service in Knowle and Dorridge then largely fell back to the traditional approach of serving the area, employing the triangle of Warwick Road, Station Road and Widney Manor Road. This must not be viewed as a complete disappointment, however, because there can be little doubt that public transport usage is healthier, particularly the railway, than would have been expected in Knowle and Dorridge, through the efforts put in by the PTE.

The two relief Dial-a-Buses, Commers 4238/ 41, found new work on an experimental service circuiting Birmingham's huge Queen Elizabeth Hospital and linking it with the Outer Circle 11 and service 21 (City – Bangham Pit). Numbered 54, the service began on 19th November 1978. However, in December, the Commers exchanged roles with single-deck Fleetlines on physically handicapped children's contracts. The Fleetline-equipped 54 service continued until the 21 itself was re-routed to circuit the hospital amongst the Harborne and Weoley service changes of August 1980.

MOTOR SHOW 1978

Of all the successes clocked up by the National Exhibition Centre, just about the biggest was to capture the Motor Show from Earl's Court, London. The Show was now to be held every two years, the first one at the NEC to be in October 1978. Here was a complete challenge – how many people would come and how would they get there?

It was calculated that many would come by rail, testing the capacity of International station to the utmost, or by coach. The remainder would come by car, at first filling the copious car parks around the NEC and, as usual, being shuttled from those points to the entrance. This shuttle service, operated by the specially-liveried PTE two-door Nationals, was already well established. However it was correctly anticipated that many more car spaces would be required, so eight overspill parks were set up with users to be shuttled free of charge to and from the Show by PTE bus. Each car park was identified by the symbol of an animal, an idea borrowed from America's Disney World and thought to be easier for the car owner to memorise. The furthest car park from the show was the Chelmsley Wood collector road but the three busiest were Packington Park, the unopened section of the M42 motorway north of the NEC, and an area adjoining the M42 at Solihull.

More than 321,000 passenger journeys over ten days were made on the park-and-ride services provided by WMPTE buses working under contract to the Show organisers, the Society of Motor Manufacturers and Traders. In addition 70,000 passengers were brought in by the normal bus facilities serving the NEC. Buses were drawn from all over the Executive and, because they would be needed throughout the day including the evening peak, the fleet had grown by around 50 vehicles, representing vehicles that should have been withdrawn since June but retained until the Motor Show. Not that the Show saw much geriatric stock – garages sent their most modern buses for the contract – older buses generally only appeared at weekends when pressure on the shuttles was at its greatest. In the event far more buses were on hand than were required; the police did such a fine job that the expected traffic congestion did not materialise. Park and ride buses were given priority and were able to get round much quicker than anticipated. Visually impressive though the bus side was, 40% of Show visitors actually came by train. More than 100 extra trains were running each day, including a ten-minute service from London at times. Nearly 400,000 people used the rail services and, although trains were rather overcrowded at times, the passengers were able to pass easily through International station and into the Show without fuss.

Exhibited in the commercial vehicle section of the show was the fifth of WMPTE's five prototype Metrobuses, 6835. Both the PTE and the manufacturers were very proud when the Metrobus won the gold award in an international coachwork competition organised by the Institute of British Carriage Automobile Manufacturers. The cynical noted the handsome moquette-covered seats sported by 6835, which contrasted with the nasty PVC standard issue in Fleetlines and the other four Metrobuses. However the cynics were to be proved wrong because the production Metrobuses would indeed blossom forth with moquette seats, both upstairs and down. It was later to be confirmed that deliberate damage was lessened when moquette was employed; it seems the more restrained end of the vandal population appreciated the PTE's consideration for its passengers.

Leyland was not to be completely outdone, however. The PTE had placed an order for five

West Midlands PTE, like many fleets, was prompted into introducing an open-top bus through accident damage. 1969 Daimler Fleetline 3867 suffered severe damage to the roof of its Park Royal body and, mindful of its age, the PTE arranged for the Moseley Road Training Centre to convert it into a permanent open-topper. The bus originally had a central exit and this was deleted at the same time. The rebuilt vehicle was painted largely blue, relieved by a black skirt and two cream bands, lined out in black. Most operators are moved to paint open-toppers in a light scheme so 3867 was a refreshing contrast. Completion of the conversion was achieved in October 1978. The bus has been found a variety of work including this tour of Coventry during a June 1983 'Shopping Week'. The tour took in the City's ruined former Cathedral, not passed by any service buses. The beauty of the old building is clearly shown — a pity the City fathers did not choose to rebuild rather than sanction the modern eyesore replacement alongside.
T.W. Moore

of the new Titan model and the first of these arrived towards the end of the show period. The bus, numbered 7001, was thus available for park-and-ride duties. Following the troubles with Leyland, the PTE was anxious to avoid being committed again to one manufacturer and orders placed at this time reflected this. The PTE intended to improve on the standards of comfort offered by the Fleetline, which was due to be taken out of production, and thus wished to order 80 Metrobuses and 80 Titans. The elected representatives, however, felt that simpler technology (and thus cheaper) buses should also be tried. Orders were therefore placed for 75 Metrobuses, 75 Titans and 10 Dennis Dominators with Willowbrook bodies.

An interesting vehicle reinstated for the Motor Show period was unsold Birmingham 'Standard' Guy 3059 but, not surprisingly, it received very little use. With the Motor Show contract out of the way, the engineers were able to indulge in a withdrawal spree towards the end of the year. Amongst types eliminated were the last ex-Wolverhampton Guys, the final survivors being 1965 Mark V models with Metro-Cammell bodies, and the last Leyland Leopards ex-Midland Red (5161 and 5212). Fleetlines on the way out were the first production batch of BCT vehicles (GON registrations), more Walsall models and further ex-Midland Red D11s and D12s. Also delicensed were a considerable number of 'Jumbo' Fleetlines, ordered by Birmingham and Wolverhampton Corporations and which had been the first vehicles received by the PTE (3881–4004). The Park Royal bodies on these giants were showing premature signs of coming apart at the seams, particularly those allocated to Selly Oak garage where they had an arduous time on the busy Bristol Road services. Some had the bodies patched up but others never ran after the end of 1978. In the

unlikely event of the cost being considered worthwhile, there was insufficient works capacity to deal with a major rebuilding exercise. In addition the mechanical reliability of the 33 feet long Fleetline chassis had never been sparkling. It was clear that some way would have to be found to replace these Jumbos prematurely.

Withdrawals of early Birmingham Fleetlines got under way in 1978 — 15 years was usual for these vehicles which were not destined to rival the quarter centuries clocked up by some of the 'Standards'. No.3284, with Park Royal body, works circular service 161/171 along Smallbrook Queensway in April. This circular, operating at its furthest point through Coleshill in Warwickshire, was one ex-Midland Red Chelmsley Wood service to retain pick-up/set-down restrictions throughout the PTE period.
M.R. Keeley

The Development of Local Railways

The launch of the Cross-City line in May 1978 was the most exciting product of a package of proposals to revitalise local rail in the West Midlands. Yet the Development Plan for West Midlands PTE, published in 1972, had to describe rail usage then as 'meagre'. Rail was carrying around 5% of work journeys and only 2% of all travel movements in the area. The railway network had been built to meet the 19th century population pattern, it was a happy accident if rail happened to run through 20th century housing developments but even then road competition was usually overwhelming.

Railways are expensive to operate but have enormous potential for the mass movement of passengers. The reverse side of the cost coin is that they enjoy their own right-of-way and have a speed potential rarely matched by bus services. The speed factor is a potent competitor to the private car. Because the latter is such an inefficient user of road space, railways are worth subsidising to avoid expensive highway construction necessary to cope with the ex-rail passengers that would turn to cars.

The PTE undertook an extensive review of the local rail system, being assisted in this respect by the transport studies of the 1960s. It was concluded that the short movements of Black Country passengers were best suited to bus. The dormitory areas in and around Birmingham, however, offered scope for rail and certain lines were identified as suitable for development into valuable parts of the public transport system. Other lines would continue to be supported for the time being pending studies into replacement facilities but, in fact, these services survive intact. Finally there were lines that the Authority and Executive chose not to support. The line between Birmingham (Snow Hill) via West Bromwich to Wolverhampton (Low Level) closed in 1972, being effectively replaced by the 79 Birmingham – Wolverhampton bus service.

The agreement with British Rail was signed in January 1973. Basically, the Executive specifies the service it requires and the fares to be charged, and British Rail supplies the trains and carries out their day-to-day management. British Rail charges the Executive the difference between the operational costs and revenue collected. The operations are not without inherent problems; on many lines InterCity trains are entitled to priority, through picking up the bulk of the costs, but an understanding of the importance of each business has minimised difficulties.

WIDENING THE MARKET

Earlier studies revealed that most existing rail users were within walking distance of their homes and the destination point of their journeys. This was insufficient to give the mass movement that rail requires so it was vital to increase its catchment areas. To achieve this, stations on lines to be developed would try to include several features, in addition to reasonable comfort and visual appeal. Free car parks would be provided to encourage park and ride. There would need to be easy access for those dropping and collecting commuters at the station – the so-called 'kiss and ride' customers. Where appropriate, bus/rail interchanges would be created and buses would become complementary feeders rather than competitors. It was reckoned that an interchange passenger would be looking for a ten-minute saving in journey time and, for this reason, inner area stations were unsuitable for development as interchanges.

It was recognised that trains should have attractive and easily memorised frequencies and that connections with buses should be good. This implies that both modes have to run to time or the interchange collapses. This aspect proved difficult in practice – the most successful interchanges are those served by high frequency bus routes. The fares policy was also designed to encourage rail travel; the evolution of the bus/rail Travelcard minimised the inconvenience of using two modes for what is really one journey and, for many years until the end of the PTE bus-operating period, there was no cost penalty for the dual-mode card. Travelcards are also valid on the fast electric InterCity trains between Coventry, Birmingham and Wolverhampton, for which that sector of BR receives compensation from the PTE.

The first lines to be improved were those via Tyseley to Solihull and Dorridge, and to Shirley. Frequencies were improved in October 1975 and journeys concentrated into Birmingham Moor Street station – hitherto many had terminated at New Street where platform space was required for other developing services. Bus/rail interchanges were created at Dorridge, Solihull, Olton and Shirley stations and car parks enlarged as much as practicable. This was a highly car-orientated area but carryings increased by 60% in three years.

The Coventry line was improved in 1976. Birmingham International station opened in January and would serve the new National Exhibition Centre whilst there were proposals to rebuild Birmingham Airport with passenger facilities facing the station – these plans did come to fruition in a slightly modified form with the airport and station linked by the Maglev people mover. Reverting to 1976, however, in May the service between Birmingham and International was doubled, employing a new turnback facility for the local trains. Bus feeders from Chelmsley Wood linked with Marston Green and Lea Hall stations.

The section on Stourbridge earlier in this book noted the retention of the Town to Junction shuttle, worked by a single diesel car, which was one of the lines originally supported only on a temporary basis. Increased car park capacity was provided at Stourbridge Junction in 1977, this was so successful that further enlargements have taken place in 1979, 1982 and 1986! The services on the Stourbridge line have been progressively improved over the years and Cradley Heath station was rebuilt as a rail/bus/car interchange in 1984.

The Cross-City line was the most startling development, however. The service north-eastwards from central Birmingham through Sutton Coldfield to Four Oaks en route to Lichfield, was still healthy. The initial plans proposed to link this Lichfield service across the City to points south-west, originally to Redditch and on a spur into the new Frankley housing estate. The redrawing of the PTA

Four class 312 electric multiple unit sets were allocated to West Midlands services in 1976. One of the sets, 312.204, received this experimental livery of yellow with blue window surrounds in the mid-1980s. WMPTE Archive

boundaries to that of the West Midlands County sadly eliminated both Lichfield and Redditch from the major upgrading, although they still continued to receive a rather less frequent BR service, and the proposed Frankley spur was abandoned. The development thus shrank to Four Oaks to Longbridge. The south-western side of the City had next to no local service and a fair amount of capital expenditure and track work was required to avoid difficulties with existing main line operations. New stations were constructed at Five Ways, serving the growing office complexes, at Birmingham University, which also serves Queen Elizabeth Hospital and at Longbridge, location of the Austin car factory. Four other stations were rebuilt including Bournville, adjacent to the Cadbury's factory. The northern side was not ignored, with car park developments at Four Oaks, Sutton Coldfield and Chester Road stations.

The original frequency for the Cross-City line, upon introduction in May 1978, was four trains per hour, increasing to six in the peaks. The scheme involved an additional 24 three-car diesel train sets, bringing the total to 76 for West Midlands operations. The line was an immediate success and, in terms of traffic diverted from the highway system, worth every penny of its £8m cost.

One line originally to have been developed was that to Derby and Leicester via Water Orton. The redrawing of the PTE boundaries excluded all stations on this line and, not surprisingly, it has not attracted support from the PTA to date. The PTA can support a line for up to 25 miles outside its boundaries but politicians are unlikely to invest ratepayers' money in this way unless a real financial return is guaranteed.

Of the lines left supported but without plans for development, the Stourbridge Town to Junction shuttle has already been mentioned. The Walsall line frequency was severely reduced in 1977 but the off-peak service was doubled to half-hourly in 1984 with successful results, thus improving its future. The peak service was then enhanced in 1986 together with that of the other line left unmentioned, that to Wolverhampton.

The bulk of the revitalisation took place in the second half of the 1970's but improvements to station facilities and car park extensions have continued. Train frequencies have been stepped up to meet the increasing demand. Most lines carry a passenger service beyond the PTE boundary and the two partners, WMPTE and BR, have agreed to convert many of the journeys extending into the shires into limited stop journeys whilst maintaining existing stopping frequencies within the PTE area. These 'express' journeys take the fullest advantage of the speed potential of rail, benefiting not only British Rail's out-county customers but also those PTE passengers served by them too.

THE FUTURE
Physical work on the long-awaited extension of the Birmingham Moor Street services through the disused tunnel to Snow Hill began in 1986, enabling trains to run from the autumn of 1987. The extension has involved the construction of new stations at both locations but will markedly improve the central penetration of the trains from Solihull/Dorridge and Shirley. Long-term plans envisage the re-opening of the formation west of Snow Hill to Smethwick West, allowing a new cross-city service from Solihull etc. in the east

to Stourbridge in the west. This would free the Stourbridge line from the constraints of the busy line via Smethwick Rolfe Street into Birmingham New Street.

ROLLING STOCK
The Coventry, Wolverhampton and Walsall lines had been converted to electric multiple units in 1967 as part of the London – North West England electrification. The bulk of the work is carried out by class 310 units, based at Bletchley, although a minority is handled by class 304 units from Longsight. Also based at Bletchley for WMPTE services are four class 312 sets, purchased for the 1976 Coventry line improvements. The class 312 units are to be replaced by further class 310 sets, however, which are being refurbished.

The remaining services continue to be worked by traditional diesel multiple units built in the late 1950s. The usual configuration has, until now, been three-car sets combined for busy journeys. Class 116 units have proved ideal for the West Midlands services but these trains have already worked beyond their expected lives due to a combination of reasons. Electrification is being considered for at least the Cross-City line; unfortunately the whole cost will have to be borne locally as BR requests for funds to electrify further InterCity services through the West Midlands have been refused by the Department of Transport. Secondly, recent diesel multiple unit designs are not suitable for intensive urban operation as the present now vintage trains. The much-maligned diesels have, in fact, served the West Midlands well, thanks to good maintenance at Tyseley depot, and the delay in their replacement must have saved ratepayers a small fortune.

The unfashionable class 116 three-car diesel multiple units have, despite their critics amongst railway enthusiasts, performed extremely well and by 1986 formed the standard allocation for West Midlands diesel services. Built by Derby Works, the 'high density' units were introduced in 1957. A class 116 in standard BR blue and grey stands at Moor Street Station, Birmingham, in August 1983 alongside a class 101 Metro-Cammell set led by M53336 bound for Stratford-upon-Avon via Shirley. The class 101 is in the short-lived impractical livery for refurbished stock of off-white with blue band. Both sets carry the WM logo M.R. Keeley

1979

January has little to commend it in any year and, in 1979, drivers had to face more than the usual amount of snow. Metro-Cammell bodied Fleetline 6782 loads at the 50 terminus in High Street on 23rd January whilst the Birmingham Co-op makes little progress with its sale bargains across the street. The Co-op store has since been demolished for a new shopping development. M.R. Keeley

The last Metro-Cammell bodied Fleetlines, in the form of 6997–7000, entered service in January. The following month Park Royal deliveries at last resumed on the remaining examples, 6661–90, of its reduced contract. This series was completed in May when 6690 went on the road from Acocks Green garage, almost three years after the first of the batch (6571). It was unfortunate that the last of so many Fleetlines to be purchased new by the PTE had such a low fleet number – 7000 would have been much more appropriate.

The remaining four Leyland Titan prototypes were also placed into service during the first couple of months of 1979. Like the prototype Metrobuses, the quintet were spread about the system, 7001–5 being allocated to Washwood Heath, Selly Oak, Walsall, Perry Barr and Harnall Lane (Coventry) respectively. Four Titans were in a very different livery to the Metrobuses but 7002 approximated quite well to the style carried by 6831–5. In due course most of the Titans had their original liveries slightly simplified and, on full repaint, all received the Metrobus layout.

The large influx of Fleetlines into the two Coventry garages towards the end of 1978 was recorded earlier. This caused a major slaughter of most of the remaining CVG6 Daimlers and a start was also made on Coventry's early rear-engine stock, both Atlanteans and Fleetlines. This modernisation was not entirely assisted by an engineering dispute which prevented certain repaired Coventry Fleetlines from operating in their home town. These buses were accepted at Selly Oak, Birmingham, where they supplemented the ailing Jumbos. Seven buses were involved and, in efficient South Division style, received proper destination blinds. The seven, 24/39/65/71Y, 360/7/70Y, were all returned to Coventry by September.

Coventry received a selection of older PTE vehicles between January and March, maintaining the momentum of replacements. Four early standard Fleetlines, 4051–4, had a sojourn in the East between service in Walsall and transfer to Coventry Road, Birmingham. These were joined by the five surviving ex-Hull Leyland Atlanteans (1145/7/52/4/6), previously at Dudley and Cleveland Road

(Wolverhampton); buses which were surprisingly acceptable to the East Division staff. With the withdrawal of the last ex-Birmingham City Transport Atlantean from Yardley Wood in March, this meant that all remaining examples of the marque were now in the East, in the shape of the Hulls and those purchased new by the former Coventry undertaking.

Well away from its former home, the last of the ex-Coventry Bristol RESLs was withdrawn in March, this being 5516 at Dudley for the Asda contract. A month earlier the last BMMO S21, 5870, had finished service whilst in April the last S22s were retired. Withdrawals of S23s continued. In the South Division, spring saw inroads into the 1964 (KOV) batch of Fleetlines and a start made on the strange single-deck Fleetlines. Coventry's unusual coach, 407Y, a Ford with semi-automatic gearbox and Plaxton body, was withdrawn in June.

The PTE was still in urgent need of new vehicles and it will be recalled that ten Dennis Dominators with Willowbrook bodies had been ordered, rather against the professional

Top **The end of an era as Park Royal belatedly delivered the final new Fleetline, No.6690, which entered service in May 1979.** M.R. Keeley

Centre **Former Coventry ECW-bodied Daimler Fleetline 24Y, temporarily working for Selly Oak, in Birmingham.** M.R. Keeley

Bottom **Whilst the Coventry trade union recoiled at operating some of their own buses, temporarily exiled to Selly Oak, these ageing ex-Hull Leyland Atlanteans were surprisingly acceptable. Roe-bodied 1152, built in 1961, loads at Bell Green.** T.W. Moore

Top **Walsall's Leyland Titan 7003, with cream band beneath the windows, heads for Birmingham along the Walsall Road, Great Barr.** R.A. Mills

Centre **The paint scheme of Titan 7001 was modified to this layout, without the cream band. There is a standing load for 7001 as it turns from Carrs Lane into Moor Street Queensway, Birmingham, in July 1979.** Alan B. Cross

Bottom **Titan 7002 was clad in this attractive Metrobus-style scheme, into which the others were subsequently repainted. This photo was taken in September 1979.** Alan B. Cross

Above **The 1964 series of Birmingham Fleetlines were now being withdrawn. No.3365 with Metro-Cammell body awaits departure time at Witton in October 1977; this route was given a 'lazy' blind which did not need changing at each terminus. Park Royal-bodied 3430 works the peak-only 30 service between the City centre and Five Ways via Holloway Head in July of the same year. This was the former Barclaycard advertisement bus and received a cream roof upon repainting into fleet livery, one of the few BCT double deckers to be so treated.** Below **New Leyland National 7009, rushed into service with all-cream paint scheme, in Summer Lane, Birmingham.** Bottom **The first ex-London Transport DMS to be received, 5501, changes drivers in Bristol Road, Selly Oak, in July 1979. Eighty such buses were eventually added to stock, all originally using the destination display area shown.** M.R. Keeley/Alan B. Cross

officers' wishes. The PTE was notified that these buses would be dearer than quoted and this provided the opportunity to cancel the order. Replacement new vehicles were found in the form of ten Leyland National single deckers for which quick delivery was available. These took the fleet numbers 7008–17 and began to enter traffic in June. Like some of the 1974 Nationals, they were rushed into service in all-cream livery, as delivered from the manufacturer, the blue relief being applied later. Unlike the earlier occasion, however, they were equipped with PTE destination gear before coming on the road.

The PTE also investigated the possibility of further second-hand purchases and, in April 1979, was informed by Ensign Bus Company, vehicle dealers based in Grays, Essex, that it was handling the sale of London Transport's 'Londoner' DMS class of Daimler Fleetlines. London Transport had purchased 2,646 of these Fleetlines, bodied by Park Royal and Metro-Cammell, with Gardner 6LXB or Leyland 0680 engines as standard power units. For reasons that baffled the rest of the industry, London Transport found itself unable to cope with the vehicles within its overhaul procedures. A minority were given light overhauls but the majority were withdrawn upon expiry of the initial Certificates of Fitness at the age of seven years, and sold through Ensign.

Ensign was thus able to offer to the PTE as many Fleetlines as could be desired. Moreover, before delivery they would eliminate the central exit, overhaul them to five year certificate standard and repaint them in WMPTE livery. They were also prepared to accept troublesome 'Jumbo' 33-feet long Fleetlines in part exchange. In view of the shortage of works capacity within WMPTE, this was an offer that proved irresistible, as it did with many other operators.

The PTE was particularly interested in the Gardner-engined, Metro-Cammell-bodied variation and, accordingly, one example was supplied suitably modified and overhauled by Ensign, entering service with the PTE in June. This was the former DMS 1257 (JGU

New destination screens with separate number boxes were quickly provided. In some cases the original blinds were employed for a time, hence the repetition of the service number 12 on bus 5524 in Colmore Row in April 1980. The location of the centre door, removed by Ensign before delivery, is made obvious by the non-standard window. No.5524 still retains engine shrouds but these were gradually removed. M.R. Keeley

A Yardley Wood DMS with four-track service numbers at Solihull Station in August 1984. Other 'customised' features on this bus, 5543, include standard PTE ventilators, trafficators, spotlamps and angled cutaway above the engine compartment. M.R. Keeley

257K), built in 1972, which became 5501 in the WMPTE fleet. There were a number of London modifications to the Fleetline chassis specification, most notably a fully automatic gearbox, but basically the bus fitted into the WMPTE fleet well. In three respects, the Londoner was superior to the standard Fleetline, possessing a higher driving position, an admirable power steering arrangement, and LT-pattern moquette seating.

The order was quickly increased several times until Ensign had been contracted to supply 80 vehicles. The escalating size of the order caused a hiccup in the numbering of the machines which had to take account of existing rebodied Fleetline 5531. The Londoners were thus numbered 5500–30 and 5532–80. Their gearboxes were converted to semi-automatic, bringing them into line with existing WMPTE stock. Delivery began in July and was spread over a year, the last few not entering service until September 1980. Ensign sub-contracted much of the modification and overhaul work and vehicles intended for WMPTE could be seen in the workshops of operators large and small all over South-Eastern England. It must be said that the quality of painting on many examples was well below that of PTE paintshops and the buses probably looked their best when the majority were repainted after three years' service in the West Midlands.

The original intention was to allocate them to three garages in the south-west of Birmingham but, in the event, a fourth (Yardley Wood) also became involved. The allocations settled down as 5500–19 to Selly Oak, 5520–30/2–40 to Harborne, 5541–60 to Yardley Wood, and 5561–80 to Quinton; this distribution being retained until their own demise began. Their arrival enabled withdrawal of 'Jumbos' to begin in earnest, although replacement was not on a one-for-one basis.

All eighty entered service with a much reduced version of the London destination display. This arrangement was hopelessly inadequate and, from the beginning of 1980, all were gradually fitted with new destination boxes, incorporating three-track number blinds. This still proved inadequate for Yardley Wood's Solihull services, involving displays such as 152E, so certain of its allocation received four-track numbers. Another significant departure from the London specification was to remove the inconvenient engine shrouds, in some cases this was done very neatly, involving triangular panels (like PTE Fleetlines) in lieu.

The London buses generally seemed to encourage touches of 'customisation' at garage level, most notably at Yardley Wood garage. Its allocation received standard PTE flashing trafficators and PTE side number boxes. A number lost their excellent London sliding ventilators in favour of the inadequate standard hoppers; in some cases only the lower deck was treated. The champions, however, were 5546 and 5552 which received almost standard PTE destination displays although it was only possible to fit three-track number blinds.

Nos.5546 and 5552 received standard PTE destination boxes. No.5546 overtakes Fleetline 6556 at Solihull Station in April 1984 — just visible is the substitution of a PTE side number box. M.R. Keeley

The transport of physically handicapped children in Birmingham was still largely carried out by ageing single-deck Daimler Fleetlines. Two Ford A models with Dormobile bodies, incorporating rear tail lifts, had been purchased in 1976 for use in Wolverhampton. These were originally numbered 6297-8 in the bus series but, in February 1979, became 501-2 in the service fleet. In May 1979 came the first of 18 further such vehicles with delivery spread over the years 1979, 1980 and 1981. No.503 joined the original pair at Wolverhampton but 504-20 would be added to the South Division and remove one of the main roles of the single-deck Fleetlines. The new Fords carried nine plus wheelchairs. No.520, built in 1981, features in this busy scene in Digbeth, Birmingham during July 1982. Other vehicles in view are Fleetlines 4582, 3868 and 4196, and National Welsh ND2576. M.R. Keeley

The Fords at Wolverhampton replaced some unusual vehicles. This 1961 Morris ambulance, registered 5999JW, survived for many years but did not receive a fleet number. M.R. Keeley

There were two of these Ford Thames buses, delivered to Wolverhampton in 1963 with Martin Walter bodies. Maurice Norton

LAST MUNICIPAL GENERAL MANAGER RETIRES

The last of the general managers of the absorbed undertakings retired at the end of June. Stan Jobling, described by James Isaac as 'his strong right arm', had begun his bus career before the Second World War as a traffic assistant in his native West Hartlepool. Wartime army service, rising to major, interrupted his career at West Hartlepool which he left in 1951 to become traffic superintendent with Bury Corporation. He joined West Bromwich in 1954 as deputy manager, becoming general manager three years later. Upon the creation of the PTE, his first role was Operations Manager for the North Division. In 1970, however, he was appointed Chief Planning Officer, becoming Director of Planning in 1973.

He will be remembered for being the last of the 'old school' managers within the PTE. His main legacy was to use his drive to ensure that his bus operating colleagues effectively designed their services to feed and not compete with the railways, whose development was one of the main remits in his Planning role. The ever-increasing loads carried by West Midlands railway lines were largely the direct result of his efforts.

LAST OF THE HALF-CABS

The end of the traditional front-engined buses officially occurred on the morning of 24th August 1979 when 327Y and 333Y made their final runs on Coventry cross-city services 9/9A (Earlsdon – Ernesford Grange/Wyken). The last one to arrive at Harnall Lane was 333Y where staff turned out in force to tow it in ceremonially. The success of the tow was initially threatened by the diversion of much of the potential labour who wished to record the event on film. Once the cameras were satisfied, however, 333Y moved much faster and made its final entrance into Harnall Lane (actually via the exit!) without too many hernias amongst its human propulsion.

The last WMPTE half-cab makes as rapid progress into Harnall Lane garage as its human propulsion can muster. The date: 24th August 1979. The bus: 333Y, Daimler CVG6 chassis, Metro-Cammell body, built for Coventry Corporation Transport in 1963. M.R. Keeley

Nos. 328–30Y actually remained licensed until October and thus were available for service; 333Y itself disappeared into the paintshop at Harnall Lane for repaint as Coventry Transport 333, prior to handing over to that city's Museum of Transport. The shop at Harnall Lane still painted by hand and enjoyed an enviable reputation at the best of times, but the staff excelled themselves with 333 which looked magnificent upon re-emergence in its original colours. The Museum, sadly, subsequently saw fit to advertise itself in large letters over the whole length of each side, ruining the effect.

Thus the half-cab era ended in the West Midlands PTE operational fleet, although the principle of front engines was maintained by the idiosyncratic Volvo Ailsas. The Coventry examples, in all fairness, could not be described as classics, although the Daimler CVG6 chassis probably would have run forever. The Metro-Cammell 'Orion' lightweight bodies had always attracted criticism for frugality of finish but even the newest examples had achieved sixteen years' service, outliving many later buses which had the advantage of being suitable for single manning. The PTE, fortunately, had recognised the value of keeping a Daimler CVG6 in preservation for itself, having set aside the former Birmingham City Transport 3225 which would re-appear in years to come, after restoration at Moseley Road Training Centre, to represent the traditional half-cab bus.

PUBLIC RELATIONS

Following a successful open day at the new Cleveland Road, Wolverhampton, garage, another was held in May 1979 at Lea Hall garage to show the Birmingham public behind the scenes. A range of current types was on view and a selection of preserved buses represented the past. Trips through the bus wash proved extraordinarily popular with the children, resulting in one exceedingly clean Fleetline with, no doubt, rather thinner topcoat than its brethren. A new feature was the over-turning and righting by breakdown crews of withdrawn Fleetline 3281; officially approved destruction enjoyed by all sections of the public, not least those enthusiasts whose love of the Fleetline had never flowered! No less than 10,000 visitors thronged the garage, and the obvious success of the day led to further events at other PTE establishments.

WMPTE still had difficulty in getting its name across, with many members of the public still referring to 'Corporation' buses, despite ten years of the West Midlands fleet-name. Some progress had been made, although perhaps not in the initially desired direction, as others corrupted the organisation's initials to 'Wumpty'. On 1st October 1979, working on the principle of 'if you can't beat them, join them', the tenth anniversary of WMPTE's creation was celebrated by the launch of 'Wumpty'. Described as a friendly little figure, he was to appear on publicity and advertising, including T-shirts, and even took multi-dimensional form as a cuddly toy. Japanese firms apparently provide an effigy of the boss for staff to work out their frustrations. The PTE did not provide a 'Wumpty' at each establishment for such a purpose, which is probably just as well. The writer knows of one instance where a frustrated employee amputated the nose of a 'Wumpty' cuddly toy with a single blow (of the fist, not the handkerchief).

METROBUSES RULE
AS THE TITAN SINKS

The PTE, pursuing its new policy of dual-sourcing, had two years' supply of new buses on order comprising 75 + 100 Metrobuses and 75 + 60 Leyland Titans. The Leyland empire had encountered increasing difficulty with its Park Royal subsidiary, hence the protracted delivery of Fleetlines 6571–6690. The Titan was assembled at Park Royal and, to the horror of the PTE, the closure of that factory meant that Titan deliveries would be out of the question for the time being. The order was thus cancelled, leaving the PTE with 135 buses missing out of its new vehicle programme. Fortunately MCW was only too pleased to increase its production Metrobus orders by 100 to a new total of 275 vehicles (to become 2001–2275), whilst for quick delivery the remaining 35 buses would be Leyland single deckers of the new National 2 design (to become 7018–52).

As the Titan was now no longer to be an important feature of the fleet, the five prototypes were concentrated at one garage; 7001–3 joining 7004 at Perry Barr, Birmingham, in November (although 7002 was actually in works with serious accident damage), and 7005 moving across from Harnall Lane, Coventry, in January 1980.

The first production Metrobuses entered service in October and November 1979, 2001–5 being part of fifteen for Selly Oak garage. Also entering service were two more prototypes, 7006–7, Metrobuses with Rolls-Royce Eagle engines, which were put to work at Perry Barr and Washwood Heath respectively. The two prototypes featured Fleetline style interiors with blue formica and red vynide seats. The Gardner-engined production buses, however, blossomed forth with orange-brown patterned moquette seats on both decks with toning formica, an improvement in seating heralded by award-winning Metrobus prototype 6835 at the 1978 Show. The driver was now protected from less desirable passengers by a perspex screen; on the debit side this was unfortunately prone to smears and fingerprints and thus reduced nearside visibility. The screen also made it impossible to work the Autofare coin drop by key in the event of electrical failure. Metrobuses for the North Division, which would receive its first in the form of 2050–75 early in 1980, would lack the screens, from which one must conclude that the Black Country does not have quite the violent element encountered in the cities of Birmingham and Coventry.

Mechanically the standard WMPTE Metrobus has a Gardner 6LXB engine rated at 170 bhp at 1850 rpm. The buses are fully automatic employing a Voith D851 3-speed gearbox. A retarder reduces the wear and tear on the air brakes, although many drivers find that the speeds at which the retarder is designed to perform makes it almost impossible to pull up smoothly. In addition the fully automatic gearbox could engage top gear with quite a kick, particularly if the vehicle was not actually accelerating, for example when increasing speed travelling downhill, and the driver would again be blamed by the passenger for poor handling. This kick persisted but has gradually improved on succeeding batches. The driver should be happier with the power steering, whilst all should feel the benefit of the air suspension which took out the worst of the shocks provided by the deteriorating state of West Midlands roads. Many Fleetline bodies were showing premature signs of age and it was felt, correctly as time

would prove, that air suspension would be worth its weight in gold.

Two unfortunate features of the Metrobus were the two-piece entrance doors, opening towards the front and vicious enough surely to loosen up the front end, and the squared-off roof profile, specified by the Metrobuses' largest customer, London Transport, an irresistible target for roadside trees which easily holed the front nearside corner. These criticisms apart, the Metrobus was to prove a relatively sound vehicle, its success being reflected by the number of repeat orders for it.

As the newcomers came in, inevitably older buses were withdrawn. Casualties at this time were the six Commers, 4236–41, whilst amongst ex-BCT Fleetlines withdrawn were the pair with experimental heating systems, 3399/400. Coventry's share of the new Metrobuses was to be 2016–31, of which the first two were in service before the end of the year, enabling withdrawal of the last ex-Hull Leyland Atlantean, 1152.

Another notable event at Coventry towards the end of the year was the renumbering of the remaining ex-Coventry double deckers. The Y suffixes were removed and 1000 added to the fleet numbers. Buses affected were 2, 3, 11, 13, 15, 20, 23–142, 338, 340–50, 352, 354–71, 373–5, 379, 380Y. From that list it can be seen that most of the 1–22Y batch of East Lancs and Neepsend-bodied Fleetlines, new in 1966, had already been withdrawn but most of the Willowbrook-bodied Atlanteans and Fleetlines of 1964–5, 338–81Y (now 1338 etc), still survived.

With the first of its new design of buses for the 1980s coming on the road, the officers of the Executive could say goodbye to the 1970s

with justifiable satisfaction. They had gone a very long way towards the aim of an integrated transport network and must have thought that politicians of all persuasions, by now, could see the advantages of the PTE concept. Indeed, surely all politicians appreciated that subsidising public transport was better than demolishing homes to achieve bigger roads? On the way the PTE had faced awesome problems like near-runaway inflation and the dilatory supply of new buses which, when they did arrive, could not be furnished with spares. The near elimination of conductors had allowed drivers to receive a better wage which, in turn, had improved the quality of the personnel and slowed the drift away from the job. The automatic question in some parts of the West Midlands (notably the ex-Midland Red areas) 'Is the last bus running tonight?' had disappeared as reliability had become taken for granted.

Yes, the PTE's officers had achieved a lot in ten years; it is good that they did not know what was ahead and that the best had already happened. With the eighties would come deepening recession and extreme political reactions to that problem, embroiling public transport. A busman in 1979 could still believe that his industry was moving towards the excellent arrangements for public transport found amongst our European partners.

The remaining ex-Coventry buses were renumbered towards the end of 1979. Most of the 1-22Y batch of Fleetlines, built in 1966, were already withdrawn but Neepsend-bodied 11Y was still running and became 1011. Some members of this batch remained in Coventry livery until shortly before the renumbering.
T.W. Moore

1980

The news that an ex-Midland Red garage was in trouble with vehicles was nothing new. Dudley, however, did suffer from one unusual quirk for an urban area. In marked contrast to, say, the Birmingham garages, there was very little difference between the numbers of buses required for service in the peak and the off-peak. Thus there was difficulty in getting hold of the buses often enough for maintenance. Additionally there were probably more buses there than could be coped with anyway. Worse still, Dudley has arguably the most punishing terrain of any PTE garage – even the bus station sits on a steep hill. Finally many of the double deckers were Leyland-engined Fleetlines whose splendid but thirstier performance made short work of Dudley's hills but logic indicated that more frugal Gardner-powered machinery would reduce the fuel bill somewhat, and be more reliable.

Dudley was to be included in the garage modernisation programme but, short-term, something had to be done about its problems. Firstly, in January, six Leyland-engined Fleetlines were exchanged for Gardner-powered specimens of a not dissimilar vintage at Cleveland Road, Wolverhampton. In February, the 238/9 (Dudley – Fatherless Barn) services were transferred to Hartshill, reducing Dudley's responsibilities and, at the same time, removing all single deckers from the garage. Finally, all the remaining Leyland-engined Fleetlines were exchanged between March and June for Gardner-equipped stock at two South Division garages, Yardley Wood and Perry Barr – bringing a permanent allocation of 63xx Fleetlines to the South for the first time.

One of Walsall's Leyland-engined Fleetlines, 6338, had been converted to Gardner in January 1979. The success of this conversion led to a general policy to replace Leyland engines in the 170 Fleetlines so equipped, using Gardner power units removed from withdrawn Fleetlines. This programme began in September 1980 and the substitution was usually carried out upon major failure of the Leyland unit or when a Fleetline with a high-mileage Leyland engine went in for mid-life overhaul. A few Fleetlines had low mileage Leyland units when overhauled and their distinctive sound could still be enjoyed as late as 1986. It was calculated that an average Gardner-engined Fleetline achieved 7.37 miles per gallon, compared to 6.28 miles of its Leyland-powered equivalent, giving some idea of the fuel savings.

The PTE wished to order further new buses for delivery in the financial year 1981–2. It proposed orders for 125 Metrobuses and 35 British Volvos, as the Volvo Ailsa was now known, thus making a second attempt at dual-sourcing. This was approved in March by the

County Council Transport Committee but ran aground with the Finance Policy and Priorities Committee who could not be persuaded that Volvos, built in Scotland, were not foreign. The engine of the Volvo was manufactured in Sweden by the parent company, but 91% of the components were made in Britain and half in the West Midlands. The Metrobus employed the German-made Voith gearbox but, nevertheless, the argument revolved around the local employment generated by

extra Metrobuses and points like dual-sourcing or price (the Volvos would have been considerably cheaper per bus) failed to convince. Thus the entire order for 160 buses eventually went to MCW; these would become 2276–435 in due course. Fortunately the Metrobus was proving a trustworthy vehicle; the Executive had a close liaison with MCW throughout the design and development stages and kept an inspection presence throughout the vehicle building process.

The evening rush period in Station Road, Solihull, and new Leyland National 2 No.7025 makes its way between the cars in May 1980. M.R. Keeley

MORE SINGLE DECKERS

With or without dual-sourcing, it was not possible for the Executive to standardise entirely on MCW products as that manufacturer did not produce a single-deck model. The 35 Leyland National saloons ordered for quick delivery as Titan substitutes entered service between March and June and were of two types. All were of the recently introduced National 2 variety with Leyland 680H engines as standard (the Gardner option was not yet available); beefy sounding machines compared to the death rattle noises of their predecessors. The radiator was moved to the front which was more bulbous to accommodate it – this took a bit of getting used to but, once accepted, looked much more jovial than the flat-faced earlier Nationals. The bodies, which included the moquette seating material favoured on Metrobuses, were finished by Duple Coachbuilders which carried out many of the minor modifications carried out at Walsall works on earlier Nationals such as a luggage pen, fitting of Autofare equipment, alterations to destination equipment, radio installation, and livery detail.

The bulk of the order, 7018–47, were longer versions of the Leyland National, as previously preferred by the PTE, and seated 50. The remaining five, 7048–52, were of the shorter option, the only ones to be purchased by WMPTE. The short length and bulbous front made them look all cab and no body. Seating 42, they were intended to replace the former Dial-a-Buses on Dorridge area services 183/4, worked from Acocks Green garage. The Fords still had some life left in them so, in the meantime, the short-length quintet were found employment at Perry Barr garage on service 39 (Birmingham centre to Witton). The 39 and 183/4 were soon to fall unexpected victims in the rapidly changing political climate but, from February 1982, the short Nationals were allocated to the 101 Birmingham Centrebus service upon which their extra manoeuvrability was a great asset.

April 1980 saw completion of the first contract of Metrobuses with 2069–75 entering service at Cleveland Road, Wolverhampton. There was a slight lull before the next batch started to arrive, 2076–9 arriving at Perry Barr in June.

Withdrawals of ex-Birmingham City Transport Daimler Fleetlines continued with these new arrivals including, for the first time, heavy inroads into the 1965–6 BON-C double deckers.

One of the short National 2 buses, 7050, at the Witton Lane terminus of service 39, complete with Bundy clock, in July 1980. M.R. Keeley

Quarry Road, in the Weoley Castle estate, was one of the least suitable roads employed by buses in Birmingham. Operation along Quarry Road ceased following the service changes brought about in the Harborne/Weoley area scheme, introduced in August 1980. Daimler Fleetline/Metro-Cammell 3726 takes up most of Quarry Road during the last week of operation. M.R. Keeley

CHASERIDER
AND OTHER AREA SCHEMES

A number of area schemes, involving widespread service revisions, reached fruition in the summer of 1980, such as Warley and Harborne/Weoley, which also embroiled Frankley, Kings Heath, Kitwell, Northfield, Selly Oak and Turves Green.

The most interesting, however, affected South Staffordshire where services were operated by both WMPTE and Midland Red, not to mention others. For the first time the primarily household-based surveys of the PTE's Field Survey Unit were directly compared with the on-bus surveys of the National Bus Company's Market Analysis Project team. The unlikely bedfellows fortunately rested easily with each other and a new South Staffordshire network was drawn up, to be known as Chaserider. Certain areas changed hands for operational convenience and to maintain the existing balance of revenue, although both undertakings made significant savings. Regular passengers benefited from the introduction of a special Travelcard ticket known as Easy Rider.

In typical Midland Red fashion of the time, the Chaserider name was added to their buses. A point of lasting historical significance is that maroon heavily featured in the publicity, this representing a mixture of WMPTE blue and the red of the NBC operator. The latter was soon to be split into several small companies with responsibility for South Staffordshire falling to the new Midland Red North undertaking. The new company favoured separate identities for each area, a coloured band for each being adopted from the established publicity. Chaserider became the fleetname for the Cannock and Stafford operations; its red vehicles being identified by a maroon band. This unintended PTE input into the Chaserider livery is probably not well known!

PTE 'DAMN NEAR BROKE'

In June the Director General, Mr James Isaac, took the hitherto unusual step of sending a personal message to every Executive employee. Entitled 'We're damn near broke!', the message made clear the serious financial position of the Executive. The causes were various; passenger ridership had gone down, inflation was running at 15% and fuel prices had increased by 60% in a year. Two damaging strikes had hit revenue. The 50% new bus grant was to be gradually phased out by 1984.

Meanwhile the County Council grant was reduced to £15.2 million, representing a dependence on the rates of 16.2% of total income. This had been reduced from the 32.7% of the financial year 1976/7.

To cope with the deteriorating financial position and reduce the rates subsidy, bus and rail fares had been increased by 16.5% in August 1979, resulting in a passenger loss of around 2 to 3%. In March 1980 there had been another increase of 15.5% and now the DG announced a package of measures, including a further 15% fares increase in August.

The DG also outlined economies within the Executive including a 10% cut in services, which would reduce markedly the overtime worked, and the loss of 170 'white collar' jobs.

The actual economy cuts to services were made public in September. The Transport and General Workers' Union regrettably reacted by threatening a £100,000 plus moneyspinner. It warned that the 125 park and ride buses scheduled for the Motor Show, to be held in October, would not be manned unless the crews were rewarded by a productivity deal and an assurance given that the Birmingham Centrebus would not be handed over to a private operator. The Motor Show organisers were livid and, although WMPTE did provide the buses, the lucrative contract went elsewhere for the next two Shows in 1982 and 1984.

The continuing delivery of Metrobuses, including 2102 with experimental Transign destination and route number displays, had allowed the fleet size to build up until the Motor Show was over. The end of October thus saw the withdrawal of a large number of buses, particularly Metro-Cammell bodied BON-C Fleetlines. Newer Fleetlines were also being withdrawn, inroads into the next batch (FOC-D/JOB-E registrations) having begun in August. The demise of 'Jumbos' continued but most surprising was the withdrawal of certain first batch Bristol VRTs. Nos. 4343–73 had been overhauled upon expiry of their certificates of fitness at seven years of age. The amount of works' time and cost involved in recertifying caused 4374 onwards to be stored upon certificate expiry, particularly in view of the impending service cuts.

South and East Divisions achieved their cuts in November whilst the North Division followed in December. Many services fell from the route map, whilst many more were revised. Large numbers of buses were withdrawn, including the last GON Fleetlines, the last Willowbrook-bodied Atlanteans and Fleetlines from Coventry, the last D11s ex-Midland Red, the sole Metro-Scania (4242) and the one-time Dial-a-Bus Fords, 4730–7. Relatively modern Fleetlines were being withdrawn, including G-suffix Coventry examples, as the fleet moved to a target 12-year maximum life.

GOODBYE TO CONDUCTORS

The East Division achieved 100% one-person operation, despite poor progress in earlier years, when its last conductors stepped down on 14th September. The last conductors of all were to be found in the North Division but, amidst the service cuts, they handed in their machines and cashbags for the last time on 13th December 1980. So ended an era.

1981

West Midlands County Council elections were due to be held in May when the Labour Party hoped to regain control from the Conservatives. Labour's transport plans were announced at the end of January. Bus and local train fares would be reduced by 25% with a freeze until at least 1985 as a step towards a 'free' fare system. There would be an immediate free fares concession for West Midlands unemployed and a flat 2p fare for schoolchildren. Services cut in the recent economies would be restored. The package was likely to increase the local rate subsidy from £15m to £100m in 1985. The Conservatives, not to say others, naturally found all this well 'over the top'. They were, nevertheless, concerned that their own reputation for frugality was losing sufficient friends to threaten success at the forthcoming elections. Therefore they sought a means that implied great benefit at little cost, reflecting the finest principles of free enterprise. Somebody at some time must have mentioned that buses carry less on Mondays than on other weekdays because, hey presto!, the Conservatives found what they were looking for. In February, the Passenger Transport Authority announced that, for an experimental period of nine weeks, a flat fare of 10p for adults and 5p for children would apply on Mondays, commencing on 2nd March.

Reactions to the 'Monday is Funday' scheme were fascinating. Exasperated Mr Ken Coleclough, the local busmen's leader of the Transport and General Workers' Union, whose membership had been battered by the Tory record of lower subsidies, higher fares and service cuts, 'blew a fuse'. He threatened, but eventually his union did not implement, a series of one-day strikes, complaining that the apparent 'U-turn' smelt of 'political jiggery-pokery'. The Birmingham Evening Mail described Mr Coleclough's condemnation as 'senseless' and 'petty'. It thundered that every shop has a sale to sell goods cheaply that will not go at a higher price, and that empty bus seats were no different. This logic is, of course, correct but no shop would sell its entire stock at minimal prices in order to shift weak lines! The Coventry Evening Telegraph considered that, whilst it was wrong of Mr Coleclough to get involved in the politics, the public had every reason to object to the £72,000 it would cost each Monday to fund the scheme. It concluded that the idea was a blatant misuse of public money.

Needless to say it was up to the professional busmen to make each Monday 'Funday' work. Certainly some empty seats were filled whilst the regular travellers (except the most loyal, the Travelcard holders) also enjoyed a cheap ride. Longer routes, however, suffered overcrowding – most notably the 159 Birmingham – Coventry service which was buried by passengers joyriding from one end to the other at a ninth of the normal price of 90p! Every bus and driver that could be found was put on the route, some running as express 959 journeys, to clear the crowds and give hope to patrons at intermediate points like Meriden that they might board a bus before Tuesday.

In April the county's transport committee voted that the Funday experiment should continue for the rest of the year. In practice, however, Labour regained control of the County Council in the May elections, and the Fundays ceased after 8th June. It was eventually determined that the experiment had cost £1.5 million, made up by £556,000 in lost Travelcard income, £675,000 in lost fares income and £280,000 in additional operating costs. Each Monday had attracted an average of 1.8 million passengers of whom 60% were farepaying, an increase of almost a third over a normal Monday, but there was evidence that some passengers had simply switched their travel from other days to take advantage of the offer.

Labour proposals to decrease fares on buses and local trains took effect in September when a reduction of around 23% was applied. At the same time a flat fare (on buses only) of 2p was introduced for children, threatening an increase in peak bus requirements to eliminate overcrowding. Drivers complained that they were being used as child minders as mothers found a cheap way of keeping their offspring from under their feet. These 'new' riders were not always well behaved, either, to the annoyance of other passengers. The rest of the Labour proposals, free fares for the unemployed and restoration of cut services, remained on the table. Before much progress was made in these areas, however, events in London's transport policy would have repercussions in the West Midlands, as will be seen in the 1982 chapter.

Future historians puzzling over the 1986 scrapping of the Metropolitan County Councils may like to study, as an example, the rival approaches to West Midlands public transport in the run up to the May 1981 elections. They may conclude that moderation and consensus would have helped both public transport and the long-term future of the County Council.

It's Monday Funday in March 1981 and the service 159 terminus at Pool Meadow, Coventry, is awash with passengers anxious to travel to Birmingham for only 10p. A line of buses has been rustled up, led by ex-Coventry 1972 Fleetline/East Lancs 1095; some to run express as service 959. M.R. Keeley

MIDLAND RED DISMANTLED

In February it was announced that Midland Red was to be split into several smaller separate operating units with support functions transferred to other National Bus Company subsidiaries. This attack on overheads meant that the Executive would no longer be dealing with one NBC subsidiary but four.

The last Midland Red built buses in the PTE fleet, BMMO S23s 5932 and 5981, had been withdrawn in January 1981. By March there were no ex-Midland Red buses of any kind at Dudley or Sutton Coldfield whilst, in June, the last D12 Fleetline (6045) was taken out of service. A study of vehicle allocations in March also reveals that ex-Birmingham City Transport buses no longer featured at Liverpool Street, Miller Street or Washwood Heath. Walsall representation was also becoming thin on the ground; by the end of the summer only 116L, in semi-preserved status, survived of that fleet. The first six months of 1981 saw the elimination of 115–121H, the ex-West Bromwich ECW-bodied low-height Fleetlines, leaving from that fleet only the slightly older MCW-bodied low-height Fleetlines, which also suffered some withdrawals. Also at West Bromwich, five of the eight Northern Counties-bodied 'Jumbo' Fleetlines were also withdrawn over the same period, although the remaining three (4005/6/8) were destined to linger on until mid-1982. April saw a major assault on the ranks of the Park Royal-bodied 'Jumbos' at Wolverhampton (3980–4004). In Birmingham, a proper start was made on withdrawing the Metro-Cammell-bodied KOX-F Fleetlines in February, with their Park Royal brethren suffering from September. Survivors of older series could still be found, however. Apart from the recently rebodied BON-C, the last of that batch (3530) continued until November, whilst the last FOC-D (3577) was not withdrawn until March 1982.

MORE NEW METROBUSES

A temporary famine of Gardner engines (a legacy of a protracted labour dispute at the Gardner factory) brought an unexpected variation in Metrobus deliveries, with Nos. 2226–45 being received between February and April with Rolls-Royce 'Eagle' power units. These twenty represented Acocks Green's share of the new deliveries and, logically, in due course were joined at that garage by the two Rolls-Royce-powered prototypes, 7006/7.

In May the first of a new contract of Metrobuses, 2276, entered service at Perry Barr garage. This was the start of 160 new Metrobuses with a simplified cooling system. They were also intended for use with a radio monitoring experiment on certain major routes in Birmingham and were thus all allocated to South Division garages. The North had, over the years, done rather better than average for new buses whilst the South garages included the legacy of long-lived ex-Birmingham City Transport vehicles. The uninterrupted influx of 160 new buses did much to restore the balance.

The success of the Metrobus was rewarded by the placing of an order for 425 vehicles of a new Mark II type. Delivery of the vehicles, which would cost around £60,000 each, would be required between April 1982 and March 1985 and would take fleet numbers up to 2860.

NEW OLDBURY BUS STATION

The town centre of Oldbury had, for many years, presented a run-down appearance with derelict buildings to be seen in every corner. Redevelopment was moving apace as the decade opened, however, including a new bus station and travel centre on a site adjacent to the main shopping area. Buses used the new facility from 29th March, the most regular visitors being Oldbury garage's allocation of Ailsa Volvos. These were joined by a further example for three months, from May to August, when a new Mark III Ailsa Volvo was received on loan. The vehicle, TGG 386W, was one of a batch built for Strathclyde Passenger Transport Executive and, although finished in WMPTE blue and cream and carrying fleet number 7053, also bore Strathclyde fleet number A10. The loan enabled the PTE to evaluate what it had missed when the politi-cians refused to allow the Volvo order the previous year. It is interesting to note that, in 1981–3, Strathclyde purchased Metrobuses and Leyland Olympians but Ailsas nevertheless outnumbered them both. TGG 386W moved on to Merseyside PTE after its three-month sojourn at Oldbury Garage.

The completed bus station and travel centre at Oldbury was opened formally in March 1982.

NEW PAINTSHOP COMMISSIONED

A major improvement in the appearance of the bus fleet, through greater painting capacity, was heralded by the commissioning on 1st August of a new paintshop at Walsall Works. A new Fibreglass Section and Plant Group workshop opening over the next couple of months were, with the paintshop, only part of a five-year modernisation of Walsall Works.

New Metrobus 2315 featured repositioned items beneath the windscreen but remained a one-off in its batch. Also visible in this August 1981 view in Bull Street, Birmingham, is the extra grille, behind the rear emergency door, fitted to 2276 onwards. M.R. Keeley

Volvo demonstrator TGG386W, actually Strathclyde PTE A10 masquerading as WMPTE 7053, was an impressive looking vehicle. The Alexander-bodied bus is seen in Spring Hill, Birmingham, in August 1981. Alan B. Cross

1982

The winter of 1981-2 was exceptionally grim. The bad weather began with this December snowstorm. The snow clung tenaciously to buildings and trees, making this view of Broadgate in Coventry particularly attractive but of little appeal at the time to busmen and those struggling home. Nearest the camera are Metrobus 2165 and three East Lancs-bodied Fleetlines. T.W. Moore

Those harbouring fond illusions that the bus drivers' lot is forever a happy one might recall the winter of 1981–2. Irresponsible users of the public highway and disagreeable passengers are daily hazards for the driver but the weather can top the lot when so inclined. Whatever the weather, road staff (including Inspectors, and engineers tending to disabled buses) have to turn out.

The bad weather began in December 1981 but snow returned with a vengeance on Friday 8th January. It snowed throughout the whole day and a strong wind caused deep drifts to form. Some Black Country services had to be withdrawn in the late evening, largely due to roads blocked by abandoned vehicles – including a gritting lorry!

Overnight winds and drifting meant some garages had to be dug out on the Saturday morning before services could start. The call on Council grit vehicles was such that some sections of bus routes could not be covered and WMPTE inspectors found themselves gritting danger spots.

By Monday morning most of the problems caused by the snow had been overcome but exceptionally low temperatures were bringing further difficulties. TV weathermen had to order new signs as overnight temperatures fell to minus 19C and never rose above freezing for over a week. Freezing fog became a further hazard, reducing visibility down to five yards. Drivers naturally worked through these appalling conditions even though heaters and demisters were often not powerful enough to clear frozen screens. Engineers had to wrestle with defects such as frozen water pumps and air systems affecting brakes and doors, the waxing of diesel fuel and fuel tank drain plugs knocked off on packed ice, not to mention a catalogue of minor bodywork damage collected on the frozen roads. Batteries were also assaulted by the extra demands placed on them and the low temperatures which reduced their charging capability.

FIRST MARK II METROBUSES ARRIVE

The last of the first design of MCW Metrobuses entered service in March 1982 when 2430–5 joined 2416–29 at Acocks Green. The first Mark II Metrobuses were placed into service in May, Oak Lane (West Bromwich) having amassed 2436–45 by June.

The Mark II is mechanically similar to the earlier Metrobuses but the body design is simplified so that the number of different parts required is substantially reduced. Glazing throughout was revised with the loss of the heavy rubber window surrounds internally. Most noticeable was the new front end with equal depth flat glass windscreens replacing the previous and more expensive asymmetric curved glass design. Improved doors were also fitted but unfortunately the nonsensical, damage-prone square roof profile remained.

The earliest Metrobuses were now falling due for repaint, and long faces were pulled at some of the complex features of their livery. No. 6834 was turned out with the grille and skirt in blue rather than matt black. The cream band below the windows was also shortened to eliminate the step towards the rear. The earliest Mark II Metrobuses were also subject to livery experiments; only one featured a black skirt and the cream band was either shortened to eliminate the step or was allowed to continue to the rear end but did not continue around the back. As a result of these experiments, the cream band was retained as before but the black skirt was dropped for future deliveries. In due course blue replaced black on the skirt on Metrobus repaints and black began to disappear quickly in some areas as most garages substituted blue to simplify retouching after minor damage.

Mark II Metrobuses were delivered at a great rate, 2594 being on the road by the end of the year. This enabled the withdrawal of many time-expired Fleetlines. The last single-door ex-Birmingham City Transport Fleetlines were eliminated in the late summer whilst withdrawals of double-door (NOV-G) examples got under way from July. Bristol VRT buses continued to be taken off the road and a quantity of the first batch was sold in the autumn to National Bus Company subsidiaries National Welsh and South Wales Transport. The second batch of VRTs was largely retained but often spent some time off the road for overhaul, although a handful of vehicles were not used again.

By the end of the year even a few standard PTE Fleetlines had been withdrawn and variety amongst absorbed stock was becoming scarce. The year end saw the demise of 1041–4, eliminating a batch of Coventry East Lancs-bodied Fleetlines, although slightly older ECW examples lingered on – 1023/38 surviving until July 1983. Notable withdrawals were 5531, the ex-BCT Fleetline rebodied as recently as 1978 with a PTE standard MCW body; 6289, the last ex-Midland Red Fleetline; and 6300, the solitary Foden. This last vehicle, new in 1977, was offered for sale as a runner and eventually was sold to a Suffolk independent operator, Goldsmith of Sicklesmere.

Other vehicular activities during the year had included the renumbering of the ex-Midland Red Leyland Nationals whose fleet numbers were spread between 102 and 154. Five thousand was added to these numbers.

The earliest Mark II Metrobuses arrived in the late spring of 1982 and featured a simplified livery. The black skirt panels were permanently dispensed with but the shortened cream band looked odd and the original design, with its step towards the rear end, returned. One of those delivered with the short band was 2445, seen here in Digbeth, Birmingham, in July 1984. This was nominally a North Division bus but was working from the South Division garage of Liverpool Street, having been exchanged temporarily for an all-over advertisement vehicle. M.R. Keeley

The small Birmingham garage at Cotteridge received a considerable number of Mark II Metrobuses in 1982, its allocation until this time consisting largely of two-door 38xx Fleetlines ex-Birmingham City Transport. Metrobus 2564 turns out of Pershore Road South, King's Norton, for Camp Lane in November. M.R. Keeley

Former WMPTE Bristol VRT 4426 at work in Barry for NBC subsidiary National Welsh. Standard NBC poppy red had been applied by the time of this July 1983 view. M.R. Keeley

The Monopolies and Mergers Commission report commented that the County Council should not have prevented the PTE from buying double-deckers from more than one manufacturer. A Leyland Olympian demonstrator, actually West Yorkshire PTE 5011, ran for some time in the summer of 1982 and returned for a shorter period the following summer. The bus loads in Corporation Street, Birmingham, whilst working from Harborne garage in July 1983. M.R. Keeley

This Alexander-bodied Dennis Dominator, built for Merseyside PTE, was operated from Harborne garage for around two months in the summer of 1982. It is seen in Paradise Circus, Birmingham, during August Alan B. Cross

MONOPOLIES & MERGERS COMMISSION REPORT

In July 1981 it had been announced that the Monopolies and Mergers Commission would investigate the efficiency of four sample bus operators – WMPTE, Bristol Omnibus, City of Oxford and Trent Motor Traction. Although the Commission would divert a considerable amount of management time during a period of heavy workload due to policy changes, Director General James Isaac welcomed the enquiry, no doubt mindful that the Commission would learn a great deal about the value of local public passenger transport.

A year later the Commission published its report, comprising 452 pages of close type. Regrettably, newspapers concentrated on the few negative aspects, notably the premium payment scheme for engineering staff. The Commission claimed that £8.7 million per year could be saved in maintenance costs, although the PTE considered that it was not fair to make comparisons with Bristol Omnibus (which had costs per vehicle hour of £3.25 compared to £3.74 of WMPTE) where only 60% of operations were urban. Despite this, WMPTE had by far the lowest cost per passenger mile of any of the operators studied.

Of 43 recommendations in the report, only five specifically criticised the PTE. It praised the Travelcard, the PTE system of budgetary responsibility, its market research unit and platform staffing levels. The Commission considered that it would not be an improvement for the PTE to become part of the County Council. It also believed that the PTA should not have interfered in the PTE's choice of vehicle suppliers, noting the overruling of proposals to buy a mixture of Leyland Olympians and MCW Metrobuses in 1982/3. It said that, in general, effective competition between suppliers is the best safeguard of the interests of purchasers and that to depend on a single supplier's designs is to take significant and avoidable risks. The Commission did, however, highly praise Gardner engines.

The Commission recommended that the PTE, having undergone continual reorganisations since 1974, should pause and limit changes to those necessary to secure specific efficiency improvements. The Executive was, at this time, devolving much of the work of the three divisional offices to individual or pairs of garages, although retaining the divisional structure. The report concluded that none of the operators was abusing any monopoly or pursuing a course of conduct which operated against the public interest. The PTE subsequently implemented the recommendations of the Commission's report.

The controversial banner surmounting County Hall dominated Birmingham's Lancaster Circus. Amidst the controversy, the driver of Metrobus 2061 continues to earn his daily bread in December 1982, without much control over the future of his job and his industry as the politicians flex their muscles. The Walsall-based Metrobus has received a mesh grille replacing the expensive slatted affair originally concocted by MCW. M.R. Keeley

LOW FARE SHAMBLES

In October 1981 the Greater London Council introduced substantially reduced fares and, as a result, was taken to court by Bromley District Council. The outcome was that, in December 1981, the House of Lords declared the GLC low fares policy unlawful.

No doubt encouraged by the Bromley success, Solihull Metropolitan Borough Council and GKN Ltd in January 1982 sought injunctions against both the West Midlands County Council and the Executive in respect of the September 1981 fare reductions. The Executive, of course, was merely carrying out the instructions of the County Council and the plaintiffs and the court supported this by discharging the Executive from the action at the actual hearing.

The County Council's supplementary rate precept, which in part was to finance the reduced fares, was withdrawn by the County Council at a special meeting the day before the court hearing. As a result of this decision, the County Council was unable to fund the low fare policy, leaving the Executive with an especially large deficit. Not only did fares have to revert to an economic level, but also the income lost since September had to be recouped.

The Executive presented the County Council with three options of which the middle course was chosen. This was to increase fares by as much as the Executive considered the market could bear. The proposed increase of 67% over September 1981 levels would not balance the books but another option, increasing fares by 78%,

threatened large passenger losses and thus serious damage to the transport system. The 67% increase was applied from 7th March and included the end of the 2p flat fare for children.

The unstable period of bus fares was now over; this was the last increase for some time as a great deal of energy was applied to promoting the network to the public, leading (after an initial fall due to the 67% fares increase) to improved patronage.

MORE POLITICS

Towards the end of the year, the Conservative central Government produced a White Paper on Transport which led to the 1983 Transport Act. Amongst the requirements of the Act was one of the recommendations of the Monopolies and Mergers Commission, i.e. that operators should produce a three-year operational plan, updated annually. Most controversial, however, was the imposition of a Protected Expenditure Limit which restricted the revenue support each Metropolitan County could provide. The PEL was the level that could not be challenged in the courts. Expenditure could be above the PEL but a ratepayer could challenge the excess, although not necessarily successfully if the County Council had a good case. The PEL for West Midlands was set at £29 million which, being the lowest per head of population of any of the Metropolitan Counties, presented the WMPTE with a tougher job to maintain standards. In effect it was being penalised for its past efficiency. The revenue support for bus and rail in the West Midlands amounted to around £11.90 per head of population, compared to an average of £29.10 in the

other Metropolitan Counties. The Labour-controlled County Council had wished to spend £42 million on revenue support.

Setting aside the unfair treatment of the West Midlands; if the local voters elect a County Council proposing, amongst other ideas, subsidised passenger transport, it is questionable whether a central government has the right to overturn the wishes of the people, although it can claim to be safeguarding against excess. County Hall, not surprisingly, reacted badly and the building quickly sprouted a 'Keep Local Transport Local' banner. This kept the rival politicians amused for a time while they debated whether the banner needed planning permission – thus a dispute sparked off by central government embroiled both County and Birmingham City councillors!

A FOR ANOMALY

Under the service numbering plan, the suffix letter 'A' was retained solely for the anticlockwise direction of circular services. Its previous use by the municipalities of Birmingham and Coventry for short workings and corridor variations had been rigorously eliminated but, no sooner had Coventry finally applied the *coup de grace*, than the 'A' suffix reappeared in December as a service variation in the South Division! In a major recast of the Yardley – City Centre – Hamstead services, the 17A was a peak-only variant along the eastern end of Garretts Green Lane. More breaches in the system followed, beginning with the introduction in February 1983 of 97A (City to Bluebell Drive, Chelmsley Wood).

1983

1980 Metrobus 2116 is overtaken by new Mark II 2612 in March 1983. The latter was one of a number of 1983 Metrobuses equipped with experimental side ventilators; this design being much neater than the standard vent. The shelters at Pool Meadow Bus Station, Coventry, are being repainted, the frequency and expense hastened by the ever increasing activities of vandals. T.W. Moore

The completion of the new £1 million bodyshop at the Executive's Birchills garage, Walsall, was the culmination of a five-year redevelopment of the works and garage at a total cost of £2.5 million.

The new bodyshop was designed from the outset with low maintenance costs and energy conservation in mind. A feature of the 23,000 square-feet insulated building was the striking double-glazed wall of glass at the Bloxwich Road end which gave natural lighting for engineers working in the vehicle lift area. Six buses could be accommodated at any one time in this area whilst a further sixteen could be dealt with at ground level in the remainder of the bodyshop.

The completion of rebuilding was celebrated with a public Open Day, the first for some years, which was enjoyed by some 20,000 visitors.

Although work at Walsall was complete, the programme of improving other garages continued – Yardley Wood and Washwood Heath in Birmingham, Park Lane in Wolverhampton, and a garage on a new site in Wheatley Street, Coventry, were all in hand or at an advanced planning stage.

DAYTRIPPER LAUNCHED
A new day ticket for individuals and families, known as the 'Daytripper', was launched in the spring with a publicity campaign embracing television, radio and newspapers. The new ticket replaced a Family Day Ticket introduced in 1980 and continued the drive to attract family travel and off-peak passengers. The ticket offered travel by bus and rail anywhere in the West Midlands, although its use was not allowed before 9.30 am on Monday to Friday. The selling price was £2 for an adult, £1 for a child, and £3 for a family of up to two adults and four children.

MID-WARWICKSHIRE MOTORS WOUND UP
In April 1983, the West Midland Traffic Commissioners revoked the licence of Mid-Warwickshire Motors following failure to pay debts of £87,000 to the Inland Revenue. Mid-Warwickshire director Mr George Day blamed incompetence by the Department of Transport for helping to drive his company out of business.

Mid-Warwickshire had leased several vehicles in the late seventies to operate a number of stage-carriage services, notably those in the Heart of England on behalf of WMPTE. A 1981 strike by civil servants delayed VAT and fuel tax repayments, the resultant strains on cash flow causing the beginning of debt with the Inland Revenue. Then, in July 1982, the Department of Transport demanded repayment of £111,000 bus grant on the grounds that the vehicles' leasing arrangements did not comply with grant conditions. The dispute was settled in February 1983 but, in the meantime, the DTp had withheld fuel tax rebate payments. This, in turn, had led to failure to pay the Inland Revenue. Mid-Warwickshire admitted insolvency and the Traffic Commissioners had to revoke the licence. They also refused an application by a sister company, Gimtool Limited, comprising directors of Mid-Warwickshire, to take over the insolvent company's operations.

WMPTE immediately stepped in on 19th April to operate the services previously worked by Mid-Warwickshire on its behalf. In an astonishing move, Gimtool also continued to run the Mid-Warwickshire services but, as it did not possess a licence, all passengers had to be carried free of charge! This was done in the hope of winning the licence but, needless to say, the PTE was less than pleased. Gimtool ceased the free service after 25th May but, in the meantime, had cultivated the image of the small man forced out by the big, bad PTE.

MUNICIPAL BUSES WITHDRAWN

The surviving ex-West Bromwich and Walsall buses, 101H and 116L, which already possessed a semi-preserved status, were withdrawn in June and earmarked for renovation. Restoration of the ex-Birmingham Daimler CVG6, 3225, had been completed during the winter and presented a fine sight; a tribute to the apprentices at the Moseley Road Training Centre.

The last ex-Birmingham bus in normal service, two-door Fleetline 3827, was withdrawn in July and, following tradition, was towed by staff into Quinton garage in a ceremony attracting the attention of television and radio. Cotteridge garage, home for many of the same batch for much of their lives, had a similar ceremony a few days earlier. Another of the batch survived in the stock list, this being the open-top conversion 3867 which remained available for special jobs.

Many ex-Coventry Fleetlines still survived but, generally, the oldest buses in stock were PTE standard Fleetlines. As new Metrobuses arrived, the earliest Fleetlines were withdrawn in quantity, together with the odd ex-London Transport DMS as these were almost as old. The withdrawal of 4021 and 4027 in August eliminated two-door double deckers, and the demise of 4033 in October finished Northern Counties representation in the bodywork range. Leyland National bodywork was proving very robust and, although there were more single deckers than was ideal, they were retained in service. Exceptions were a pair of the unpopular two-door variety built for work at the National Exhibition Centre, 4798–9. These were considered suitable as WMPTE promotion vehicles, in view of their low floor and two doors, but in the event conversion was never completed.

More surprising withdrawals in August were the five Leyland Titans, 7001–5. Their demise in mid-month indicated that a buyer was interested; this was subsequently revealed to be London Transport, customer for nearly all of the modern Titans built, although it was May 1984 before they took delivery.

OFF-PEAK FARES REDUCED

To encourage further the use of buses and trains in off-peak periods, and to assist the unemployed, a package of reductions was introduced in October, whilst keeping the

25th May 1983 and the bus war in Solihull draws to a close — at least for the time being. In the background, Leyland National 2 No.7021 loads on a replacement service for a Mid-Warwickshire route — surprisingly it has been given a Wolverhampton area number (555). Ahead, a Lincoln Alexander-bodied Bristol RELL operated by MWM successor Gimtool sets off along Poplar Road in pursuit of another WMPTE National working replacement service 557. M.R. Keeley

Well away from the war games in the Solihull area, the Executive's image was being improved in Cradley Heath. Certain routes traditionally had terminated in a side street alongside the dilapidated railway station. The land formerly occupied by a goods yard adjacent to the station, however, offered potential as a car/bus/rail interchange and, in June, buses began to use a new bus station alongside; the official opening taking place in August. The railway station was also being replaced by a pleasant new structure with a generous car park alongside. The whole complex cost around £250,000. This reminder of the previous arrangements at Cradley Heath Station shows ex-Midland Red Fleetlines 6203 and 6071 in Chester Road alongside crumbling railway buildings in October 1978. M.R. Keeley

ordinary fare scale and Travelcard prices at the March 1982 levels. The reductions comprised a maximum 32p fare for adults (16p for children) on bus services, cheap day rail return tickets, and reductions in the price of off-peak Travelcards and Daytripper tickets. An exception was the Birmingham – Coventry 159 service, upon which the maximum off-peak fare became 64p. To advertise and sell the revised PTE tickets, four time-expired Fleetlines, 4078/80 and 4109–10, were used as Travelcard promotion vehicles prior to

disposal. Despite the recession, promotions and the reductions in fares assisted in a 3% growth in passenger carryings during the financial year 1983–4.

The County Council took a further gamble when, at Christmas, it extended the hours of pensioners' free passes to include the evening peak period on Monday to Friday. There was a great risk of extra buses being required to clear the longer queues but, fortunately, the peak had some spare capacity due to the recession.

1984

The last of many Fords for Central Coachways were delivered in 1981 and featured the style of Duple coachwork shown on THA405W, a design, associated with the Scottish Bus Group and usually found on heavyweight chassis for motorway express work. Only one coach came in 1982 and broke new ground in being a Bedford YNT. Duple coachwork of orthodox styling was fitted to JVJ511Y, seen at the NEC in June 1984. A945MDH was one of two Plaxton Paramount-bodied Bedford YNT coaches purchased as part of the modernisation promised under the WMPTE aegis.
Maurice Norton/M.R. Keeley

With the withdrawal of 4725 from Wolverhampton in December 1983 for overhaul, all operational Bristol VRT vehicles were now concentrated at Walsall. The return to service of Bristols after overhaul, plus the allocation of new Metrobuses 2742–4 enabled all standard Fleetlines to be removed from Walsall by the end of May 1984. The year would also see commencement of withdrawal of the overhauled first batch of VRTs, 4343–73.

The ex-Midland Red garage at Sutton Coldfield closed in January and its work was distributed to Lea Hall, Perry Barr, Miller Street and Walsall. The garage allocation had included 23 Ailsa Volvos of which 4768–72 joined the bulk of the others at Oldbury, whilst 4527–9 and 4773–87 moved to Perry Barr which had operated the three prototypes when they were new. The second coming of 4527–9 to Perry Barr proved to be short-lived, however, as the trio ceased to be used after June. The bulk of Sutton's Metrobus allocation passed to Miller Street, whilst Nationals went to Lea Hall and Perry Barr. Miller Street also sent its Nationals to Perry Barr, all its single-decker work having been transferred in the reallocation of work or converted to double deck.

CENTRAL COACHWAYS PURCHASED

The Executive extended its field of operations into the coaching market by the March purchase of Central Coachways (Walsall) Ltd from the West Midlands Co-operative Society Ltd. The Executive was already in the private-hire market but all existing vehicles were dual-purpose versions of standard buses, and were generally not available if the hire coincided with the weekday peaks.

Central Coachways contributed thirteen full luxury coaches comprising eleven Fords, a Bedford YNT and an AEC Reliance, employed on excursions, tours, contracts and private hire. The Executive intended to keep the Central operation as a separate subsidiary, invest in new garage premises and upgrade the fleet. The operation was, in fact, moved to premises off Lords Drive in Walsall, and fleet modernisation was quickly begun with two new Bedford YNT vehicles with Plaxton Paramount 3200 49-seat bodies. These were in a livery of dark and light green, white and gold, a refreshing variation on the colours of the acquired fleet. The Bedfords were soon followed by two Bova Europa coaches to a high specification, including video, toilet and light refreshment facilities. The two Bovas were actually second-hand, being purchased in December from Bebb of Llantwit Fardre, but at eight months of age were hardly elderly.

WHITE PAPER THREATENS PTE

As the year progressed, many local councillors and WMPTE staff viewed with increasing concern the Conservative central Government plans for de-regulating bus services. The Government was already proposing to scrap the metropolitan county councils and the local politicians were already engaged in that battle, leaving little energy and time to struggle on behalf of the PTEs.

At the core of the alarm was the 'Buses' White Paper which proposed the abolition of road service licensing outside London, following the moderate success of deregulated coach services and the more dubious results of deregulated buses in Trial Areas (of which none was in a dense urban area). The proposals would enable operators to run any services they wished provided they registered the route and timetable with the Traffic Commissioners. Adequate notice of withdrawal from a service would be required. After half a century of regulation, the proposals opened the door for rival operators to compete over the best routes. To compete on equal terms, this meant that the PTE would no longer be able to cross-subsidise loss-making routes or weak times of the day – under the proposals such journeys would have to be put out to competitive tender and be awarded to that requiring the lowest subsidy. The scenario thus threatened a free-for-all on the best routes together with considerable job losses where routes were lost. The demise of the integrated approach to bus and rail services, so carefully built up since 1969, was inevitable.

BARMY WAY TO RUN A BUS SERVICE

In January the West Midland Traffic Commissioners had granted licences to both WMPTE and Heart of England Services Ltd to replace services previously operated by the defunct Mid-Warwickshire Motors in the Meriden and Balsall Common areas. Heart of England, managed by Mr George Day, was a direct successor to Mid-Warwickshire.

Licences for additional services were sought in the spring, and both operators made allegations about the other's tactics and/or shortcomings. Commissioners' Chairman, Mr Ronald Jackson, commented that they had a duty to co-operate with one another in the co-ordination of services. Operating services in front of one another was 'a barmy way to run a bus service,' he said. The licences were granted but would expire in November, at the same time as those granted in January.

Events took an unexpected turn, however, in August when the Executive's licence for one of the two groups of services involved was revoked by the Secretary of State, following an appeal by Heart of England Services. The Secretary of State had decided that, as the PTE received a network subsidy, it was cheaper for the public purse if the unsubsidised Heart of England Services ran these routes.

The Executive and the County Council made two important contributions in 1984 to easing the public transport problems of handicapped people. In February tactile plates with distinctive raised symbols were added to bus doors so that blind and partially sighted passengers could immediately identify the layout of the bus interior. This was followed in May by the introduction of buses specially designed to meet the needs of the wheelchair-bound and the less mobile. Known as 'Easibus' in Wolverhampton and 'Easy Rider' in Coventry, ten routes were introduced in each town, operating on particular days of the week. The buses employed were four converted Leyland Nationals, 6844/5/7/9, which were extensively modified to provide lift facilities for wheelchairs through an extra door in the centre, and anchorage points for the chairs once aboard. Boarding and alighting was assisted by couriers. Penetration of certain side roads in Coventry was not possible with the Nationals, and two Duple-bodied Dennis Lancets of shorter length were on order but, unfortunately, did not arrive until 1985. One of the long-awaited Duple-bodied Dennis Lancet buses for Coventry's 'Easy Rider' services discharges its appreciative passengers in Broadgate. The fleet number 7053 (previously applied to Volvo Ailsa demonstrator TGG386W) was not carried for long; all except the oldest single deckers receiving numbers in the 1xxx series in the spring of 1985. T.W. Moore

The Mid-Warwickshire Motors liking for AEC vehicles continued with Heart of England Services. The latter operated a number of these ex-London Country Park Royal-bodied AEC Reliances. JPA 115K performs on former WMPTE service 196 following the Secretary of State for Transport's ruling. It is pursued along Station Road, Solihull, in March 1985 by JPA 174K en route for Leamington. M.R. Keeley

The first travellers on the special silver Metrobuses intended for the guided busway were visitors to the International Rotary Convention, held in June 1984. No.8104 leaves the grounds of the NEC. M.R. Keeley

GUIDED BUSWAY

The biggest WMPTE exercise of the year was the International Rotary Convention, the first to be held in England, which took place at the National Exhibition Centre in June. The Executive was responsible for all the local transport arrangements for the 22,500 Rotarians attending. No less than 33 shuttle bus routes were operated between the NEC and 200 hotels throughout the Midlands, as far afield as Shrewsbury, Derby, Cheltenham and Newport Pagnell. At the busiest times two hundred buses were involved, of which many were hired from other operators.

The demand for extra PTE vehicles on the Convention services was partly met by operating the special Metrobuses already built for the 'Tracline 65' guided busway service. They were being stored until the busway was opened and their use on the Convention services was as low-key as their distinctive silver livery and Tracline lettering allowed. The Tracline Metrobuses were numbered in a special series, 8101–14.

The guided busway itself was opened with enormous publicity on 9th October. The busway was constructed in Streetly Road, Short Heath, and formed the final 600 yards of the 65 service from Birmingham city centre. Each track of the busway was formed from concrete slab with steel guide rails. The buses were equipped with special guidance arms and horizontal guide wheels. Upon entering the busway, the driver was instructed to bring the

offside guide wheel into gentle contact with the leading guide rail. After a short distance the bus engaged the nearside guide rail, and from then on, the driver no longer needed to steer the bus.

The bus drivers who were not required to steer gave local comedians plenty of new material. Nevertheless the Passenger Transport Authority was proud to possess the first double-deck guided buses in the world (single deckers so equipped already existed abroad).

Because the guide system confined the bus to a limited track, it was estimated that it used 25% less road space than a conventional bus. This would have obvious benefits in congested areas, particularly as the reserved track permitted faster timings and improved punctuality. The same advantages apply to reserved track tramways but the guided busway had the advantage of being cheaper, could be built progressively as finance permitted, and the buses could be used both on or off the guideways.

The problems of guideways on corners was still to be solved and the straight former tramway reservation in Streetly Road was ideal for the experiment. Nevertheless the residents were considerably, and understandably, upset at the loss of the broad grass reservation and forty to fifty mature trees. 145 new trees and 2,000 hedging and other plants were provided to lessen the blow.

The 14 special 'Tracline 65' Metrobuses, as recorded earlier, bore a special silver livery. The silver was combined with black skirt panels, a combination which looked most striking when fresh but promised exceptional drabness after a couple of years. Electronic dot destination indicators of two types were fitted. Nos. 8101–7 displayed only one line upon

which the destination and 'via' were shown in an alternating display, while 8108–14 showed both in a single steady two-line display. A standard Metrobus, 2791, which entered service at Walsall in September, also had the latter style of destination indicator. There was a fifteenth guided Metrobus, bus 2686, which had acted as prototype during early testing of the system. Although in standard blue and cream livery it was also used on 'Tracline 65' whilst one of the regulars was used for experiments. The guide wheels on 2686 were subsequently removed and the bus entered normal service.

The guided bus trackway was only one of a number of important route enhancement features in the 'Tracline 65' project. Conventional bus-only lanes were incorporated elsewhere along with changes in road priorities to improve traffic flow. Passengers further benefited from a better design of bus shelter, in the same idiom as the bus livery, including some with tip-up seats and improved information displays.

After one year 'Tracline 65' had increased its carryings by 29%, an increase out of all proportion to the importance of the final 600-yard stretch of trackway. It was clear that the other route enhancements and the publicity had generated a considerable number of passengers. Setting aside the guided bus project, 'Tracline 65' had provided valuable knowledge in other respects. Early in 1986, the Executive reported to the PTA that up to £500,000 would be required to experiment with curves and other situations not encountered on the existing track. The Executive therefore recommended that any money available for experimentation should be concentrated on Light Rapid Transit.

The opening of the guided busway on 9th October 1984 and there are plenty of silver Metrobuses on hand for the visitors, press and, of course, the day-to-day custom on service 65. This is the final section of the guideway in Streetly Road, Short Heath. WMPTE 'Fare'

Blue and cream Metrobus 2686 acted as prototype guided bus, and was used on 'Tracline 65' for a time. The guide wheels ahead of the front axle are highlighted by snow in February 1985. The bus is loading at the Bull Street terminus in central Birmingham — the 'Tracline 65' logo is visible on the passenger shelter. M.R. Keeley

1985

The three-year contract for 425 Metrobus Mark II double deckers, which had begun with 2436, was completed by the entry into service of 2837–60 in January. A further 100 MCW Metrobuses had been ordered but the uncertainty of the future, and the loss of the grant for new buses, caused delivery of these to be required over two years, fifty per year; a considerable reduction in the intake of vehicles. The first of the new contract, 2861–4, entered service in April and delivery of the fifty proceeded slowly with 2907–10 coming on the road in December.

The new Metrobuses had a modified type of hopper ventilator which both let in more air and streamlined the appearance considerably. Three, 2862–4, also had modified emergency exits at the rear of the upper deck; the exits were entirely glazed in lieu of the usual window set into an opening panel. The East Division was still running many ageing ex-Coventry Fleetlines and received twenty of the new Metrobuses (2862–8/77–9/85–6/91–8), a much higher proportion than usual of the deliveries.

Also received at Coventry were, at last, the two Duple Dominant-bodied Dennis Lancet buses, designed with 23 dual-purpose seats and accommodation for five wheelchairs for the 'Easy Rider' services of the handicapped and less mobile. They were delivered as Nos. 7053–4 and entered service in April. These numbers were not carried for long as, with effect from April 1st, all single deckers except the ageing ex-Midland Red Nationals had the first digit of their fleet numbers renumbered into the 1xxx series. Nos. 7053–4 thus became 1053–4 in an exercise which some took to be an elaborate April Fools Day hoax!

Many PTE Nationals were approaching the end of their lives and the two Lancets would show the adequacy of the model for general fleet replacement. With the same view in mind, orders were placed for six Alexander-bodied Volvo Citybus underfloor-engined single deckers and six of the new Leyland Lynx rear-engined model. These were required by the end of October, causing MCW to decline to submit a prototype to the trials although, in the event, the Citybuses and Lynxes were several months late.

EXISTING BUSES MODIFIED

As the proportion of Metrobuses in the fleet increased, the shortcomings of the ageing Fleetlines became more apparent. A package of improvements for the 635 later examples, 6301–6800 and 6866–7000, was therefore evolved. Each Fleetline received power steering, separate heating for the cab, and the driver's seat re-upholstered in moquette, replacing the sweaty plastic used hitherto.

There were periodic purges to persuade drivers to use the side and rear service number boxes, all too often left blank or, worse still, incorrect. One set of vehicles which did not lend themselves to this discipline were the Ailsa Volvos. Due to the engine alongside the driver, that worthy had to leave the vehicle through the driver's door and reboard the bus through the passenger entrance to get at the side and rear number boxes. Not surprisingly, at times of pressure (which are frequent) the driver felt justified in omitting this exercise. Ailsas 4738–87 were therefore fitted at Walsall Works with electronic route numbers, eliminating the need for the driver to leave the cab.

Above Right **The last Bristol VRT to be overhauled re-entered service in December 1984, some months behind the previous vehicles. The latecomer was 4714 and its delay was caused by the application of South Staffordshire Tramways livery, celebrating one hundred years of public transport in Walsall. Its appearance was, quite simply, magnificent and showed how good a modern bus could look when given a flattering livery. The colours were maroon and cream, lined in yellow, with a white roof.** M.R. Keeley

Right **The loss of the two small grilles under the windscreen is a certain indication that Fleetline/ Metro-Cammell 6533 has received separate heating for the cab as part of the package of improvements for 6301-6800 and 6866-7000. The substitution of a plain front panel permitted the application of the full fleetname. No.6533 was one of several Fleetlines loaned to the then National Bus Company subsidiary Cheltenham & Gloucester in March 1985 for Cheltenham Races. The buses between the Station and the Racecourse were under particular pressure on this, Gold Cup day.** M.R. Keeley

Below **Oldbury-based Ailsa 4752, with electronic service numbers, waits as a passenger unloads shopping in Abbey Road, Warley, in August 1985.** M.R. Keeley

Metrobus 2393 was one of several to receive this striking 'Threatened' scheme based on a background of cream and red. WMPTE 'Fare'

OPPOSITION TO TRANSPORT BILL

The Transport Bill had its second reading in Parliament on 12th February. It was broadly unaltered from the White Paper, despite 8,000 largely critical responses from the public, operators, local authorities and other interested parties. It then entered the committee stage where its various provisions would be debated. It is clear from a document, published by WMPTE in January appraising the proposals, that the PTE found the competitive tendering acceptable but only within a regulated framework which would retain the benefits of co-ordination and integration.

The Executive itself launched a massive campaign in the spring, spearheaded simply by the word 'Threatened', in an attempt to alter the bill and advise the public of its effects. The campaign included a family of leaflets, giving details of the Executive's achievements and then dealing with individual topics affected by the Bill. Metrobuses in all-over 'Threatened' livery were backed by large side advertisements on 300 other buses and a video. A telephone 'hotline' number was included in the advertisements and leaflets. Whilst much previous effort had been made through talks with the Department of Transport, and through the Bus and Coach Council and the Association of Metropolitan Authorities, it was clear that most of the PTE's 1.4 million passengers per day had no idea of the effects of the Bill. The 'Threatened' campaign hoped to mobilise their support.

Behind the scenes the Executive was having to plan, not only to defeat the Bill but also to cope if it was enacted and the buses, unsubsidised, left dependent on earnings from fares and contracts. It was also limbering up to make the mental leap from co-ordinating to competing. Nevertheless in the summer of 1985 there were a number of joint innovations with potential future competitors. In May, 'Southern Rider' day tickets were introduced giving freedom of WMPTE and Midland Red South services whilst the existing 'Daytripper' tickets were extended to include certain points outside the County accessible by British Rail. In July a 'Leisure-link' summer Sunday service X1 was introduced between Brownhills and Stourport, jointly operated with Midland Red West.

The Annual Report for the year ended 31st March 1985 covered the many achievements of the PTE over the years but recognised that the changed political climate saw less need for strategic planning; the Government regarding public transport as a commercial commodity.

The achievements were summarised as follows:
– Maintained overall ridership at mid-1970s levels, arresting a decline between 1980–2.
– Invested £120 million on public transport.
– Achieved 100% one-person operation.
– Introduced and expanded Travelcard, now used by 200,000 holders within the integrated bus and rail fares structure.
– Increased local rail travel by over 100% to 24 million passengers per year.
– Introduced 35 major bus network improvement schemes.
– Introduced 19 centres where bus and train services are linked.
– Installed 3,500 new passenger shelters.
– Built or significantly improved 14 rail stations.
– Provided 2,627 free car parking spaces at 29 rail stations – 89% used daily.
– Built 5 new bus stations with 2 more on the way.
– Encouraged development of locally built buses specifically designed to meet passenger needs.
– Introduced special buses for the disabled.
– Built or significantly improved 10 bus garages.
– Experimented with Dial-a-Bus and the guided busway.
– Developed consistent industrial relations policies.
– Introduced comprehensive training and development policies.
– Achieved all this with the lowest costs in the country for public transport services in a Metropolitan area.

Heart of England Tours acquired Ailsa double deckers to meet their increased fleet requirements. At the other end of the scale was YHA392J, a Plaxton-bodied Ford, new to Midland Red and one of several shortened by them to midibus dimensions. The Ford passes the Bulls Head, Meriden, on 22nd February 1986 — the next significant date for Heart of England operations. M.R. Keeley

Less management time was now available for evolving major service revisions, although much had been achieved already. Nevertheless, in April, one of the biggest investigations bore fruit when services in Coventry were extensively revised. This followed three years of intensive study using market research and the latest computer techniques to bring the pattern of services into line with changes in demand. The public consultation stage had included an exhibition touring 25 locations in the City.

Every Coventry household received a free newspaper containing new timetables for all the City's services, and a 'hotline' telephone enquiry number was maintained for two weeks.

HEART OF ENGLAND DISPUTE CONTINUES

The convoluted saga of the routes in the Heart of England continued in 1985, with further applications and hearings before the Traffic Commissioners. It will be recalled that, at the beginning of 1985, WMPTE was operating one set of services, between Solihull and Coventry, and Heart of England Services the other, linking a number of villages with Solihull.

At a hearing in March, Heart of England assured the Commissioners that it would continue to operate its set of services. However, three hours later, the operator announced withdrawal of the services, claiming that the PTE had failed to hand over money due for pensioners' concessionary fares. The services were again taken over by the PTE, who claimed that it had merely refused to increase the offered subsidy.

The hearings continued and, in August, the Traffic Commissioners granted licences for all services in the area to Heart of England Tours, an associate company of Heart of England Services. Proprietor Mr George Day had claimed that he could serve the area at less cost than the PTE provided he was sole operator. He would not have been prepared to run if the PTE was also granted licences. The PTE maintained that the past history of the independent did not guarantee continued operation and the PTE would again have to pick up the pieces. The Commissioners decision, however, was influenced by that of the Secretary of State for Transport the previous year, ie that it was against the public interest for WMPTE to provide services subsidised from public funds when another operator was prepared to provide equivalent services without County Council subsidy.

The new arrangements began at the beginning of the new school term in September. Two interesting innovations for Heart of England Tours were the introduction of double deckers (three prototype Ailsas originally built for Tyne and Wear PTE) and the extension of the services from Solihull into central Birmingham. Despite the advertised timetable, it was actually several weeks before Heart of England buses operated the extension. The workshops and two coaches had been destroyed by fire at the Water Orton base in July, hours before a planning inquiry to hear an appeal against council action to stop the premises being used as a depot. This had followed a mystery blaze, engulfing seven vehicles, the previous November leaving the independent short of vehicles.

With this difficult background, residents' complaints of unreliable and decrepit vehicles were numerous, and backed by Solihull council. Ministry of Transport inspectors immediately had a field day, banning four buses from the road. The prospects were not good for Heart of England Tours and its passengers.

BUS FLEET PROGRESS

By 1985 the Executive's objective of a modern bus fleet, with buses running for around twelve years, had been achieved. Ex-Coventry Fleetlines were being replaced by new Metrobuses in the East whilst the South Division was disposing of ex-London Transport DMS buses and making inroads into the 4243 batch of Fleetlines. The North Division was withdrawing survivors of the first batch of Bristol VRT buses and, by the autumn, was taking second batch examples off the road. Surplus single deckers, in the shape of ex-Midland Red and two-door Nationals, were being stored. The last normal example of the huge 4036–4235 contract was withdrawn in July (4214). However, in May, 4069 had returned to the fray after being converted to an opentopper for the North Division. It was accompanied by 116L, thoroughly renovated although painted in WMPTE rather than its original Walsall Corporation blue. Wolverhampton also gained a 'vintage' Fleetline in July, in the form of 4041, fully repainted including a khaki roof as originally applied when new. The other original component of the North Division, West Bromwich, returned 101H to service in October; this squat, low-height bus in WMPTE's modified livery for such vehicles looked particularly alien in the mid-1980s.

MINIBUSES INTRODUCED

Ten minibuses had been allocated to the Central Coachways subsidiary for operation from its Walsall base. The vehicles were Ford Transits with bodies converted to bus standard by Carlyle, the former central works of Midland Red which was now handling 'outside' work to ensure its survival. The Transits bore registration numbers B55–64 AOP, indicating they were originally intended to have fleet numbers 7055–64 but actually carried identifications M1–10.

Their first regular employment was on a new service, introduced on 14th October, linking the previously impenetrable further reaches of Pheasey to Kingstanding Circle and thence to Old Oscott. This was followed on 25th November by services from West Bromwich Bus Station to Europa Village and to Stone Cross via the Wigmore Farm estate, plagued by narrow roads. The new services were distinguished by a 'Shuttlebus' fleetname and the publicity made much of the friendly nature of the small buses, an advantage identifed in minibus schemes recently introduced by other operators around the country. The services were operated by Central Coachways under contract to the PTE.

MORE GARAGE CLOSURES

Two more bus garages were closed in 1985. The garage at Stourbridge closed in January whilst the October demise in Birmingham of Coventry Road, which had been listed for closure for some years but like Houdini had previously always wriggled free, was enabled by the £2 million extension and refurbishment of Washwood Heath garage.

The Stourbridge work and allocation was spread widely but that of Coventry Road was more straightforward. Its work passed to Lea Hall, Liverpool Street and Washwood Heath which also received some of Lea Hall's existing responsibilities.

The prototype Ford Transit minibus in April 1985, in the car park at WMPTE Summer Lane headquarters — due to height restrictions, this was the only PTE bus capable of such a feat! The fleet number 7055 with matching registration indicates that the Fords were originally to be 7055-64. Note the fleetname, which did not find favour. M.R. Keeley

In the event the Ford minibuses were numbered M1-10 and carried the Shuttlebus name. Legal ownership was Central Coachways Ltd. M10 prepares to turn right out of Collingwood Drive, Pheasey, in June 1986. M.R. Keeley

TRANSPORT ACT BECOMES LAW

The controversial Transport Act became law on 30th October 1985. The PTE now knew the path to take. No-one could predict what would be at the end of the path leading to deregulation although there were many prepared to guess, usually without optimism. The timetable of the run-up to deregulation was also known and it was tight. The most critical task was to identify which services could be operated without subsidy and therefore registered as commercial services by the required date of 28th February 1986. The decision of which routes to register was not simply an accountancy exercise – many loss-making services could be turned into profit by amalgamation or by deletion of early, late and Sunday journeys. Such decisions had to be made, however, against the unknown threat of competition over the same roads and abstracting vital revenue.

These commercial services would not be run by the West Midlands Passenger Transport Executive, however. The Executive was required to form a Company which would conduct the bus operations in the new unsubsidised environment. All traffic, engineering and many centrally-based office staff would be transferred to the new Company by Deregulation Day, which was to be 26th October 1986. This new Company would be owned by the Passenger Transport Authority and capable of being split into smaller competitive parts, reflecting the Government's desire to sell eventually the bus industry into private hands. The Passenger Transport Authority was presently the West Midlands County Council, due to be abolished on 31st March 1986. The new Authority, already being set up in readiness for 1st April, would consist of councillors appointed by each of the seven Metropolitan District Councils within the West Midlands.

The remaining office staff would transfer to a restructured Executive which would have much revised roles. These included identifying public transport needs not met by the commercial network, managing the tendering of the socially desirable bus network, securing the provision of local rail services, administering concessionary fares schemes, generally promoting public transport through information and marketing, and managing bus stations, bus/rail interchanges and station car parks.

The transfer was not straightforward because both organisations would be attempting to operate with the minimum of staff. Many employees enjoyed the opportunity to take early retirement or voluntary redundancy but for others it was a worrying time. Compulsory redundancy for some was a possibility and morale was poor as 1986 began, the last year of WMPTE as a bus operator.

As the industry moved into a year of the most radical change in decades, Director General James Isaac became President of the Bus and Coach Council, the body representing all interests in the bus and coach industry. The BCC obviously recognised the strengths of the man at this most critical time but, at the same time, it guaranteed him an even more strenuous 1986.

THE RAPID TRANSIT PROJECT

The West Midlands had become the largest urban area in Western Europe without a rapid transit system. The West Midlands County Council and the Executive thus appointed a joint team and consultants to undertake a comprehensive study into the potential for rapid transit. The feasibility study of transportation consultants Halcrow Fox, reporting in June 1984, concluded that a viable system was both practical and justifiable. The report of economic and planning consultants Roger Tym & Partners on the planning implications supported the conclusion.

The study eliminated guided busways, as having inadequate capacity, and automated transit, as costing twice as much as the favoured system known as Light Rail Transit. Light Rail is to be found in many European cities where, generally, it has evolved as a natural development of traditional tram systems. Although similar to a conventional railway, its lightweight nature makes it equally at home underground, overground on its own right of way or, where unavoidable, sharing the streets with other vehicles. Stops are approximately 650 metres apart, slightly less frequent than buses and maximising the potential for the rapid acceleration of Light Rail vehicles.

Rapid transit investment elsewhere has had a dramatic upward effect on public transport demand and has been an important element in packages of measures aimed at regenerating cities. Recession-hit Birmingham, mindful of the successful Tyne and Wear Metro in Newcastle, needed a catalyst for regeneration and a commitment of confidence, not to mention a fast, efficient network for its passengers.

The Rapid Transit team recommended a total network of ten lines, linking across central Birmingham. An initial network of four lines was proposed, serving West Bromwich, Kingstanding, Sutton Coldfield and Chelmsley Wood, involving two underground routes in Birmingham centre. The County Council approved a proposal to start with an East-West route across Birmingham and that a Parliamentary Bill be sought to secure powers of construction. Transit consultants Kennedy, Henderson and Maunsell were appointed to undertake detailed alignment studies with a view to lodging a Parliamentary Bill in November 1985.

The East-West proposal was a surface route from Coleshill Road, Hodge Hill, via Washwood Heath and Saltley, dipping underground at Gosta Green to travel beneath the City centre to Five Ways, a distance of around six miles. The County Council, not long off abolition, regarded Light Rail as a priceless gift to the City that could be picked up and developed.

The scheme offered West Midlanders a fast and effective public transport system for the 21st century that was not dependent on hydrocarbon fuel. Like all major advances, however, there was some pain to suffer in order to secure the long-term future. The underground section was very costly but, of course, involved minimal surface disturbance in the City centre. Road widths on the surface section between Gosta Green and Saltley were adequate to accommodate Light Rail. Some demolition became necessary along Washwood Heath Road between Saltley and the Fox & Goose but the properties concerned were mostly elderly and many owners seemed satisfied with the compensation offered. The introduction of a further underground section in the Fox & Goose area deflected a lot of potential criticism. The proposals east of the Fox & Goose caused stiff opposition, however, where they would require demolition of good quality housing along Coleshill Road.

The Coleshill Road residents formed a highly effective action group which became known as SMART (Solid Majority Against Rapid Transit). This group effectively alarmed residents in roads surrounding Coleshill Road that railcars rumbling at high speed through the neighbourhood would both be more dangerous and dramatically reduce house values, against clear evidence from abroad that Light Rail improved the status of a community. SMART thus gained more supporters and then mobilised Castle Bromwich as logical next point on the line through to Chelmsley Wood. Negligible demolition would have been required in Castle Bromwich, although there would be environmental damage in the form of lost mature trees. Threats of hazard and demolition were sufficient to elicit support in Castle Bromwich and, before long, SMART leaflets were dropping through letterboxes all over Birmingham and even into obscure Black Country estates that eventually may just have seen Light Rail over a distant horizon.

Public protests outside County Hall and the Council House, Birmingham, were very well supported and councillors and relevant MPs began to get worried. The 'front man' of the scheme, West Midlands County Councillor Philip Bateman, Chair of the Passenger Transport Committee, found himself with an increasingly uphill struggle. Public meetings to discuss the Light Rail proposals turned ugly and the opportunity to explain the advantages was drowned.

As the deadline to get a Bill before Parliament by 27th November 1985 drew near, SMART stepped up its campaign. Birmingham City Council on November 5th chose to object to the Bill as SMART demonstrated in considerable numbers outside the Council House. Two days later, Councillor Bateman, on a fact-finding visit to the West German city of Hanover and with the pros and cons of Light Rail staring him in the face, accepted that the scheme had failed to win the backing of residents, Birmingham City Council and West Midlands MPs. He therefore announced that the route would be halved to run from Five Ways to Saltley only, thus reprieving all but ten of the 172 properties threatened with demolition. This left the most expensive but critical central core of the route intact and reduced the project cost from £130 million to £95 million. Political colleagues challenged the purpose of the shortened route and continued to insist on the full scheme, despite the risk that its likely failure could lose the project for ever. By the time County Hall policymakers had decided to go for the full six miles, professional officers had to declare that there was insufficient time to table the Bill.

Thus it seemed that Birmingham's big chance for Light Rail had gone; the West Midlands County Council was to be abandoned in March 1986 and would not be replaced by any body of such strength. The new Passenger Transport Authority, however, retained the existing joint team to ensure that the initiative and knowledge would not be lost. The properties in Washwood Heath and Hodge Hill remained blighted until, early in 1986, the new PTA abandoned the initial route but without prejudice to future plans in the county.

One of the rapid transit cars of Hanover, West Germany, considered an ideal model for future transport in Birmingham. Mark Alexander

De-Regulation Year

West Midlands PTE opened 1986 with a completely new structure. The former North, South and East Divisions, loosely based on the old municipal boundaries, were swept away. Coventry remained a separate district but the North and South Divisions were reorganised into three new areas, each led by a Group General Manager. These groups were on a geographical basis, segments radiating from central Birmingham, that deliberately managed to avoid the territorial boundaries of the old undertakings. The new structure was as follows:

Coventry	Western
Harnall Lane †	Cleveland Road
Sandy Lane*	Cotteridge*
	Dudley
Eastern	Harborne*
Acocks Green	Hartshill
Lea Hall	Park Lane*
Liverpool Street	Quinton
Washwood Heath	Selly Oak*
Yardley Wood	
Northern	
Hockley	
Miller Street*	
Oldbury*	
Perry Barr	
Walsall	
West Bromwich	
Central Coachways	

*Closed before De-regulation Day. Part of Miller Street re-opened as Newtown minibus unit.
†Replaced by new Wheatley Street garage in 1986

Each of the new groups, except for Coventry, started off with around 550 buses. A further general manager was appointed to deal with Works Functions and, subsequently, another for central operational services. These senior managers continued the process of slotting personnel into the new structure and preparing for de-regulation on 26th October. Above this level, the Executive continued to be managed by the professional Directors and, of course, the political Passenger Transport Authority.

All services to be commercially operated had to be registered with the Traffic Commissioners by February 28th. An operator was allowed to make increases to frequencies after that date but any other alterations had to be agreed with the Traffic Commissioners and the Tendering section of the on-going Executive. The Traffic Commissioners were required to publish all registrations by April 1st, and

then the Tendering section could begin the long job of establishing gaps in the commercial network. These gaps, which may only exist at certain times of the day, had to be placed in an order of priority of tendering – the cost of the tenders affected how far the money available for tendered services would stretch.

The proprietor of Heart of England Tours, Mr George Day, finally ceased bus operations after Saturday 22nd February 1986. He had recently faced a court hearing, brought by the Traffic Commissioners, resulting in fines and solicitors' fees. Speaking with the local press, Mr Day claimed continuous harassment from ministry officials and, whilst he was pleased to have had a go, he was now ready for a quiet life. Thus on Monday 24th February, WMPTE buses resumed operating the two groups of services covering the Heart of England area.

Ex-employees of Heart of England Services and Tours had already formed a new bus company, Solihull District Omnibus, operating other one-time H of E services. SDO had registered some services for the post-October situation and would also be tendering for socially desirable routes.

LONDON LINER LAUNCHED
On 17th March the Executive moved into a completely new field of operation by launching an express coach service between Birmingham and London, known as London Liner.

The Executive was looking for new business to make up for what was to be trimmed under bus service de-regulation. It was felt there was a market for rail quality of travel at a price around that offered by National Express Rapide coaches. Coaches could not compete with rail on speed but they could equal it on comfort and beat it on penetration of the two

City centres. There was a concentration on crew training, the steward/drivers being tutored by British Airways staff to give a first-class service to the passengers.

At the Birmingham end, passengers could board in Colmore Row and outside the Albany hotel on Smallbrook Queensway; both locations considerably more useful than the Digbeth terminus of National Express. Passengers buying their London Liner tickets in advance could use them on the local bus network to get into central Birmingham without charge, another advantage over National Express. In London, passengers would be set down at Marble Arch and the Wilton Road, Victoria, coach station of London Buses.

The service was operated jointly by Central Coachways, on behalf of WMPTE, and London Buses. The coaches of each operator had identical lettering with gold and white lining. The base colour was quite different, however, the PTE vehicles being in French blue, and the London ones in their traditional red. The elegant restraint of the livery emphasised the high class nature of the London Liner at a time when the motorways were filled with coaches plastered in tasteless stripes.

The initial PTE contribution was two new Bova Futura coaches registered C903–4 JOF – Bova coaches already featured in the Central Coachways fleet. London Buses used Duple-bodied DAF coaches. These vehicles were only temporary, however, as both operators were expecting striking new MCW 'Metroliner' double deckers. Three were on the way for WMPTE/Central Coachways; the vehicles, C900–2 JOF, entering service in May and June. The restrained London Liner livery looked even more tasteful on these magnificent 69-seaters. The displaced Bovas joined the general Central Coachways fleet but retained French blue, partially re-lettered 'Central Liner'. Mobile recruitment Fleetline bus 245 DOC was withdrawn in April and, in August, its 'ageless' registration was transferred to Bova C904 JOF.

One of the two Bovas, always kept in immaculate condition, prepares for a London Liner journey in May 1986. C904JOF was subsequently re-registered 245DOC, receiving the mark from a superannuated Fleetline. M.R. Keeley

EXPERIMENTAL SINGLE DECKERS ARRIVE

The overdue experimental single deckers, viewed as possible Leyland National replacements, entered service in March and April. The six Volvo Citybuses with underfloor engines and Alexander bodies were numbered 1055–60 and carried a livery of off-white with two blue bands. The turbocharged Gardner rear-engined Leyland Lynx buses, the manufacturer's replacement for the National, were numbered 1061–6. Neither bus had much going for them in the styling department but for sheer untidyness the Lynxes, clad in white with a confusion of dark blue stripes, had to win. The dozen were allocated to Cleveland Road, Wolverhampton, replacing double deckers, initially on services 500/501 to Perton via Tettenhall but later employed more equitably.

NEW NAME AND LIVERIES

In view of their appearance, it was not surprising that the Leyland Lynx buses were being repainted into PTE colours as early as May, and these were followed by the Volvo Citybuses. The layout was new, however, resembling the Metrobus scheme and in the shade of blue employed on those vehicles, but with cream applied to the roof as well as beneath the windows. This very attractive scheme was adopted for all single deckers and a programme began of repainting as many as possible before the new operating company took over on 26th October.

The new company name had now been announced as West Midlands Travel Limited. The blue and cream livery was to be retained, having built up a reputation with the travelling public over many years. It was to be updated for single deckers as described above and for Fleetlines. The Fleetline layout was not altered but repainting of the lower panels into Metrobus blue commenced at garages in an endeavour to cover those Fleetlines expected to continue in service after 26th October. This embraced the upgraded Fleetlines 6301–6800 and 6866–7000. Deletion of West Midlands fleetnames began in May.

A new livery was sought for buses operating 'Timesaver' limited stop services, to be greatly expanded after 26th October. The fifty MCW Metrobus double deckers on order, 2911–60, were to be fitted with a much higher quality interior trim, virtually to coach standard, for use on 'Timesaver' services. A small number of the existing dual-purpose Leyland Nationals would also continue on limited stop work, although some were destined for the new bus

Alexander-bodied Volvo Citybus 1056, in original livery, passes through Queen Square, Wolverhampton, in May 1986. The Leyland Lynxes were a painter's nightmare — 1066 does battle on the previously double-decked 500 service in Darlington Street, Wolverhampton, also in May 1986. The rear view of Leyland Lynx 1062 is in Lichfield Street, Wolverhampton. The skirt panels are grey on this vehicle. Leyland Lynx 1061 is shown at Wolverhampton Bus Station in July 1986, repainted in the livery that became standard for West Midlands Travel. The Citybuses and Lynxes all had nearside destination blinds — the Lynx location was more noticeable although the size of lettering was somewhat inadequate. M.R. Keeley

Dudley garage was well advanced with the substitution of Metrobus blue on its Fleetlines by July 1986 when No.6543 was loading with other Fleetlines and ex-Midland Red National 5119 in the town's new Bus Station. The National still carries WMPTE insignia and would be sold upon de-regulation. M.R. Keeley

livery for ordinary services. Dual-purpose National 1861 was painted in a livery of cream with blue skirt, waistband and roof but did not have the required impact. Instead a livery of silver, relieved by red and blue stripes, was chosen. There was no great desire to promote the new name prior to the big launch but 1863 did receive in mid-summer West Midlands Travel fleetnames and Timesaver lettering for publicity shots. A double-deck version was required to act as prototype for the new Metrobuses. The guided buses were already in silver so it was no problem to give 8101 a fresh coat and apply the red and blue relief colours (a great improvement on the black of the guided buses) and Timesaver lettering, the vehicle appearing in July.

NEW COVENTRY GARAGE

On 29th March 1986, the old Coventry Transport premises in Harnall Lane East closed and, from the next day, a new garage off Wheatley Street took over. The development on a 4.1-acre site had cost £8 million and, whilst Harnall Lane was situated in a predominantly residential area, the new garage was adjacent to Pool Meadow Bus Station, linked by a bus-only road.

Wheatley Street garage was designed to hold 140 buses and includes a two-storey office block to accommodate garage and district administration, welfare facilities and ancillary workshops.

DUDLEY BUS STATION

A number of photographs in this book show the hazardous nature of the old Dudley Bus Station, situated on a steep hill. The answer was to rebuild the Bus Station so that buses loaded on the almost level east-west axis. The Bus Station re-opened in 1986, being in use some time before the official ceremony on 30th September. In place of the tatty old worn-out shelters, the new Bus Station offered an even greater standard of appearance and comfort than previous constructions.

GARAGES CLOSE

A number of former Birmingham City Transport garages were closed in the spring and summer of 1986 in the run-up to de-regulation. Harborne closed on the 12th April, most of its work and buses going to Quinton, Perry Barr and Acocks Green. Miller Street followed on the 31st May with work and buses mostly moving to Perry Barr, Hockley, Walsall and Lea Hall. The 'Tracline 65' guided buses passed to Hockley. Selly Oak finished on 2nd August, the bulk of the work passing to Liverpool Street but its single-deck services went to Yardley Wood.

Earlier in the year saw the closure of Oldbury, whose work passed to Dudley and West Bromwich. A substantial part of the Oldbury allocation consisted of Ailsas 4738–72. These moved to Walsall where a few Ailsas had been evident since the autumn for driver familiarisation. The influx of Ailsas to Walsall permitted the withdrawal of a considerable number of Bristol VRT buses including 4347, the last of the first hundred.

Apart from the 'Jumbo' Fleetlines sold prematurely, few former WMPTE buses have run for another stage carriage operator. Amongst the exceptions is one-time 5502, working a Burton-upon-Trent local service in July 1986 for Stevensons, the Staffordshire independent. This Metro-Cammell bodied Daimler Fleetline was new in 1973 as London Transport DMS1259, and joined many similar vehicles in the Stevensons fleet. M.R. Keeley

FIRST TENDERS

A trial run for the tendering procedure took place with the Heart of England services. The tender of Midland Red Coaches was accepted, introducing that relatively small, coaching only, offshoot of the once mighty Midland Red to bus operation. Midland Red Coaches took over from WMPTE vehicles with effect from 16th June, using its own Leyland Leopard/ Willowbrook coaches, which had bus doors, and elderly former Fife Scottish Alexander-bodied Daimler Fleetlines acquired for the purpose. Midland Red Coaches developed a close relationship with Midland Red West as de-regulation approached and the latter's single deckers were frequently seen in the autumn.

The Passenger Transport Authority made £3.6 million available for socially necessary bus services by competitive tender for the period from 26th October to 31st March 1987. The tendering process began in earnest on 4th July when the first 69 services were put out to tender. The amount of work won by West Midlands Travel would have a direct influence on the number of jobs saved.

All WMPTE tender contracts are what is commonly known as 'bottom line'. Each operator quotes the subsidy required for the contract and, if successful, is allowed to keep all the income. The lower the tender, the greater the chance of winning the contract – but also the greater the commercial risk.

Some encouragement to WMT staff was provided by the winning of tenders offered in advance of national de-regulation by Hereford & Worcestershire, giving the fledgling company influence in new areas. The contracts were worked out of Liverpool Street and Hartshill garages using, initially, Leyland Lynxes and a silver dual-purpose National. Executive drivers found themselves in unfamiliar territory such as Bromsgrove but particularly on Sundays when the X92 to Ludlow and Hereford was operated.

The cost of the PTE restructuring in human terms was felt most severely by works staff at all levels. It was necessary to bring works capacity into line with the future level of operations and the reduced need for maintenance of modern buses – for instance, it was not necessary to give Metrobuses a mid-life overhaul and nearly all Fleetlines had already been handled. All works facilities were to be concentrated at Tyburn Road, Birmingham, so the jobs of 181 employees at Walsall Works, 79 at Sandy Lane, Coventry, and around 40 in other engineering departments had to go. Voluntary redundancy was first available to those at Walsall and Coventry and then at Tyburn Road, to allow transfers to the latter. Closure of the two works was to be achieved by 5th September. Some idea of the human problem will be gained by the fact that the loss of 300 jobs left only around 400 employed at Tyburn Road, a cut in works staff of 40%.

The final exercise to match garages to the future level of operation meant the closure of three more premises after service on 25th October. The garages to be closed, on the last day of WMPTE bus operations, were Cotteridge (Birmingham), Park Lane (Wolverhampton) and Sandy Lane (Coventry). The cost in drivers' jobs, as many by voluntary redundancy as possible, was high. By the end of July the worst was known and those who were to leave and those who remained prepared to face their individual futures.

The story of the Heart of England services received another twist when Midland Red Coaches took over their operation upon winning the first tendered services in the West Midlands. Willowbrook-bodied Leyland Leopard 535 unloads in Poplar Road, Solihull, in October 1986. M.R. Keeley

Midland Red Coaches covered journeys requiring double deckers with former Fife Scottish Alexander-bodied Daimler Fleetlines. No.59 (RXA59J) pulls away from Solihull Station in August 1986. M.R. Keeley

National 1822 received the silver livery for 'Timesaver' services but, in September 1986, was working from Hartshill on one of the successfully won tendered journeys offered by Hereford & Worcestershire. No.1822 performs a journey from Bromsgrove Bus Station on the 318 service, basically a Midland Red West operation. M.R. Keeley

NEW IMAGE PREPARATIONS

At the very end of September, the first buses began to appear with West Midlands Travel fleetnames and the intention was that the entire fleet surviving de-regulation would be equipped by 26th October. The new fleet-names, mostly cream but with a touch of red, looked most attractive. It was now known that the Volvo Ailsas would be retained and these too began to receive the fleetnames and, in some cases, the lighter blue panels. Ailsas at Perry Barr garage also began to appear retouched into a pseudo-Metrobus livery; this great improvement being applied if the vehicle was under repair for a long enough period to allow the extra painting time.

Amongst the many personnel receiving redundancy was 'Wumpty', the figure used on advertising for a number of years. He was replaced by a bee – a lot of the WMT publicity revolved around the word 'buzz' – patronising the Brummies' pronunciation of bus. The advertising included a superb television commercial which showed West Midlands Passenger Transport Executive buses rushing back to the 'hive' (garage), staff busy as bees working on them, and then the vehicles rushing out again as West Midlands Travel buses. Local rail threatened to be buried by the focus of media attention on the buses so it was re-launched as 'Midline', again employing press and TV advertising, covering an area rather larger than the West Midlands. 'Midline' publicity was able to emphasise that, whatever else was changing, local rail was still there to serve its existing and any new passengers. Its slogan was 'Simply the Better Way'.

By the 25th October the central streets of West Midlands towns were full of buses wearing the new fleetnames. The image was strong, imposing a similar impression of the new operating company. Any other operators prepared to take on West Midlands Travel were brave indeed.

Above **As de-regulation and the change from WMPTE to WMT approached, it was possible to see together vehicles with old and new lettering. At Lea Hall Station on October 4th, Fleetline 6900 still retained its PTE fleetnames whilst Metrobus 2368 is ready for the new era.** M.R. Keeley

Ailsa 4784 blossomed forth in this revised livery, markedly reducing the amount of unrelieved cream on these particular vehicles, and was accompanied by other similarly retouched Ailsas before the end of the PTE era. It proceeds along Birmingham's Queensway, passing Moor Street Station, on October 3rd. M.R. Keeley

The traditional WM symbol survives on buses in concessionary pass notices and also, in this case, on the destination blind of this WMPTE-sponsored service. The legend reads 'Service sponsored by WM'. West Midlands Travel Leyland National 1471, at Solihull station in August 1987, was new as WMPTE 4471. It was one of the few by this date to retain this livery style although the blue had been retouched into the WMT shade. M.R. Keeley

Epilogue

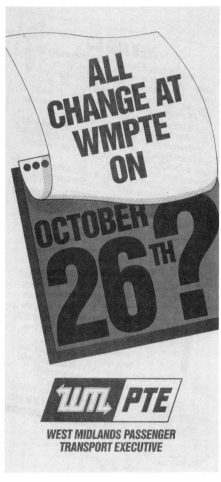

Front cover of a blue and pink leaflet produced by West Midlands PTE explaining the changed status of the Executive and the setting up of West Midlands Travel. The leaflet emphasised the things that were not changing, such as concessionary fares and 'most of the familiar blue and cream buses'.

The staff of West Midlands Travel and the ongoing West Midlands Passenger Transport Executive went their separate ways with effect from Sunday 26th October 1986. For a time there was an overlap of Directors, for example Mr James Isaac was PTE Director General and WMT Managing Director until Mr Bob Crawford, previously PTE Director of Planning & Engineering, was appointed acting Director General of the PTE.

Around 150 buses in service at the beginning of October did not pass to West Midlands Travel. These were surplus to the reduced requirements and were thus sold immediately before the changeover by the Passenger

Mr James Isaac, PTE Director-General at the time of the 1985 Transport Act, had to switch his management skills from integration of bus services to competition, an atmosphere for which he was well trained earlier in his varied career. He subsequently became Managing Director of West Midlands Travel.

Transport Executive so that the ratepayers benefited from their resale value. On the credit side, West Midlands Travel was immediately able to place into service large fleets of Metrobus II luxury double deckers for 'Timesaver' limited-stop services and 'Minibuzzes' for operation in Solihull, Sutton Coldfield, Stourbridge and Cradley Heath. Despite the number of buses not transferred from the Executive, the new intake immediately enabled WMT to create a reserve fleet.

Amongst vehicle types eliminated on the changeover were the ex-Midland Red and two-door Nationals, the ex-London Fleetlines, and the Bristol VRTs – with the exception of 4714, the South Staffs liveried example which went into store. All the remaining 4243–4342 Fleetlines were sold, along with nearly all the 4530–79 series. The last ex-Coventry Fleetlines went, 1135–6, along with the largely intact batch of almost identical vehicles, 4447–66. The only bus from municipal days to survive into the WMT fleet was open-topper 3867. WMT was able to rationalise double-decker allocations so that Walsall and Liver-

pool Street (renamed Birmingham Central) were intended to be entirely Metrobus. Perry Barr also lost its Fleetlines to become entirely Metrobus and Ailsa, all fifty of 4738–87 being concentrated there.

On the operational side, no WMT commercial services entered the Bull Ring Bus Station, Birmingham, completing a process of withdrawal begun some years previously. WMT had won 82% of the tenders for socially necessary services, the remainder passing to Midland Red West, Midland Red North, Midland Red South, Solihull District Omnibus, Vanguard Coaches and Tarnbrook Ltd, trading as Invincible. The 'Tracline 65' service, which included the guided busway, was not registered commercially on Sundays by WMT. The Sunday contract was won by Midland Red West who, naturally, had to operate along the normal highway. WMT received a grant to continue operating the special Metrobuses but, in January 1987, the Passenger Transport Authority agreed to close the subway later in the year, the experiment having achieved its aims. The busway closed after service on 26th September and work quickly began on restoring the central reservation. The fourteen special Metrobuses equally quickly lost their guide wheels and were repainted by WMT into standard livery with fleet numbers 2961–74 (2961 retained its prototype Timesaver scheme).

Light Rail Transit is considered by many to be the next stride forward in public transport and fortunately the concept was not killed in the Hodge Hill debacle. The joint West Midlands PTA/PTE team investigating LRT's potential relaunched it as 'Midland Metro' in September 1987.

West Midlands Travel had a number of problems to iron out with its post-deregulation network but those amendments, successfully accomplished, are part of a new story. Change is rapid and even some of the developments covered in this epilogue are already history. WMPTE achieved a most effective monopoly in December 1973 and the legacy has given West Midlands Travel exceptional strength. This very strength ironically may lead to the enforced dismantling of WMT by central government to ease its sale into private hands and encourage greater competition.

The story of the West Midlands Passenger Transport Executive also continues but it is a new beginning with changed objectives and its activities shared without discrimination between all public transport operators in the West Midlands. So former colleagues, who had worked alongside each other to create the integrated network of the old WMPTE, are now in quite separate organisations. The minority remaining with the Executive have had to learn to live without the family.

Service Vehicles

Ex-Birmingham AEC Matador 117 was transferred to Coventry. The recovery crew hitches up Fleetline/East Lancs 87Y, failed in Fairfax Street in August 1977. T.W. Moore

Left **A venerable Bedford oil tanker, 116 (MUL 450) contributed by Birmingham, performs at Selly Oak in September 1974.** Right **A 1959 Ford Thames 4D lorry, 114 (XOG 714) ex-Birmingham, at the Fox & Goose, Ward End, in January 1973.** Paul Gray

Left **A 1959 Ford Thames 5-cwt van, 115 (XOG 715), still in Birmingham's dark blue, parked at Perry Barr garage in June 1972.** Right **Austin A35 140 (GOG 340D), one of 13 passed to the PTE by BCT, at Miller Street 'light cars' garage in June 1972.** Paul Gray

Left **The newest BCT service vehicles were four attractive BMC 30-cwt vans, including 141 (NVP 341G), at Perry Barr garage in June 1972.** Right **Arguably the most unusual service vehicles taken over by the PTE were the two BMMO D7 towing vehicles from Midland Red, part of a fleet of such machines converted by them from double-deck buses. No.219 was originally new in 1956 as Midland Red 4531 and is seen at Sutton Coldfield garage in July 1974.** Paul Gray/Alan D. Broughall

Left **This 1958 AEC Mercury tower wagon, TXV 906, had been purchased by Walsall from London Transport. It was still finding employment in January 1973, long after the Walsall trolleybuses had been scrapped.** Right **Wolverhampton contributed two relatively rare Guy Warriors. WDA 301 was a breakdown tender dating from 1958. It is seen at Park Lane garage, Wolverhampton, in April 1974.** Paul Gray

Left **The ex-Coventry Ford Transit, 408Y, photographed in December 1978.** Right **This Kenex bus conversion of a Ford Thames van, contributed by Walsall, was new in 1962. It is seen in the vehicle park opposite the St Paul's Street offices in November 1974.** M.R. Keeley/Paul Gray

Left **This ex-Coventry Bedford RL breakdown tender, dating from 1955, migrated to Stourbridge as seen in October 1978. Shortly afterwards it was repainted from Coventry to PTE colours.** Right **A 1973 Ford Transit pick-up, 160 (GVP 207L), delivers shelters being erected near Moor Street Station in November 1978.** M.R. Keeley/Alan B. Cross

1975 Ford D series 411 (HOA 97N) features a hydraulic crane. It is seen at Walsall Bus Station in August 1980.
Alan B. Cross

A 1959 Daimler CVG6, ex-Coventry 290, was converted to a towing vehicle in 1978. On tow is Fleetline 139Y. T.W. Moore

Left **The PTE was particularly proud of its Foden recovery vehicles. No.102 was in attendance to the many buses shuttling to and from the 1978 Motor Show at the National Exhibition Centre.** Right **1962 Daimler Fleetline 3245 became this striking driver recruitment vehicle. It is seen at Paradise Circus in September 1979, not long after conversion, and survived until 1986 when its 'ageless' registration number was transferred to a Bova coach.** M.R. Keeley/Alan B. Cross

Appendix: Buses Operated by WMPTE

Buses acquired from Birmingham City Transport 1.10.1969

2181x2230	JOJ 181x230	1949-50	Leyland PD2/1	Park Royal	H29/25R
2231x2260	JOJ 231x260	1950	Leyland PS2/1	Weymann	B34F
2426x2525	JOJ 426x525	1950	Crossley DD42/7	Crossley	H30/24R
2526x2625	JOJ 526x625	1950-1	Guy Arab IV 6LW	Metro-Cammell	H30/24R
2626x2775	JOJ 626x775	1951-2	Daimler CVD6	Metro-Cammell	H30/24R
2776-2900	JOJ 776-900	1952-3	Daimler CVG6	Crossley	H30/25R*
2901x2999	JOJ 901x999	1952-3	Guy Arab IV 6LW	Metro-Cammell	H30/25R*
3000	LOG 300	1953	Guy Arab IV 6LW	Metro-Cammell	H30/25R
3001	LOG 301	1952	Guy Arab IV 5LW	Saunders-Roe	H30/25R
3002	LOG 302	1954	Daimler CLG5	Metro-Cammell	H30/25R
3003x3102	MOF 3x102	1953-4	Guy Arab IV 6LW	Metro-Cammell	H30/25R
3103x3227	MOF 103x227	1953-4	Daimler CVG6	Crossley	H30/25R
3230	460 MTE	1960	Leyland PDR1/1	Metro-Cammell	H43/33F
3231-3240	231-240 DOC	1961	Leyland PDR1/1	Metro-Cammell	H43/33F
3241-3250	241-250 DOC	1962	Daimler CRG6LX	Metro-Cammell	H43/33F
3251-3300	251-300 GON	1963	Daimler CRG6LX	Park Royal	H43/33F
3301-3350	301-350 GON	1963	Daimler CRG6LX	Metro-Cammell	H43/33F
3351-3400	351-400 KOV	1964-5	Daimler CRG6LX	Metro-Cammell	H43/33F
3401-3450	401-450 KOV	1964	Daimler CRG6LX	Park Royal	H43/33F
3451-3474	BON 451-474C	1965	Daimler CRG6LX	Marshall	B37F
3475-3524	BON 475-524C	1965	Daimler CRG6LX	Park Royal	H43/33F
3525-3574	BON 525-574C	1965-6	Daimler CRG6LX	Metro-Cammell	H43/33F
3575-3612	FOC 575-612D	1966	Daimler CRG6LX	MCW	H43/33F
3613-3625	FOC 613-625D	1966	Daimler CRG6LX	Park Royal	H43/33F
3626-3650	JOB 626-650E	1967	Daimler CRG6LX	Park Royal	H43/33F
3651-3662	JOL 651-662E	1967	Ford R192	Strachans	B46F
3663-3674	KOX 663-674F	1967	AEC Swift MP2R	MCW	B37+30D
3675-3680	KOX 675-680F	1967	AEC Swift 2P2R	MCW	B37+39D
3681-3730	KOX 681-730F	1967	Daimler CRG6LX	MCW	H43/33F
3731-3780	KOX 731-780F	1968	Daimler CRG6LX	Park Royal	H43/33F
3781-3880	NOV 781-880G	1968-9	Daimler CRG6LX	Park Royal	H43/29D†

x = Incomplete series:
The following operated for WMPTE: 2229/36-7/49/60, 2471, 2505/26-84/6-93/5-603/6-10/2-26/30/2-3/7/40-1/3-5/7-9/51/5-6/9/62/4-6/8-71/4-5/7/9/81/3-4/9-94/6-9/704-7/9-11/3-6/8-25/8-35/7-45/7-50/2-62/4-5/7-71/3-2923/5-3078/80-217/9-27.

The following were loaned to PMT but did not run for WMPTE: 2247/52/6-9 (2247 was used for one PTE private hire).
The following were acquired but did not run in service: 2190-1, 2202/9/11/3-4/8/23-4/6/8/31-2/4-5-8-46/53-5, 2468/72/5-7/9/82-7/92/9-500/2-4/6/9-12/4-7/9-21/4/94, 2604-5/11/36/46/53/63/73/6/80/5-8/95, 2701-3/17/26/36/46/51/63/72.

*2847 was H30/25RD; 2926 was H32/25R
†Autofare equipment reduced capacity of 3781-3880 to H43/28D; No. 3867 was converted to O43/22F in 1978.

WITHDRAWAL DATES
1969: 2229/36-7, 2471, 2505/27/81, 2603/10/33/7/51/9/62/4/9-70/83-4/91/7, 2704-6/22/42-3, 3385
1970: 2249, 2574, 2643/5/56/68/714-5/7/81/92/4, 2707/9-10/5/20-1/3/84/41/5-8-50/7/60/4/73-4
1971: 2563/70/5/7/9, 2623/6/30/2/40-1/4/7-9/55/65-6/79/89-90/3/6/8-9, 2711/3-4/6/8-9/24-5/9-35/7-40/4/7/52-6/8-9/61-2/5/7-8/70/1/5/82/93/9, 2807/28/51/76-9/83-4/9/91-2/4-5/7-2900/9-19/29/44/54/68/71-5/82/8-92/7-
3000/23/32/6/9/43-50/64-5/7/9/77/85, 3103/9/17/68-9, 3222, 3531 (rebuilt as 5531 q.v.)
1972: 2260, 2539/41/5/8/51/3-6/60/2/6-9/71-3/6/8/82/4/6-91/3/5/6-8, 2601-2/7-8/16, 2789/97-8, 2800-1/3-6/12/5-6/8-20/7/30/9/49/54-7/63-6/8/75/80/5-8/90/3/6, 2920-3/6/8/42/6/59/76-8/81/3-5/7/93-6, 3001-2/42/52-3/6/
78/83/6, 3104/10-3/6/8/22-4/32/6/41-4/6/9/56-7/9/62/72/4/7-9/81/4/7/9, 3201/7-8/10/7, 3417, 3533, 3751
1973: 2526/8/31-2/5/7-8/57/99, 2620, 2796, 2802/9-11/3/29/37/73, 2927/30/5/47/50, 3006/20/66/70-5/80-2/4/7/9-98, 3101-2/39-40/5/7-8/50-4/8/60-1/3-5/7/70-1/3/5/80/2-3/5-6/8/93-6, 3202-4/9/11/6/9/26
1974: 2530/42/4/7/59/64-5, 2776-7/9/87, 2835/8/42/4/67/9, 2904/55-6/63/7/70/80, 3026-7/9/34/8, 3126, 3445
1975: 2534/52/61/83, 2612/21-2, 2780-1/3/5-6/91, 2808/25/33-4/6/40-1/3/50/2/82, 2907/33/6-8/41/5/66/86, 3009-10/3-4/6/8-9/28/33/40-1/55/62/76, 3125/30-1/5/76/90/2/8, 3200/5/13-4/24, 3303
1976: 2529/36/40/3/6/9-50/80/80, 2606/13-4/8-9, 2778/84/8/90/2/4-5, 2814/21-2/4/31-2/45/8/58/60-2/70-2/4/81, 2908/32/48-9/52-3/60/2/5, 3004/8/12/7/21/5/30/51/4/7-8/60-1/3/88, 3105-8/14/27/33/7-8/97/9, 3215
1977: 2533/92/7, 2600/9/15/7/24-5, 2817/23/6/46-7/53/9, 2901-3/5-6/25/31/4/9-40/3/51/7-8/61/4/9/79, 3003/5/7/11/5/22/4/31/5/7/68/99-3100/15/9-21/8/9/34/55/66/91, 3206/12/20-1/3/5/7/32-3/5-8-40/2/5-53/60/2/5, 3316,
3508, 3651-80
1978: 3059, 3230/4/6/54/63/8/73/8/88/94-5/7-8, 3300/4/8-12/4/8-9/22/4/8/30-1/4/62/74, 3448, 3504
1979: 3237/7/41/3/55-7/70-14/7/80-7/9-91/6/9, 3325/7/9/32-3/5-7/9-41/3-4/6-55/7-8/60-1/4-5/7-71/3/7-83/6-9/99-402/4-5/8-10/2-6/9-29/31-2/4-5/7-9/41/6-7/51/3-4/8/62/7/93
1980: 3244/58-9/61/4/6-7/9/72/9/92-3, 3301-2/5-7/13/5/7/20-1/3/6/38/42/5/56/9/63/6/72/5-6/84/90-8, 3403/6-7/11/8/30/3/40/2-4/9-50/5-7/9-61/3/5-75/85/7-92/4-503/6-7/9-29/32/4-53/5/8/60/2/4-5/7-8/71-3, 3602-10/2-6/8/
20-15/9-30/6/42-3/7/9/83/7/95/7/9
1981: 3436/52/66/8-74/86, 3505/30/54/6-7/9/61/3/6/9-70/4-6/8-94/6-601/11/7/9/22-4/6-8/31-5/7-41/4-6/8/50, 3681-24-6/8-94/6/8, 3700-16/8-22/7-9/31-3/7/40-4/6/50/2-4-5/9/61/5/73, 3834
1982: 3577/95, 3717/23-6/30/4-6/8-9/45/7-9/53/6-8/60/2-4/6-72/4-90/4/7-9, 3801/3/5-8/10/2-5/7/9/22-4/8-31/33/5/9-40/7-8/50-1/6-60/3-6/72-4/6-9
1983: 3791/3/5-6, 3800/2/4/9/11/6/8/20-1/5-7/32/6-8/41-6/9/52-5/61-2-8-71/5/80.
Transferred to WMT 10/86: 3867

Buses acquired from Walsall Corporation 1.10.1969

Fleet No	Registration	Chassis	Year	Body	Type
1L	ODH 76x88	Leyland PD2/1	1951	Park Royal	FH30/26R
2L	ODH 89x100	Guy Arab III6LW	1951	Park Royal	FH30/26R
3-18L	ODH 297x309	Guy Arab III6LW	1951	Park Royal	FH30/26R
19-24L	ODH 801x812	Leyland PD2/1	1951	Park Royal	FH30/26R
25-30L	1 UDH	Daimler CRG6LX	1962	Northern Counties	H37/27F
31-35L	2272 DH	Daimler CRG6LX	1963	Northern Counties	H41/29F
36-55L	ADH 119-124B	Daimler CRG6LW	1964	Northern Counties	H41/29F
56L	BDH 425-430C	Daimler CRG6LW	1964	Northern Counties	H41/29F
61-75L	EDH 631-635C	Daimler CRG6LW	1965	Northern Counties	H41/29F
76-90L	EDH 936-955C	Daimler CRG6LW	1965	Northern Counties	H41/29D
91-105L	XDH 56G	Daimler CRC6-36	1968	Northern Counties	H51/34D
106-119L	761-775 UDH	Daimler CVG6	1963	Metro-Cammell	H37/28F
	KDH 876-90D/E	Daimler CRG6LW	1966-7	Northern Counties	H41/29D
	RDH 91-105F	Daimler CRG6LX	1968	Northern Counties	H41/29D
	XDH 506-519G	Daimler CRG6LX	1968-9	Northern Counties	H41/27D
201L	KYY 543	Leyland 7RT		Park Royal	H30/26R
203-204L	OLD 596, 601	Leyland 7RT		Park Royal	H30/26R
400L	TDH 99	Daimler CVG5	1954	Northern Counties	H32/28R
401L	YDH 401	Daimler CVG5	1956	Walsall/Met Sec	H32/27R
800L	600 DDH	Dennis Loline II	1958	Willowbrook	H41/29F
801-805L	PDH 801-805	Leyland PSU1/13	1952	Leyland	B44F
806-810L	PDH 806-810	Leyland PSU1/13	1953	Park Royal	B42F
811-820L	RDH 501-510	Leyland PD2/12	1953	Roe	FH33/23RD
821L	TDH 673	Daimler CVG5	1954	Northern Counties	H37/28R
822L	TDH 769	AEC Regent V	1954	Park Royal	H33/28R
823L	TDH 770	Leyland PD2	1954	Metro-Cammell	H32/28R
824L	YDH 224	Daimler CVG6-30	1956	Willowbrook	H41/33R
825L	YDH 225	AEC Bridgemaster	1956	Crossley	H41/31R
826-840L	WDH 901-915	Daimler CVG6	1956	Willowbrook	H37/29RD
841L	841 FDH	Leyland PDR1/1	1959	Metro-Cammell	H40/34F
842-849L	242-249 HDH	Dennis Loline II	1960	Willowbrook	H44/30F
878-884L	878-884 HDH	Dennis Loline II	1960	Willowbrook	H44/30F
885L	885 LDH	Dennis Loline II	1960	Willowbrook	H44/30F
886-890L	886-890 MDH	Daimler CVG6-30	1961	Metro-Cammell	H41/31F
891-895L	891-895 MDH	AEC Regent V	1961	Metro-Cammell	H41/31F
896-900L	896-900 MDH	AEC Regent V	1961	Willowbrook	H41/31F

x = Incomplete series:

The following operated for WMPTE: ODH77-89/91-2/5, 100, 297, 300/4/7, 801/4-5/7-8/10-2 with fleet numbers 237, 120-31/3/73/6/83/7, 217/26/30/4, 197, 233/5-6/8-40L.
The following were acquired but not run in service: ODH 306/8 (fleet numbers 229/31).

Notes

17L, 24L had been rebuilt to H41/29D by Northern Counties in 1968 and 1965 respectively.
2/4-13/5-6/8-23/5-30L were rebuilt to H41/29D by Lex Garages (Stour Valley) Ltd. 1971-2.
8L had a Perkins V8 engine 1967-70.
120/5, 237L (ODH 78/83/77) had been upseated to FH38/27R in 1959-60.
201/3/4L were ex-London Transport Executive in 1959. Due to LTE overhaul procedure, it is likely that vehicles basically dated from 1949, despite age of registrations.
The body of 401L was built by Walsall Corporation on Metal Sections frames.
801/2/5L had been converted to B43F; 808L to DP40F; 810L to DP36F.
811-3L had been lengthened and rebuilt to FH39/32F by Willowbrook 1959-60.

WITHDRAWAL DATES

1970: 3, 14, 801-3/6/13-4/84L
1971: 120-1/3-30/3/73/83/97, 201/3-4/17/26/30/3-7/40, 400-1, 809/11-2/7/9-20/2/5L
1972: 122/31/76/87, 238/9, 804-5/7/26/8/49/78-83/5, 900L
1973: 69, 800/8/10/5-6/8/21/3-4/39/46-8L
1974: 1, 56, 827/9-38/40/2-5/96/8-9L
1975: 15, 62, 71/3, 892/5L
1976: 2/4/6-9/11/2/9-20/8-30/3/5/8/43/4/6/61/4-5/72/85, 888/91/3-4/7L
1977: 5/10/3/6/21-3/5-7/31-2/4/6/9-41/5/7-52/63/6-8/70/4-7/84, 841/86-7/9-90L
1978: 17-8/37/42/53-5/78-83/6-91/6/7/9, 102-5/15L
1979: 94/5, 101L
1980: 24/92/3/8, 100/6-9/12-4L
1981: 110/1/7-9L
1986: 116L

Trolleybuses acquired from Walsall Corporation 1.10.1969

Fleet No	Registration	Chassis	Year	Body	Type
303-304	BDY 806, 808	Sunbeam W	1947	Weymann	H30/26R
306-310	BDY 812-4/6/9	Sunbeam W	1947	Weymann	H30/26R
338-342	NDH 955-959	Sunbeam F4	1951	Brush	H30/26R
344-347	ADX 193-196	Sunbeam F4	1950	Park Royal	H30/26R
351-353	ADX 189-191	Sunbeam F4	1950	Park Royal	H30/26R
850	HBE 541	Crossley TDD42/3	1951	Roe	H29/25R
851-865	TDH 901-915	Sunbeam F4A	1954-5	Willowbrook	H36/34RD
866-872	XDH 66-72	Sunbeam F4A	1956	Willowbrook	H36/34RD
874-877	GFU 692-695	BUT 9611T	1950	NCB	H28/26R

A further Crossley trolleybus was acquired in withdrawn condition: 873 (HBE 542)

Notes

303-4/6-10 were ex-Maidstone & District in 1959 (new to Hastings Tramways).
342 had been rebuilt and lengthened to H34/31R in 1965.
344-7/51-3 were ex-Ipswich Corporation in 1962.
850/73-7 were ex-Grimsby-Cleethorpes Transport in 1960 (new to Cleethorpes Corporation); 875-7 being rebuilt and lengthened to H39/30F (875-6) or H37/30F (877) before entering service in 1962-3.
866 had been rebuilt to H37/34F in 1969.
All were withdrawn in 1970.

Buses acquired from West Bromwich Corporation 1.10.1969

Fleet	Registration	Year	Chassis	Body	Seating
*101H	NEA101F	1968	Daimler CRG6LX	MCW	H42/31F
*102-114H	KEA 102-114E	1967	Daimler CRG6LX	MCW	H42/31F
*115-121H	TEA 115-121G	1969	Daimler CRG6LX	ECW	H45/28F
157x176H	GEA 157x176	1952	Daimler CVG6	Weymann	H30/26R
177-186H	KEA 177-186	1955	Daimler CVG6	Metro-Cammell	H32/26R
187-198H	PEA 187-198	1957	Daimler CVG6	Willowbrook	H34/26R
199x210H	SEA 199x210	1957	Daimler CVG6	Metro-Cammell	H37/26R
214-219H	UEA 214-219	1958	Daimler CVG6-30	Metro-Cammell	H41/32R
220-225H	YEA 220-225	1959	Daimler CVG6-30	Metro-Cammell	H41/32R
226-227H	YEA 226-227	1960	Leyland PSUC1/4	Roe	B43F
228-232H	YEA 228-232 DEA	1960	Daimler CVG6	Metro-Cammell	H37/29R
+233H	MXX341	1953	Guy Special	ECW	B26F
234-237H	734-737 FEA	1961	Daimler CVG6-30	Metro-Cammell	H41/33R
238-244H	238-244 JEA	1962	Daimler CVG6-30	Metro-Cammell	H41/33R
245-249H	245-249 NEA	1963	Daimler CVG6-30	Metro-Cammell	H41/33R
250-251H	250-251 NEA	1963	Leyland PSUC1/4	Roe	B43F
+252H	MXX340	1953	Guy Special	ECW	B26F
253-258H	253-258 TEA	1964	Daimler CVG6	Metro-Cammell	H37/29R
259-265H	CEA 259-265C	1965	Daimler CVG6-30	Metro-Cammell	H41/33R

x = Incomplete series:
The following operated for WMPTE: 159-68/72-5, 199-201/3-10H
The following were acquired but did not run in service: 157/70-1
*101-121H were low height and carried special liveries with West Bromwich and WMPTE.
+233H and 252H were acquired from London Transport Executive in 1961.

WITHDRAWAL DATES
1969: 162-4H
1970: 160/6-8H
1971: 161/5/72/5/90, 227H
1972: 159/80/8-9/96-7, 201/26/8/33H
1973: 173-4/7/91/9-200/3-10/29-32/43/52H
1975: 178/81-6/93-5/8, 215H
1976: 179/87/92, 218/20/34/6/8-9/44/50/4/6-8H
1977: 214/6-7/9/21-5/35/7/40-2/5-9/51/3/5H
1978: 259-65H
1981: 105/8/10/4-21H
1982: 102-4/6-7/9/11-3H
1986: 101H

Buses acquired from Wolverhampton Corporation 1.10.1969

Fleet	Registration	Year	Chassis	Body	Seating
1-18N	SUK 1-18	1957	Guy Arab IV*	Metro-Cammell	H33/27R
19N	WUK19	1958	Guy Arab IV 6LW	Burlingham	FH41/27F
20-39N	YDA 20-39	1959-60	Guy Arab IV 6LW	Metro-Cammell	FH41/31F†
40-69N	4040-69JW	1961	Guy Arab IV 6LW	Metro-Cammell	FH41/31F
70N	4070JW	1961	Guy Wulfrunian	East Lancs	H42/30F
71N	4071JW	1962	Guy Wulfrunian	East Lancs	H40/31F
72-111N	7072-111UK	1963	Guy Arab V 6LW	Weymann	H41/31F
112-121N	7112-121UK	1963	Guy Arab V AEC	Weymann	H41/31F
122-146N	122-146 DDA	1963-4	Guy Arab V 6LW	Park Royal	H41/31F
147-156N	DDA 147-156C	1965	Guy Arab V 6LW	Strachans	H41/31F
157-181N	GJW 157-181C	1965	Guy Arab V 6LW	Metro-Cammell	H41/31F
182-186N	HJW 182-186D	1966	AEC Renown 3B2RA	MCW	H40/32F
187-217E	MDA 187-217E	1967	Guy Arab V 6LW	Strachans	H41/31F
384x398N	FJW 384x398	1948-9	Guy Arab III6LW	Brush	H29/25R
500x535N	FJW 500x535	1948/50	Daimler CVG6	Brush	H29/25R
536x538N	FJW 536x538	1949	Guy Arab III6LW	Brush	H29/25R
539x560N	FJW 539x560	1950	Guy Arab III6LW	Park Royal	H28/26R
571-577N	KJW 571-577	1953	Guy Arab III6LW	Roe	H31/25R
578-584N	KJW 578-584	1954	Guy Arab IV 6LW	Metro-Cammell	H31/25R
585N	NUK 585	1954	Guy Arab IV 6LW	Park Royal/Guy	H33/28R
703-704N	7894-5 UK	1963	Ford Thames 529E	Martin Walter	B19F
705-707N	705-707 CDA	1963	AEC Reliance 2MU2RA	Park Royal	B40D
708-713N	NJW 708-713E	1967	AEC Swift MP2R	Strachans	B54D
714-719N	NJW 714-719E	1967	Daimler SRC6	Brush	B54D
720N	KUK 720D	1966	Ford R226	Strachans	B54D‡
721N	LUK 721E	1967	Ford Transit	Martin Walter	12

x = Incomplete series:
The following operated for WMPTE: 392-3N, 511-2/4-5/7-20/2/4-5/7-20/2/4-5/7-20/2/4-5/7-8/50-1N
The following were acquired but did not run in service: 386/90-1/4, 507/36-7
*1/3-5/13-8N had Meadows 6DC engines; 2/6-12N had Gardner 6LW engines.
*22N was H41/31F
†720N was B52D between 1969-72, and was renumbered 1720 in 1975.

WITHDRAWAL DATES
1969: 392, 518-9/22/49N
1970: 70, 135, 393, 512/4-5/7/27/9-31/3/8/42/5/7-8/50-1N
1971: 511/20/4/6/40-1/6/53-60/71-85, 714N
1972: 1/3-5/7/9/11/3-7/30, 155/6/90/2/8, 207/9/11/4-7, 708/11N
1973: 2/8/10/2/8/33/43/63/71/7/83/93, 124/39/82/7-9/91/3-7/9-202/4/10/2-3, 705/13/5N
1974: 19/32/4-5/72-3/87-8/96-7, 102/4/13/5/7-8/21/5/7/32-4/6/8/40/8/69/74/84/6, 203/5-6/8, 706/9-10/2/8N
1975: 20-2/8-9/31/6-8/41/50-1/9/61/4-5/9, 112/4/6/9-20/2-3/6/8-31/7/41-6/50-1/83/5, 707/16-7/9N
1976: 6/23-7/39-40/2/4-9/52-8/60/2/6-8/9, 103/6/47/52-4/7/62/7/76, 720-1N
1977: 74/6/9-82/4-5, 101/5/8-10/49/58-61/4-5/70-1/3/7-81, 703-4N
1978: 75/8/86/90-2/4-5/8-100/7/11/63/6/8/72/5N

Buses purchased new by WMPTE 1969-74

Fleet	Registration	Year	Chassis	Body	Seating
3881-3980	SOE 881-980H	1969-70	Daimler CRG6LX-33	Park Royal	H47/33D*
3981-3999	TOB 981-999H	1970	Daimler CRG6LX-33	Park Royal	H47/33D*
4000	TOB 400H	1970	Daimler CRG6LX-33	Park Royal	H47/33D*
4001-4004	TOC 1-4H	1970	Daimler CRG6LX-33	Park Royal	H47/33D*
4005-4012	TOC 5-12H	1970	Daimler CRG6LX	Northern Counties	H45/31D
4013-4027	VOH 13-27J	1970	Daimler CRG6LX	Northern Counties	H45/27D
4029-4035	YOX 29-35K	1971	Daimler CRG6LX	Northern Counties	H43/33F
4036-4060	XON 36-60J	1971	Daimler CRG6LX	Park Royal	H43/33F
4061-4135	YOX 61-135K	1971	Daimler CRG6LX	Park Royal	H43/33F†
4136-4235	YOX 136-235K	1971-2	Daimler CRG6LX	MCW	H43/33F
4236-4241	EOF 236-241L	1972	Commer	Rootes	B19F‡
4242	EOF 242L	1973	Metro-Scania	MCW	B47F
4243-4303	EOF 243-303L	1973	Daimler CRG6LX	Park Royal	H43/33F
4304-4342	NOB 304-342L	1973	Daimler CRG6LX	Park Royal	H43/33F
4343-4361	EOF 343-361L	1972-3	Bristol VRT/SL6G	MCW	H43/33F
4362-4424	NOB 362-424M	1973-4	Bristol VRT/SL6G	MCW	H43/33F
4425-4442	TOE 425-442N	1974	Bristol VRT/SL6G	MCW	H43/33F

* Autofare equipment reduced capacity of 3881-4004 to H47/32D
†4069 was converted to O43/30F in 1985
‡4240-1 were B18F; 4238/41 were rebuilt to B15F in 1976

WITHDRAWAL DATES
1972: 3907
1977: 3932
1978: 3940-1/5-6/51-2/4/6/8/63-4
1979: 3882-3/6, 3912/4/7-23/5/9/31/3-4/7-8/42/7-8/53/7/9/61-2/7, 4236-41
1980: 3881/4-5/8-91/3-8, 3900-6/8-11/5-6/26-8/30/5-6/43-4/9-50/5/60/5-6/70/8, 4242, 4374-88/90-5/7/9, 4439
1981: 3887/92/9, 3913/24/39/68/71/4-7/80-1/3/5/9/91-5/7/9-4001/3-4/7/9-12/23, 4261, 4389/96/8, 4400-19/25/8/30-3/6/8/40-2
1982: 3969/72-3/9/82/4/90/6/8, 4002/5-6/8/15/8-9/24/6/46/56/84, 4133/41/67, 4420-4/6-7/9/34-5/7
1983: 4013-4/6-7/20-2/5/7/9-40/2/4-9/52-8/60/2/6-8/9, 4109-11/4-6/8/20-9/31-2/4/7/44/50/98, 4234
1984: 4044/50/67-8/70/3/81/3/9/91-2/6-7, 4100-7/13/7/9/35-6/8-40/3/7-8/83/5-6/8/91-7/9-4200/4-6/9-11/3/8/21-5/8-32/5, 4348/50/3-5/64/6/8-9/72-3
1985: 4054/65-6, 4108/12/30/42/5-6/68/70/2/5-6/84/7/90, 4201-3/7-8/12/4-7/9-20/6-7/33/44/7-8/58/62-3/6/8-72/87-8, 4330/5/8/43-6/9/51-2/6-63/5/7/70-1
1986: 4041, 4243/5-6/9-57/9-60/4-5/7/73-86/9-4329/31-4-6/7/9-42/7
Transferred to WMT 10/86: 4069

Buses acquired from Midland Red 3.12.1973

Fleet	Registration	Year	Chassis	Body	Type
*101x158	HHA 101x158L	1972-3	Leyland National	Ley Nat	B51F
4849x4942	849x942 KHA	1960-1	BMMO D9	BMMO	H40/32RD
4945x5044	2945x3044 HA	1961-3	BMMO D9	BMMO	H40/32RD
5094x5144	5094x5144 HA	1962-3	BMMO S16	BMMO	B52F
5145x5169	5145x5169 HA	1962-3	Leyland PSU3/4R	Weymann	B53F†
5170x5244	5170x5244 HA	1962-3	Leyland PSU3/4R	Willowbrook	B53F†
5245x5294	5245x5294 HA	1963	Daimler CRG6LX	Alexander	H44/33F
5296x5378	6296x6378 HA	1963-4	BMMO D9	BMMO	H40/32RD
5379x5394	AHA 379x394B	1964	BMMO D9	BMMO	H40/32RD
5395x5404	BHA 395x404C	1965	BMMO D9	BMMO	H40/32RD
5405x5445	EHA 405x445D	1966	BMMO D9	BMMO	H40/32RD
5446x5511	6446x6511 HA	1963-4	BMMO S17	BMMO	B52F
5512x5545	6512x6545 HA	1964	BMMO S16	BMMO	B52F
5546x5595	AHA 146x195B	1964	BMMO S17	BMMO	B52F
5596x5645	BHA 596x645C	1965	BMMO S17	BMMO	B52F
5675x5700	CHA 675x700C	1965	BMMO S17	BMMO	B52F
5701x5721	DHA 701x721C	1965	BMMO S17	BMMO	B52F
5725x5773	EHA 725x773D	1966	BMMO S17	BMMO	B52F
5849x5868	JHA 849x868E	1967	BMMO S21	BMMO	DP49F‡
5869x5878	LHA 869x878F	1967	BMMO S21	BMMO	DP49F
5879x5903	MHA 879x903F	1968	BMMO S22	BMMO	DP45F
5904x5915	PHA 904x915F	1968	BMMO S22	BMMO	DP45F
5916x5939	RHA 916x939G	1968-9	BMMO S23	BMMO	B51F
5940x5991	UHA 940x991H	1969-70	BMMO S23	BMMO	B51F
5992x6041	GHA 392x441D	1966	Daimler CRG6LX	Alexander	H44/33F§
6042x6091	JHA 42x91E	1967	Daimler CRG6LX	Alexander	H44/33F
6092x6140	LHA 592x640F	1967	Daimler CRG6LX	Alexander	H44/33F
6156x6190	SHA 856x890G	1969	Daimler CRG6LX	Alexander	H45/30D¶
6191x6225	UHA 191x225H	1969	Daimler CRG6LX	Alexander	H45/30D¶
6261x6293	YHA 261x293J	1970	Daimler CRG6LX	Alexander	H45/30D¶

All incomplete series. The following operated for WMPTE: 102-19/31-2/5/7-41/8-54, 4849/53/6/8/63/5-6/8/71-2/4-6/9-80/3/7-8, 4900/2/5/18-21/3/6/8/38/42/5/7/9/53/7/62/8/78/81-2/4-5/7/95/7, 5000/2/14/22-3/36/44/96, 5104-5/16/28/36/44/8/60-3/73/5/7/95/8, 5200-1/12/23/5/32/9/43-4/6-7/51-3/5-6/9/61/8/70/2/5/7/9-80/3/6-8/91, 5304/21-2/6-7/40/2/4/6-50/2-3/9/63-5/8/73/8/92/7-8, 5400-1/3/7/17/9/22/6-7/38-9/43-4/56/8-9/63-4/7/9/74-5/83/8/91/3-4/7, 5502/7-8/28/30/3-4/6/41/3/6-7/9-51/3/6/8/61/3-6/8-9/72/4/85/8/94, 5598-5601/3/8/22/33-4/6-9/43/78-9/82-3/6/92/5, 5705/9/15/7/9-21/5/7-8/32/5-6/42-3/54/8/61-2, 5849-53/9/70/6-7/86/9/99, 5902-3/8-11/25/9/32/4/8/45-6/50-1/4-5/8/62/8-70/2-3/5/81-4/6/93/6, 6005/9/12/20-4/40/5/8-50/6/8/63-6/9-80/2/4/92/4/7-8, 6101-3/5/8-12/4/8-22/4/6-7/9/31-3/7-40/56/9-60/6-7/74/86-9/98-6200/2-4/10-5/9-20/3-4/61-70/8-83/6-93.

*102-112/4-9/31-2/5/7-41/8-54 renumbered 5102 etc in September 1982.

†5148/60-3/73/5/7/98, 5200-1/12/23/5/32/9/43-4 to B51F 1976-7.

‡5849-50 had been reseated to B51F; 5852 reseated to B52F 1974.

§6023 had been converted to H43/28D.

¶6156/9/60/6-7/74/88-9, 6203/14-5/9-20/4/61-7/9-70/8-9/82-3/6/90-3 converted to H45/31F 1975-8.

WITHDRAWAL DATES

1974: 113, 4875-6, 4905/57/62/84-5/97, 5000/2/22/96, 5105/16/36/44, 5530/3-4/43, 5705

1975: 4863/8/80/7, 4919/21/47, 5104/28/63, 5246, 5340/8/65/97, 5494, 5528/72, 5683

1976: 4849/56/8/66/72/88, 4918/20/3/6/8/38/42/5/9/53/78/82/7/95, 5195, 5327/44/7/53/63/8/73/8/92, 5400/3/7/19/27/58-9/63/7/74-5/83/8/91/3/7, 5502/7-8/36/41/6/9-51/6/8/61/3-6/8-9/74/85/8/94/8-5601/3/8/22/33-4/6-9/ 43/78-9/82/6/92/5, 5709/15/7/9-21/5/7-8/32/5-6/42-3/54/8/61-2, 5902/62

1977: 4853/65/71/4/9/83, 4900/2/68/81, 5014/23/36/44, 5162, 5201/23/43/59/61/75/80, 5304/21-2/6/42/6/9-50/2/9/64/98, 5401/17/22/6/38-9/43-4/56/64/9, 5547/53, 5759, 5850/9/76-7/86

1978: 5148/60-1/73/5/7/98, 5200/12/25/32/9/44/7/51/36/70/79/83/8, 5849/51-3/89/99, 5903/8-9/25/34/8/45/50-1/4/68/70/83-4/93/6, 6005/12/21-4/50/8/72, 6269

1979: 5286, 5870, 5910-1/46/55/8/72/5/82, 6020/40/8-9/63/5-6/71/5/82, 6120/87, 6264

1980: 5252/5/68/72/87/91, 5929/69/73/86, 6056/64/9-70/3-4/6-80/4/92/4/7-8, 6101-3/5/8-12/4/8-9/21-2/4/6-7/9/31-3/7-40/74/86/98, 6211/91

1981: 5932/81, 6009/45, 6156/9-60/7/88-9/99, 6200/2-4/10/2-5/9-20/3/61-3/5-7/70/8-83/7-8/92-3

1982: 6166, 6224/68/86/9-90

1983: 102

1986: 103-12/4-9/31-2/5/7-41/8-54

Buses acquired from Coventry Corporation 1.4.1974

1-22Y	CKV 1-22D	1966	Daimler CRG6LX	East Lancs	H44/31F
23-40Y	KWK 23-40F	1968	Daimler CRG6LX	ECW	H44/28F
41-58Y	KKV41-58G	1969	Daimler CRG6LX	East Lancs	H45/27D
59-75Y	SWK 59-75J	1970	Daimler CRG6LX	Park Royal	H45/27D
76Y	SWK 76J	1970	Daimler CRG6LX	East Lancs (1972)	H44/30F
77-94Y	YHP 477-94J	1971	Daimler CRG6LX	East Lancs	H45/27D
95-122Y	YVC 95-122K	1972	Daimler CRG6LX	East Lancs	H44/30F
123-142Y	See Footnotes	1973	Daimler CRG6LX	East Lancs	H44/30F
211Y	SKV 211	1957	Daimler CVG6	Metro-Cammell	H33/27R
216x265Y	VWK 216x265	1958	Daimler CVG6	Metro-Cammell	H33/27R
266-290Y	XVC 266-290	1959	Daimler CVG6	Metro-Cammell	H33/27R
291x312Y	291x312 RW	1961	Daimler CVG6	Metro-Cammell	H34/29R
313-337Y	313-337 CRW	1963	Daimler CVG6	Metro-Cammell	H34/29R
338x359Y	CDU 338x359R	1964	Leyland PDR1/2	Willowbrook	H44/32F
360-381Y	CRW 360-381C	1965	Daimler CRG6LX	Willowbrook	H44/32F
407Y	YVC 407L	1972	Ford R226	Plaxton	C49F
408Y	GWK 508L	1973	Ford Transit	Deansgate	12
5516-5518	KHP 516-518E	1967	Bristol RESL6G	ECW	B44F
5519-5521	KHP 519-521E	1967	Bristol RESL6G	ECW	B42D

x = Incomplete series:

The following operated for WMPTE: 216/20/3-37/9-40/2/5-61/3-90/2-337/8/40-59Y
The following were acquired but did not run in service: 238/43-4/91 (243-4 became tuition buses and 291 a tree cutter).

Notes
211/6/20/3-37/42/5/7-8/50-2/60/3, 360-4Y renumbered 1211/6 etc in 1974-5.
5516-21 were numbered 516Y, 4443-4, 519Y (later 519), 4445-6 until September 1976.
1360-4 reverted to 360-1Y, 362, 363Y, 364 in 1978.
2-3/11/3/5/20/3-142, 338/40-50/2/4-71/3-5/9-80 renumbered 1002-3/11 etc. in November 1979.
1-5/9-11/3/6-8/22Y had bodies by East Lancs subsidiary Neepsend.
23-40Y were originally H45/27D, being rebuilt in 1973-4.
41-58/77-94Y were converted to H44/29F in 1974-9 and 70Y to H44/24F in 1975.
59-69/71-5, 338/40-59Y lost one upstairs seat upon fitting with periscopes in 1976-7.
123-5/33/5/40Y were registered PDU123-5/33/5/40M, and 126-32/4/6-9/41-2 were registered GWK 126-32/4/6-9/41-2L.
WITHDRAWAL DATES
1975: 223/6-8/31/7/60Y
1976: 216/30/6Y
1977: 211/20/4/32/4-5/42/5/7-8/50/2/63/7-77/80-7/9-90/3, 309/11Y
1978: 225/9/33/9-40/6/9/51/3-9/61/4-6/78-9/88/92/4-308/10/2-24/31/5-6/51/3/76-8/81Y, 5517-21
1979: 1/4-10/2/4/6-9/21-2, 325-30/2-4/7/72.. 407Y, 5516
1980: 47/50/2/6/62, 139, 338/40-50/2/4-71/3-5/9-80Y
1981: 2/3/11/3/5/20/30/7/45-6/8-9/51/3-5/7-8/64/6/8/70/2/4, 141Y
1982: 24-9/31-6/44/59-61/9/71/3/5, 126Y, 408Y
1983: 23/38/63/5/7/78/80/4/6/92/4/6Y
1984: 76-7/9/81/3/5/7-8/90/3Y
1985: 82/9/91/5/7-104/6/8/10/2-3/5-20/2/4-5/8/31/3/7-8/42Y
1986: 105/7/9/11/4/21/3/7/9-30/2/4-6/40Y

Secondhand buses purchased by WMPTE

1142-1146	6342-6346 KH	1960	Leyland PDR1/1	Metro-Cammell	H44/31F
1147-1149	2347-2349 AT	1960	Leyland PDR1/1	Roe	H44/31F
1151-1156	2351-2356 AT	1960	Leyland PDR1/1	Roe	H44/31F
5500-5530		1972	Daimler CRG6LX	MCW	H44/27F
5532-5580		1972-3	Daimler CRG6LX	MCW	H44/27F

Notes
1142-9/51-6 were ex Kingston-upon-Hull Corporation 1975.
5500-30/2-80 were ex London Transport Executive 1979-80.
5500-28 were registered JGU 255/7/9-62/4/8-73/6-81/5/7-90/2/4-7K
5529-30/2-80 were registered MLH 299, 300/5/8/10-4/7-31/3/6-8/40-1/4-6/9-51/4-8/60-8, 463L
WITHDRAWAL DATES
1976: 1153
1977: 1143-4/6
1978: 1142/8-9/51/5
1979: 1145/7/52/4/6
1983: 5504-5/9-13/8/22/6/8/50/6/65/76/9
1984: 5500-3/7/14-7/9-21/4/32/40-1/4-5/54/7/60-1/6-9/71/3/5/8
1985: 5506/8/23/5/7/9-30/5-6/8-9/42-3/7-9/51-3/8-9/62-4/70/2/7/80
1986: 5533-4/7/46/55/74

Vehicles acquired with business of Central Coachways 3.1984

TDH 232R	1977	Ford R1014	Plaxton	C45F
YNX 446-447S	1978	Ford R1114	Duple	C53F
FFD 968T	1979	AEC Reliance	Duple	C53F
GEA 733-734T	1979	Ford R1114	Duple	C53F
LHA 451-452V	1980	Ford R1114	Duple	C45F
OHA 465W	1980	Ford R1014	Duple	C45F
*OWK 661W	1980	Ford Transit	Dormobile	16
THA 404-405W	1981	Ford R1114	Duple	C53F
JVJ 511Y	1982	Bedford YNT	Duple	C53F

*OWK 661W was acquired from Bonas, Coventry, in 1984
WITHDRAWAL DATES
1984: TDH 232R, YNX 446-447S, FFD 968T
1986: GEA 733-734T, LHA 451-452V, OHA 465W, OWK 661W

Vehicles acquired for Central Coachways during WMPTE control

	A945-946 MDH	1984	Bedford YNT	Plaxton	C49F
	A735-736 HFP	1984	Bova	Bova	C49FT
M1-10	B55-64 AOP	1985	Ford Transit	Carlyle	B16F
	C900-902 JOF	1986	MCW DR130/30	MCW	CH53/16DT
	C903-904 JOF	1986	Bova	Bova	C49FT

Notes
M1-10 renumbered 555-64 from September 1986.
A735-736 HFP were acquired from Bebb, Llantwit Fardre, in 1984.
C904 JOF was re-registered 245 DOC in 1986.

Buses purchased new by WMPTE 1974-1980

Fleet Nos	Registration	Year	Chassis	Body	Code
4447-4451	ROK 447-461M	1974	Daimler CRG6LX	East Lancs	H44/30F
4462-4466	TOE 462-466N	1974	Daimler CRG6LX	East Lancs	H44/30F
4467-4476	ROK 467-476M	1974	Leyland National	Ley Nat	B50F
4477-4526	TOE 477-526N	1974	Leyland National	Ley Nat	B50F
4527-4529	TOE 527-529N	1974	Ailsa-Volvo	Alexander	H44/35F
4530-4579	GOG 530-579N	1975	Daimler CRL6	Park Royal	H43/33F
4580-4605	GOG 580-605N	1975	Daimler CRG6LX	Park Royal	H43/33F
4606-4629	JOV 606-629P	1975	Daimler CRG6LX	Park Royal	H43/33F
4630-4464	GOG 630-684N	1974-5	Bristol VRT/SL6G	MCW	H43/33F
4685-4729	JOV 685-729P	1975	Bristol VRT/SL6G	MCW	H43/33F
4730-4737	JOV 730-737P	1975	Ford A	Alexander	B23F
4738-4787	JOV 738-787P	1976	Ailsa-Volvo	Alexander	H44/35F
4788-4799	KOM 788-799P	1976	Leyland-National	Ley Nat	B46D
5531	BON531C	(1978)	Daimler CRG6LX	MCW	H44/33F
6300	ROC 300R	1977	Foden	Northern Counties	H44/33F
6301-6375	KON 301-375P	1976	Leyland FE30ALR	MCW	H43/33F
6376-6420	NOC 376-420R	1976	Leyland FE30ALR	MCW	H43/33F
6421-6500	NOC 421-500R	1976-7	Leyland FE30AGR	MCW	H43/33F
6501-6570	SDA 501-570S	1977	Leyland FE30AGR	MCW	H43/33F
6571-6580	MOM 571-580P	1976	Leyland FE30AGR	Park Royal	H43/33F
6581-6610	NOC 581-610R	1976	Leyland FE30AGR	Park Royal	H43/33F
6611-6660	SDA 611-660R	1977-8	Leyland FE30AGR	Park Royal	H43/33F
6661-6690	WDA 661-690T	1979	Leyland FE30AGR	Park Royal	H43/33F
6691-6720	SDA 691-720S	1978	Leyland FE30AGR	MCW	H43/33F
6721-6745	NOC 721-745R	1977	Leyland FE30AGR	East Lancs	H43/33F
6746-6760	SDA 746-760S	1977-8	Leyland FE30AGR	East Lancs	H43/33F
6761-6800	SDA 761-800S	1978	Leyland FE30AGR	MCW	H43/33F
6801-6815	OOX 801-815R	1977	Leyland National	Ley Nat	B50F
6816-6830	OOX 816-830R	1977	Leyland National	Ley Nat	DP45F
6831-6834	SDA 831-834S	1978	MCW DR102/1	MCW	H43/30F
6835	WDA 835T	1978	MCW DR102/1	MCW	H43/30F
6836-6850	TVP 836-850S	1978	Leyland National	Ley Nat	B50F
6851-6865	TVP 851-865S	1978	Leyland National	Ley Nat	DP45F
6866-6905	TVP 866-905S	1978	Leyland FE30AGR	MCW	H43/33F
6906-6999	WDA 906-999T	1978-9	Leyland FE30AGR	MCW	H43/33F
7000	WDA 700T	1979	Leyland FE30AGR	MCW	H43/33F
7001-7005	WDA 1-5T	1978-9	Leyland TNLXB1RF	Park Royal	H47/26F
7006-7007	BOM 6-7V	1979	MCW DR104/4	MCW	H43/30F
7008-7017	AOL 8-17T	1979	Leyland National	Ley Nat	B50F
7018-7047	DOC 18-47V	1980	Leyland-National 2	Ley Nat	B50F
7048-7052	DOC 48-52V	1980	Leyland-National 2	Ley Nat	B42F

Notes

4467-4526, 4788-4797, 6801-26/8-30/6-65, 7008-7052 renumbered 1467-1526, 1788-1797, 1801-26/8-30/6-65, 1008-1052 in April 1985
4503/5/7/10-1/7/9-21/3, 7008-17 entered service as B52F in all-cream livery
4518 was registered GOK618N
4530-4579, 6301-6420 converted to Gardner engines between 1979 and 1986
4730-7 re-seated to B22F 1976; 6831 originally seated H43/33F; 6844-5/7/9 to B22DL 1984
5531 used the 1965 chassis from bus 3531.

WITHDRAWAL DATES

1980: 4730-7
1982: 4454, 4705/7/28, 5531, 6300
1983: 4702/6/15/98-9, 7001-5
1984: 4527-9, 4639/61/81, 6827

1985: 4514, 4631/3-5/43-4/7-8/52/8-9/70/4/6/85
1986: 4447-53/5-66, 4530-60/2-4/6-8/71-6/9, 4630/2/6-8/40-2/5-6/9-51/3-7/60/2-9/71-3/5/7-80/2-4/6-4701/3-4/8-14/6-27/9/88-97
Transferred to WMT 10/86
4467-4513/5-26/61/5-9/70/7-8/80-4629, 4738-87, 6301-6826/8-7000/6-52

Buses purchased new by WMPTE 1979-86

Fleet Nos	Registration	Year	Chassis	Body	Code
2001-2075	BOK1-75V	1979-80	MCW DR102/12	MCW	H43/30F
2076-2090	BOK 76-90V	1980	MCW DR102/18	MCW	H43/30F
2091-2225	GOG 91-225W	1980-1	MCW DR102/18	MCW	H43/30F
2226-2245	GOG 226-245W	1981	MCW DR104/8	MCW	H43/30F
2246-2275	GOG 246-275W	1981	MCW DR102/18	MCW	H43/30F
2276-2325	KJW 276-325W	1981	MCW DR102/22	MCW	H43/30F
2326-2435	LOA 326-435X	1981-2	MCW DR102/22	MCW	H43/30F
2436-2475	NOA 436-475X	1982	MCW DR102/27	MCW	H43/30F
2476-2610	POG 476-610Y	1982	MCW DR102/27	MCW	H43/30F
2611-2667	ROX 611-667Y	1983	MCW DR102/27	MCW	H43/30F
2668-2735	A668-735 UOE	1983	MCW DR102/27	MCW	H43/30F
2736-2772	A736-772 WVP	1984	MCW DR102/27	MCW	H43/30F
2773-2795	B773-795 AOC	1984	MCW DR102/27	MCW	H43/30F
2796-2860	B796-860 AOP	1984	MCW DR102/48	MCW	H43/30F
2861-2886	B861-886 DOM	1985	MCW DR102/48	MCW	H43/30F
2887-2910	C887-910 FON	1985	MCW DR102/48	MCW	H43/30F
2911-2929	D911-929 NDA	1986	MCW DR102/59	MCW	DPH43/23F
8101-8114	A101-114 WVP	1984	MCW GR133/1	MCW	DP23DL
1053-1054	B53-54 AOC	1985	Dennis Lancet	Duple	B50F
1055-1060	C55-60 HOM	1986	Volvo YV31MEC	Alexander	B48F
1061-1066	C61-66 HOM	1986	Leyland LX112	Leyland	

Notes

2686 was prototype for 'guided buses' 8101-8114.
2911-2929 were the first of 50 Metrobuses for WMT 'Timesaver' services. They were licensed, along with many new minibuses, prior to transfer but did not enter general service.
1053-1054 were delivered as 7053-7054 and renumbered in April 1985.

Welfare Buses purchased by WMPTE

Fleet Nos	Registration	Year	Chassis	Body
501-2	NRF 172/7P	1976	Ford A	Dormobile
503-8	AOE 503-8T	1979	Ford A	Dormobile
509-13	EJW 509-13V	1980	Ford A	Dormobile
514-20	HOC 514-20W	1981	Ford A	Dormobile

501-2 were numbered 6297-8 until February 1979

WITHDRAWAL DATES

1985: 501
1986: 502-3
504-20 were sold to Birmingham Education Department in September 1985 but continued to be operated by WMPTE. They reverted to WMPTE in July 1986 but were not used again as welfare buses.

An adventurous move towards the end of the PTE's existence as a bus operator was the purchase of three Metroliner double-deck coaches for the London Liner service introduced in conjunction with London Buses Ltd in March 1986. Tastefully painted in a French blue livery lined in gold and white, the vehicles were operated by the Central Coachways subsidiary. WMPTE